RECONSTRUCTING
MARXIAN ECONOMICS

RECONSTRUCTING MARXIAN ECONOMICS

Marx Based upon
A Sraffian Commodity
Theory of Value

Spencer J. Pack

PRAEGER SPECIAL STUDIES • PRAEGER SCIENTIFIC

New York • Philadelphia • Eastbourne, UK
Toronto • Hong Kong • Tokyo • Sydney

Library of Congress Cataloging in Publication Data

Pack, Spencer J.
  Reconstructing Marxian economics.

  Bibliography: p.
  Includes index.
  1. Marxian economics. 2. Value. I. Title.
II. Title: Commodity theory of value.
HB97.5.P227 1985   335.4   84-26279
ISBN 0-03-003092-7 (alk. paper)

Published and Distributed by the
Praeger Publishers Division
(ISBN Prefix 0-275)
of Greenwood Press, Inc.,
Westport, Connecticut

Published in 1985 by Praeger Publishers
CBS Educational and Professional Publishing
a Division of CBS Inc.
521 Fifth Avenue, New York, NY 10175 USA

© 1985 by Praeger Publishers

56789 052 987654321

Printed in the United States of America
on acid-free paper

To
Dr. ROBERT F. BARLOW
in gratitude and admiration

CONTENTS

RECONSTRUCTING
MARXIAN ECONOMICS

INTRODUCTION

The purpose of this work is to show that the basic architectonics of Karl Marx's analysis of capitalism are sufficiently independent of Marx's labor theory of value to survive the replacement of the labor theory of value by a commodity theory of value as presented by Piero Sraffa. This work argues that Marx's analysis of the theoretical genesis of capital does not necessarily depend upon the *labor* theory of value. The theoretical genesis of capital as demonstrated by Marx can be based upon a Sraffian commodity theory of value. Thus, even if the labor theory of value is *replaced* with a commodity theory of value, this essential aspect of Marx's theory of capital will remain intact.

This work raises important issues for Marxian economics in particular and for economic theory in general. Recently, writers have used Sraffa's work to criticize Marx's labor theory of value.[1] In a seminal work presenting many of these criticisms of the labor theory of value from a Sraffian perspective, Ian Steedman has gone so far as to argue that

> It can scarcely be overemphasized that the project of providing a materialist account of capitalist societies is dependent on Marx's value magnitude analysis *only* in the negative sense that continued adherence to the latter is a major fetter on the development of the former.[2]

Here, Ian Steedman joins hands with Joan Robinson who has long argued that "no point of substance in Marx's argument depends upon the labor theory of value."[3] Note, however, that Steedman actually goes farther than Robinson by arguing that not only does Marx's analysis of capitalism not depend upon the labor theory of value, but that continued adherence to it actually hinders the development of analyses of capitalism. This sort of position has given rise to a new school of economists. As de Vroey has noted in a recent article in *Capital and Class*:

> Until recently, to assert at the same time adhesion to the Marxian
> paradigm and rejection of the labour theory of value would have been
> considered blasphemy. . . . Nowadays this view is gaining strength and
> is defended by many of the brightest young left economists. Sign of suc-
> cess, they have their own label: Sraffian Marxists.[4]

The Sraffian Marxists, or neo-Ricardians, as they are more generally
called,[5] assert that one can (and indeed ought) to do a Marxian-type analysis
of capitalism without using the labor theory of value. This work will show
how one can do this by basing Marx's account of the theoretical development of capital upon a commodity rather than upon the labor theory of
value.

The subject matter of this study is very controversial. This study will
not *directly* discuss the advantages and disadvantages of using a commodity
versus Marx's labor theory of value. Instead, it will merely be shown that
much of Marx's analysis (particularly his development of the concept of
capital, contained in the first several hundred pages of Volume I of *Capital*)
is not materially affected by basing his analysis upon a Sraffian commodity
theory of value rather than upon his labor theory of value. However, it may
be noteworthy to point out that many economists would argue that a major
advantage of using the commodity theory of value is the by-passing of the
notorious transformation problem which arises when one uses Marx's labor
theory of value. Hence, as Bandyopadhyay has argued,

> The upshot of adopting the post-Sraffa analysis is there is no transfor-
> mation problem of the sort Marx confronted and which was a boon to
> critics of Marx . . . it [the transformation problem] appears to be a
> wholly self-inflicted conundrum created by Marx's starting point and
> the particular account of valuation and exchange valuations with which
> he concluded his beginning.[6]

The major point of this work is that basically nothing is lost by ground-
ing Marx's work upon a commodity rather than upon the labor theory of
value. However, it should be noted here that something is gained, namely
the avoidance of any kind of transformation problem which results from
the need to transform Marxian values into long-run prices of production
when using the labor theory of value.[7] Thus, it is true that this work will not
directly enter into the controversies over the validity, nature, scope, or purposes of Marx's labor theory of value.[8] However, it indirectly contributes to
that controversy by showing how much of Marx's work may be
reconstituted by basing it upon a commodity theory of value rather than
upon the labor theory of value.

The ideas upon which this work are based are very tightly interelated. In
a sense, the work in itself should almost be seen as a system of simultaneous

equations. Everything fits together very tightly, thus making the order of the presentation of ideas a problem.

Before undertaking this work, the following assumptions were made; the study ultimately rests upon these basic assumptions.

1. It was assumed that there must be some kind of theory of value. As Joseph Schumpeter has argued, "economic phenomena and problems form a coherent set and . . . it is the theory of value which unifies them."[9] Because of this,

> the problem of value must always hold the pivotal position, as the chief tool of analysis in any pure theory that works with a rational schema.[10]

This assumption implies that if the labor theory of value were to be discarded, then it must at the same time be replaced by another theory of value.

2. It was assumed that Marx's labor theory of value is meant to be in some sense "scientific"; that is, the labor theory of value is supposed to have something to say about how capitalist societies actually work, and it is supposed to have some kind of predictive power. It was assumed that Marx's theory of value is not *merely* a normative theory which is designed to "move the masses." This "Sorellian" interpretation of the labor theory of value, that it is some kind of necessary myth which is needed in Marxist theory for purposes of political agitation, is a misuse of Marx's labor theory of value.[11] Instead, the general approach which was taken to Marx's work is the same as that which Schumpeter took. For Schumpeter, as for us,

> We shall not chant *O Altitudo* each time Marx's name turns up in the following pages; but neither do we put him out of court *a limine*; we simply recognize him as a sociological and economic analyst whose propositions (theories) have the same methodological meaning and standing and have to be interpreted according to the same criteria as have the propositions of every other sociological and economic analyst. . . .[12]

3. It was assumed that Marx's labor theory of value is a *theory* about value, and is not something which is simply true by definition.[13] Thus, the labor theory of value (as with *any* theory of value) must in some way be related to prices and profits. Moreover, the labor theory of value is not *only* an arbitrary definition used for purposes of aggregation and measurement problems.[14]

4. It was assumed that Marx's understanding of and development of the concept of capital does not result from a simple arbitrary definition. Marx's conception of capital developed out of his analysis of commodities, money, and commodity fetishism. Thus, in order to analyze whether Marx's conception of capital is independent of the labor theory of value,

it was assumed that Marx must be followed in his analysis of commodities, money and commodity fetishism. This assumption was equivalent to assuming that there is an inherent logic and order to Marx's presentation of economic categories; hence, it is not possible simply to rip out a definition of capital from Marx's theoretical system. Rather, Marx must be closely followed as he seeks to uncover the mysteries of capital and find out how capital necessarily evolves out of the commodity form of value.

5. It was assumed that Marx's understanding of what capital is and the theoretical genesis of capital is an important aspect of Marx's work, meriting detailed investigation. It was assumed that Marx was interested in capital and that he wanted to *theoretically* explain how there developed

> a mode of production in which the labourer exists to satisfy the needs of self-expansion of existing values, instead of on the contrary, material wealth existing to satisfy the needs of development on the part of the labourer.[15]

6. Closely related to assumption 4, it was assumed that Marx's theoretical system is not a "smorgasbord" which can be disassembled and put back together "holding onto or discarding constituent components according to his or her particular tastes."[16] Thus, it was assumed that the discarding of the labor theory of value could conceivably have led to profound modifications in Marx's entire theoretical system.

Based upon the above assumptions, it was decided to reconstruct Marx's analysis of the theoretical genesis of capital, based upon a commodity theory of value. This reworking brought up various controversies. First, it necessitated the reading and interpretation of Marx's *Capital,* a work which is not without its ambiguities and obscure points.[17] Second, it necessitated the reading and interpretation of Sraffa's work. This also presented problems, primarily because Sraffa writes in a very terse, abbreviated style. However, difficulties also arose because Sraffa presented his work in the form of a prelude to a critique of neoclassical theory, rather than as either a critique of Marx' work, or as an independent theory which can stand up on its own.[18] The reading of Sraffa suggested that Sraffa is actually using what may be termed a commodity theory of value.[19] Within Sraffa's framework, commodities have value because they are produced by other commodities. Surplus value may be said to arise when commodities produce more commodities as outputs than are used up as inputs. This theory is very similar to Marx's labor theory of value. With Marx, only labor power creates value;[20] labor power does this when it actually labors. For Marx, labor power, and the exploitation of this labor power is the source of surplus value. The interpretation offered here is that for Sraffa any commodity when used to create other commodities may be said to create value, and surplus value may be said to arise when commodities as a group (including the commodity labor power) can produce more commodities as outputs than are used up as inputs.

The organization of the study is as follows. Due to the complex nature of the subject matter, Chapters 1–5 can *all* be considered to be introductory chapters to the problem at hand. Chapter 1 gives the theoretical background to the problem at hand and gives a short account of the history of value theory in economic thought, with special reference to how value theory may relate to capital theory. The purpose of this chapter is primarily to place the study within the overall development of economic thought and to show why the issues which this work deals with are important and interesting ones.

Chapter 2 gives an account of and an interpretation of Sraffa's work with reference to value theory and the creation of surplus value. Chapter 3 discusses a few of the theoretical implications resulting from what is here being called the commodity theory of value. This is where there is a presentation of how the commodity theory of value has been used to criticize the labor theory of value when that theory of value is used to help determine such things as relative prices and the rate of profit.[21] Chapter 4 continues that discussion by considering a model of a fully automated society.[22] This model casts additional (though by no means definitive) doubt on the usefulness of the labor theory of value when that theory is used to help determine relative prices and the rate of profit. Perhaps more importantly, it further *dramatizes* that there is a difference between Marx's labor theory of value and the commodity theory of value which may be found in Sraffa's work and which is being used in this work.

Chapter 5 discusses some of the theoretical and historical assumptions concerning the capitalist mode of production. This is followed by Chapters 6–10 which actually rework Parts I and II of Volume I of *Capital* using a commodity theory of value in place of the labor theory of value.

Various obstacles and issues crop up along the way when doing this analysis. These include, but are not limited to:

(a) the distinction between what is meant by "to create" versus "to determine" value;

(b) the absence of a clear and satisfactory definition of the concept mode of production, which is nowhere defined consistently in Marx;[23]

(c) the question as to where Marx begins his analysis, at the realm of production (be that either capitalist production or simple commodity production) or at the realm of circulation;

(d) the relationship between Marxian economics and what is known as general equilibrium theory;

(e) the reason for the *relatively* impoverished analysis which Marx gives concerning money in Volume I of *Capital*;

(f) the general lack of a monetary analysis in both the development of the commodity theory of value and in Volume I of *Capital*.

These various questions and puzzles are briefly dealt with where appropriate in the main text, in footnotes, and, where extended discussion appears warranted, in appendices. In spite of these controversies and the unsettled nature of many of these issues, the main hypothesis of the study is upheld: one may indeed rework Marx's account of the theoretical genesis of capital based upon a commodity rather than upon the labor theory of value.

For convenience to the reader, each of the chapters which rework Marx using a commodity theory of value contains a listing of how the substitution of a commodity theory of value for the labor theory of value changes important points in Marx's theory. This may serve as a guide for future research on the full implications of the changes wrought by the substitution performed in this study.

Previous authors have shown how one may rework various aspects of Marx's theory without reference to the labor theory of value. This includes, among others, a reworking of Marx's theory of history;[24] the handling of exploitation;[25] the effects of lengthening the hours of work, and the intensifying of the pace of work, speed-ups, etc., on relative prices and the rate of profit;[26] and crises of disproportionality.[27] The distinguishing characteristics of this study are that:

(a) it clearly and consciously elaborates on the fact that Sraffa is using a theory of value which is distinct from both the Marxist labor theory of value and neoclassical theories of value;

(b) nonetheless, it is posited that the theory of value which Sraffa uses (and which is here called the commodity theory of value) is so similar to the labor theory of value that it may be used in place of the labor theory of value in Marx's analysis of capitalism;[28]

(c) Marx's account of the theoretical genesis of capital is reconstructed upon the basis of this Sraffan commodity theory of value rather than upon the labor theory of value.

Thus, this study lays a firm groundwork upon which future economists may build upon. It shows how Marx's analysis of capitalism may be reconstructed, but using a commodity rather than Marx's labor theory of value as the foundation upon which to build an analysis of capitalism. It is shown that very little is changed by building Marx's analysis upon a commodity rather than the labor theory of value.[29]

NOTES

1. Piero Sraffa, *The Production of Commodities by Means of Commodities,* (Cambridge University Press, 1960).

2. Ian Steedman, *Marx After Sraffa,* (New Left Books, 1977), p. 207.

3. Joan Robinson, *An Essay on Marxian Economics,* 2nd edition, (Macmillan, 1966), p. 22. For a more recent statement of Robinson's position, see "The Labor Theory of Value," *Monthly Review* **29**, 7 (1977): 50–59.

4. de Vroey, "On the Obsolescence of the Marxian Theory of Value: A Critical Review," *Capital and Class* (Summer 1982): 34.

5. Actually, this group of economists is so controversial that there is even a controversy over what to call them. Although they are generally called neo-Ricardians, the term Sraffian Marxists would seem to be more appropriate. On the controversy over "the labelling process," see Pradeep Bandyopadhyay, "Who's Afraid of the 'Neo-Ricardians?': Some Notes on the Jousting," unpublished, pp. 3–4.

6. Bandyopadhyay, "Looking for Social Abstract Labour," unpublished, p. 35.

7. For Marx's account of how this may be done, see *Capital,* Vol. III, Parts I and II.

8. The literature on this subject is enormous. Let the reader who wishes to embark upon a study of this literature be forewarned: much of it is marked by a high level of mathematical sophistication and/or dialectical subtleties. The best introduction to this subject is probably still Ronald Meek's *Studies in the Labor Theory of Value,* 2nd edition (New York: Monthly Review Press, 1976); this second edition contains an introduction which attempts a synthesis of Sraffa and Marx. The "classic" criticism of Marx's labor theory of value is Bohm-Bawerk's "Karl Marx and the Close of His System"; the "classic" defense of this theory is Rudolf Hilferding's "Bohm-Bawerk's Criticism of Marx." Both of these are reprinted, along with an excellent introduction by Paul Sweezy in *Karl Marx and the Close of His System* (New York: Augustus M. Kelley, 1966). Criticisms of Marx's labor theory of value from a Ricardian (or what may now be termed a Sraffian) perspective were first put forth (although largely implicitly) by the obscure Russian economist, V. K. Dmitriev, *Economic Essays on Value, Competition, and Utility* (Cambridge University Press, 1974); (see especially the first essay). These criticisms were developed in the work of the German economist, Ladislaus von Bortkiewicz, "On the Correction of Marx's Fundamental Theoretical Construction in the Third Volume of Capital," 1907, reprinted in English in the above-mentioned E. von Bohm-Bawerk in *Karl Marx and the Close of His System*, edited by Paul Sweezy; but see, also, the more obscure but no less important paper "Value and Price in the Marxian System," reprinted in English in *International Economic Papers* No. 2, 1952. Paul Sweezy's *The Theory of Capitalist Development* (New York: Monthly Review Press, 1942) is noteworthy for (among many other things) containing an early attempted defense of the labor theory of value while taking into account the work of Bortkiewicz. (Dmitriev's work was apparently unknown to Sweezy — it has only recently been translated into Western languages.)

The publication of Sraffa's *Production of Commodities by Means of Commodities* has helped spark renewed interest in Marx's labor theory of value, and at this particular time the literature on this subject seems to be growing exponentially. Among other recent publications, the following may be cited: The Summer 1982 issue of *The Review of Radical Political Economics* is a special issue devoted to value theory; the December 1982 issue of the *American Economic Review* contains an article by Wilfried Parys on "The Deviation of Prices from Labor Values"; and *Studies in Political Economy,* a new Canadian journal, promises a forthcoming article by Gilles Dostaler, "Labour Theory of Value." For a useful review of the literature on this subject since the publication of Sraffa's aforementioned work, see the work of Bandyopadhyay, "The Renewal of Marx's Economics," *Catalyst* No. 12 (1978): 22–40; "Further on the Renewal of Marx's Economics: A Reply to Thompson," *Catalyst* No. 14

(1981): 72–91; and "In Defense of a Post-Sraffian Approach," in I. Steedman, P. M. Sweezy, et al., *The Value Controversy* (London: New Left Books, 1981), pp. 100–129. Bandyopadhyay is essentially critical of the labor theory of value; it may be usefully balanced by a study of Laibman's work, "Values and Prices of Production," *Science and Society* (Vol. 37, Winter 1974, pp. 404–436); "Controversies in the Theory of Surplus Values: A Comment," *Science and Society* (Vol. 38, Winter 1975, pp. 482–487); and "Exploitation, Commodity Relations, and Capitalism: A Defense of the Labor-Value Formulation," *Science and Society* 44, (Fall 1980); 274–288. See, also, Anwar Shaikh's work (Shaikh is perhaps the most vociferous of the orthodox defenders of the labor theory of value), "Marx's Theory of Value and the Transformation Problem," in Schwartz, *The Subtle Anatomy of Capitalism* (Santa Monica, Calif.: Goodyear Publishing Company, 1977), pp. 106–139, and "Neo-Ricardian Economics: A Wealth of Algebra, A Poverty of Theory," *Review of Radical Political Economics* 14, No. 2 (1982): 67–83.

Mention should also be made of the fact that there have been a number of attempted reformulations of the labor theory of value to take into account perceived problems of Marx's labor theory of value. This further complicates issues in that it is often not clear what these attempted reformulations have to do with *Marx's* labor theory of value, other than the name. For more on this subject, see Chapter 3.

9. Schumpeter, *History of Economic Analysis*, p. 513.

10. Ibid., p. 588.

11. This is a popular misconception of the purpose of the labor theory of value. In a related vein, the American economist Thorstein Veblen ["The Socialist Economics of Karl Marx," in *The Portable Veblen* edited by Max Lerner (New York: Viking Press, 1948), pp. 275–296)] asserted that Marx felt laborers had a claim to the whole product of their labor. Recently, Peter Drucker ["Toward the Next Economics," *Public Interest* Special Issue (1980) 4–18] made the same assertion. For Marx's objection that this is a misuse of the labor theory of value, see "Critique of the Gotha Program" in *Karl Marx on Revolution*, edited by Saul Padover (New York: McGraw-Hill 1971), pp. 488–506; see also, Engels' "Preface to the First German Edition" of Marx's *The Poverty of Philosophy* (1884).

12. Schumpeter, *History of Economic Analysis*, p. 385; emphasis in original.

13. As held by, e.g., Thomas Sowell in *Say's Law: An Historical Analysis* (Princeton University Press, 1972), p. 186. On this point, see G. A. Cohen, "The Labor Theory of Value and the Concept of Exploitation," *Philosophy and Public Affairs* No. 4 (1979).

14. On this point see Schumpeter: "In itself, the choice of hours or days of labor as units by which to express commodity values or prices . . . no more implies any particular theory of exchange value on price than the choice of oxen as units by which to express commodity values implies an ox theory of exchange value or price." [History of Economic Analysis, p. 188 fn.]; Schumpeter repeats this point on p. 310.

15. Marx, *Capital*, Vol. I (Charles H. Kerr and Co., 1906), pp. 680–681.

16. Paul Sweezy, "Marxian Value Theory," *Monthly Review* 31, No. 3, (1979): 3.

17. Marx, *Capital*, Vol. I (Charles H. Kerr and Co., 1906). I used Marx's *A Contribution to the Critique of Political Economy* (International Publishers, 1970) and especially his *Grundrisse: Foundations of the Critique of Political Economy* (Random House, 1973) to help in interpreting *Capital*. Among the secondary sources, I leaned most heavily upon Kozo Uno's *Principles of Political Economy: Theory of a Purely Capitalist Society* (Sussex, 1980). A note on Uno: apparently, approximately one-half of the academic economists in Japan are Marxists, and of these, approximately one-half are followers of Uno. For a useful introduction to Uno, see Thomas Sekine, "Uno-Riron: A Japanese Contribution to Marxian Political Economy," *Journal of Economic Literature* 13, No. 3 (1975): 847–877. Uno's *Principles* has only recently been translated into English; the unfortunately high price charged by the publisher is no doubt inhibiting the dissemination of this remarkable work in the English-speaking world. An excellent textbook on Marxist economics is the little-known work by

William Blake, *Elements of Marxian Economic Theory and its Criticism* (New York: Cordon, 1939)—this work has also been marketed under the rather uninspiring title of *An American Looks at Karl Marx.*

18. Sraffa, *Production of Commodities by Means of Commodities.* Important secondary sources which were consulted were Luigi Pasinetti, *Lectures on the Theory of Production* (New York: Columbia University Press, 1977), and Alessandro Roncagcia, *Sraffa and the Theory of Prices* (New York: Wiley, 1978). This latter work contains a complete bibliography of Sraffa's writings. My reading of Sraffa is also heavily influenced by the work of Dmitriev, the obscure Russian mathematical economist who may be viewed as a forerunner to Sraffa. For a convenient introduction to Dmitriev, see Paul Samuelson, "Review of Economic Essays on Value, Competition and Utility by V. K. Dmitriev," *Journal of Economic Literature* **XIII** (1975): 491–495.

19. It has not been widely understood that Sraffa has been using what may be termed a commodity theory of value, and there has been some confusion on this point. Ian Steedman, for example, calls Sraffa's approach a "physical quantities" framework (See Steedman, *Marx After Sraffa,* pp. 65–67; p. 78.) This is slightly misleading, since Sraffa is dealing with the production of *commodities* by means of *commodities.* While it is true that commodities are physical quantities, they are more than that. This is an important distinction to keep in mind, particularly with reference to a Marxian-type analysis. As Harry Braverman has pointed out, "the first volume of *Capital* may be considered a massive essay on how the *commodity form* in an adequate social and technological setting, matures into the form of capital . . . " [Harry Braverman, *Labor and Monopoly Capital,* Monthly Review Press, New York, 1974, p. 20, emphasis added.] This issue is more fully discussed in Chapters 6 and 8. Incidentally, this may be a convenient place to state my methodology with respect to interpreting various writers. Wherever possible, I have tried to give as *literal* and *clear* an interpretation as possible as to what the authors are saying. This sort of reading and exposition may have the disadvantage of *appearing* to be "naive."

20. "Human labour-power in motion, or human labour, creates value, but is not itself value." [*Capital,* Vol. I, p. 59.] "The purely natural material in which *no* human labour is objectified, to the extent that it is merely a material that exists independently of labour, has no *value,* since only objectified labour is value; . . ." [*Grundrisse,* p. 308; emphasis in original]. References to Marx's theory that only labor power creates value are scattered throughout the *Grundrisse.* See, among other places, pp. 224, 225, 272, 296, 308, 453, 543, 548, 553, 612, 670, 674, and 767 fn.

21. No attempt is made to critically evaluate the validity of these criticisms of the labor theory of value. In the past Sraffa's work has frequently been used to attempt to *disprove* the validity of the labor theory of value. Since one can always resort to ad hoc hypotheses to save any theory, it is not clear whether one can definitely disprove any theory of value. However, one may propose and develop alternative theories of value and see how fruitful these alternative theories are. The basic approach taken in this work is that Sraffa and the Sraffian-based critiques of the labor theory of value are indeed employing an alternative theory of value, one which is very close to but not the same as the labor theory of value.

22. This discussion is continued at a more general level in Appendix C.

23. See Pradeep Bandyopadhyay, "New Methods on Modes of Production," paper presented to *Graduate Seminar, Depart of Anthropology,* University of Toronto, Toronto, March 1978.

24. G. A. Cohen, *Karl Marx's Theory of History: A Defense* (Princeton, N.J.: Princeton University Press, 1978).

25. See, e.g., Joan Robinson and Amit Bhaduri, "Accumulation and Exploitation: An Analysis in the Tradition of Marx, Sraffa, and Kalecki," *Cambridge Journal of Economics* **4**, No. 2 (1980): 105–106; Geoff Hodgson, "A Theory of Exploitation Without the Labor Theory of Value," *Science and Society* **XLIV**, No. 3 (1980): 257–273; Arun Bose, *Marx on Exploita-*

tion and Inequality (Oxford University Press, 1980); and John E. Roemer, *A General Theory of Exploitation and Class* (Cambridge, Mass.: Harvard University Press, 1982). An excellent nonmathematical introduction to this latter work is contained in John E. Roemer, "New Directions in the Marxian Theory of Exploitation and Class," *Politics and Society* 11, No. 3 (1982): 253–288.

26. Steedman, *Marx After Sraffa,* Chapter 6, pp. 77–87.

27. David Hawkins, "Some Conditions of Macroeconomic Stability," *Econometrica* 16 (October 1948: 309–322. This is an important early article using what is essentially a commodity theory of value in a dynamic framework showing the likelihood of a crisis of disproportionate development even when starting with the assumption of full employment. For Hawkins' interpretation of the relationship between his model and Marx's models of extended reproduction, see footnote 6, pp. 320–321. Possible ways to theoretically treat disequilibrium aspects of this model, with various assumptions about the role of market price flexibility, the transfer of capitalist ownership between different sectors of the economy, and the nature of the production function are briefly discussed in pp. 321–322. These important suggestions into how economists may study the dynamics of capitalism when essentially using a commodity theory of value have never been satisfactorily pursued.

28. It is an interesting question, although outside the scope of this work, as to exactly why this is so. My own interpretation may be briefly stated as follows. I think that Ricardo really had a commodity theory of value although he thought that he had a labor theory of value. Marx took Ricardo at his word, that he (Ricardo) had a labor theory of value, and sought to develop and perfect it. For support of the position that Ricardo really had a commodity theory of value, see Dmitriev. The commodity theory of value that Sraffa uses is so similar to Marx's labor theory of value because of their common Ricardian roots. It is largely for this reason that one can reconstruct Marx's theoretical apparatus based upon a commodity theory of value; in so doing, as this work will show, very little of Marx's work needs to be changed.

29. For the same sort of approach as that attempted in this work, see Geoff Hodgson, "Marx Without the Labor Theory of Value," *Review of Radical Political Economics* 14, No. 2 (1982): 59–66. Hodgson covers much of the same material as this work, although much more briefly. As Hodgson explains, "it has not been the intention of this paper to add to already existing critiques of the labor theory of value. The main aim here has been to show that it is possible to 'read' Marx without the labor theory of value, and still derive Marx's central conclusions. This article is intended to start a debate, not to finish one" [p. 64]. This work is conducted in much the same spirit. However, in this study it is not merely a question of reading Marx without the labor theory of value, but of replacing the labor theory of value and reading Marx with a Sraffian commodity theory of value.

1

THEORETICAL BACKGROUND

As is well known, Marx held that commodities in a capitalist society only have value insofar as they contain embodied labor.[1] On the basis of this labor theory of value Marx developed a concept of capital as self-expanding value, that is value which creates more value.[2]

Now, in recent years, Marx's labor theory of value has come under increasing attack. Much of this attack has been inspired by Piero Sraffa's *Production of Commodities by Means of Commodities*.[3] In a sense, this is rather ironic, since Sraffa's work was intended to be the prelude to a critique of *neoclassical* economic theory.

The interpretation offered here is that Sraffa's work can be used to attack *both* neoclassical and Marxist economic theory partly because he is using *neither* a labor theory of value nor a "subjective" theory of value (upon which traditional economic theory is largely based). Instead, Sraffa is using what may be called a commodity theory of value. Within Sraffa's theoretical framework, commodities have value because they are produced by other commodities.

Now, a peculiarity of this theory of value is that it is so similar to Marx's labor theory of value that much of work (particularly the qualitative aspects of his analysis, i.e., those parts which do not depend upon the precise quantitative determination of such things as, among others, relative prices and the rate of profit) can be based upon a properly specified commodity theory of value instead of the (controversial) labor theory of value. Indeed, in a certain sense the commodity theory of value can be viewed as a generalization of the labor theory of value. In the labor theory of value only one commodity, labor power, can create value. In Marxian theory, labor power is the worker's capacity to produce. In capitalist society labor power is a commodity which is bought and sold in the marketplace. A worker hires herself/himself out to a capitalist. The capitalist then sets the worker (or labor power) to work, creating both new commodities as well as new values.

In contrast, using a commodity theory of value, *any* commodity which is used to make other commodities creates value. Note that this commodity theory of value has a certain degree of circularity to it.[4] The answer to the question as to what makes commodities is simply that commodities make commodities. The theory literally refers to a society where commodities are produced by means of commodities. Within this theoretical framework, labor power can be treated as any other commodity, which, when used to create other commodities, can be said to create value.

Marx's analysis of capital and capitalism is based upon the labor theory of value. However, the commodity theory of value is so similar to the labor theory of value that a great deal of Marx's work can also be based upon the commodity theory of value. Specifically, this study shows that Marx's development and conception of capital as self-expanding value can be based upon a commodity theory of value. The hypothesis may be presented diagrammatically as in Figure 1.[5]

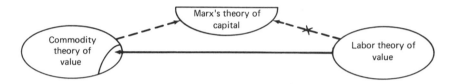

FIGURE 1. Value Theory and Marx's Theory of Capital

Marx has a well-developed theory of capital which rests upon the labor theory of value. This study substitutes a commodity theory of value for the labor theory of value (as shown in the above diagram).[6] Then the study will redevelop Marx's theory of capital as self-expanding value (i.e., I and II of *Capital*) based upon the commodity theory of value.

The rest of this chapter will present a brief history of value theory. Its purpose is not to present any new material unknown to economists.[7] Rather, its aim is simply to:

1. illustrate why value theory is an interesting and important area of study;

2. help to position the material contained in the rest of this book within the overall development of economic thought; and,

3. point out that the issues dealt with in this study are not merely some kind of minor left-wing controversy or obscure squabble between extremists, Marxists and "neo-Marxists." Rather the issues dealt with in this study are of such importance that they are (or ought to be) of concern to all economists.

Value theory has had a long and interesting past.[8] Gone are the days (if there ever really were any) when one could agree with John Stuart Mill that "happily, there is nothing in the laws of Value which remains for the present or any future writer to clear up; the theory of the subject is complete."[9] Indeed, behind the solemn pages of basic introductory price theory textbooks (largely using basic algebra and graphs), intermediate price theory textbooks (coming more and more to use the tools of calculus and matrix algebra), and advanced "highbrow" textbooks (relying upon topology and other arcane mathematical tools) lie some fundamental disagreements over what causes goods and services to have value.[10]

The classical theorists rooted their analysis of value, or what enables a good to have a price, and what determines relative prices largely on the side of supply. Thus, Adam Smith was largely concerned with the "costs of production" and felt that a good's value was in the long run determined by its costs of production. David Ricardo felt that a good's value was largely dependent upon the amount of labor used to produce it and that

> this is really the foundation of the exchangeable value of all things, excepting those which cannot be increased by human industry. . . . If the quantity of labour realised in commodities regulate their exchangeable value, every increase in the quantity of labour must augment the value of that commodity on which it is exercised, as every diminution must lower it.[11]

On this issue, Karl Marx can be squarely placed in the classical tradition, as he held that the value of a good depended upon the amount of embodied labor which it contained.

It can be argued that the classical economists had a view of the economy as one which produced and reproduced itself over time.[12] The classical economists were largely concerned with economic growth, and, given the proper institutional requirements, the economy would grow over time and the wealth of nations would expand.[13]

With their emphasis on reproducing (and hopefully expanding) the goods in society, in retrospect it seems only natural that they would place their emphasis on the determinants and cause of value on the side of production. For them, although demand and the utility of a good was largely responsible for the quantity of the good produced (and was a necessary prerequisite for the good to be produced), utility and demand did not determine a good's value, so that "utility then is not the measure of exchangeable value, although it is absolutely essential to it."[14]

The classical economists were largely concerned that the resources of society be used productively, that is, that they be used to create more goods. In this sense, classical economics is supply side economics. For them, capital was a *particular* way of using commodities. Thus, for example, Adam Smith held that capital was that part of a person's stock used to make more money:

> His (the capitalist's) whole stock, therefore, is distinguished into two parts. That part which, he expects, is to afford him this revenue, is called his capital.[15]

For Ricardo:

> Capital is that part of the wealth of a country which is employed in production, and consists of food, clothing, tools, raw material, machinery, etc., necessary to give effect to labour.[16]

Hence, capital is a certain way of using a nation's stocks; it is using stock in such a way as to support and enable workers to produce.

In this theoretical framework, capital is not conceived of as an independent "factor of production" which is rewarded according to its contribution to production. Instead, with Smith and particularly with Ricardo, capital is a way of using "stocks" productively, and the owner of the stocks receives the value of what is left over after all necessary costs are paid. Profits, the return to capital, is thus a residual category representing the value of the output of the production process after all neceasary costs (including wages paid to workers) are deducted. On this basis, abstracting from the problem of rent, assuming technology to be known, and the iron law of wages to prevail, Ricardo was able to construct a logically consistent theory of the determination of the relative prices and the rate of profit,[17] thus, in a sense, representing the high point of classical economic theory.[18]

It is now generally agreed that there was a major shift in economic theory in the later part of the 19th century,[19] given rise to what is now known as neoclassical economics. A major difference between classical and neoclassical economics consists in their handling of value. Indeed, in the *Foundations of Economic Analysis*, Paul Samuelson suggested that

> If one were looking for a single criterion by which to distinguish modern economic theory from its classical precursors, he would probably decide that this is to be found in the introduction of the so-called subjective theory of value into economic theory.[20]

The subjective theory of value holds that the value of a good is determined largely by the use value or utility which people *perceive* they can obtain from that good. Here, what is important is the marginal utility which people perceive they can obtain from a good. This marginal utility largely determines relative price so that in equilibrium $Px/Py = MUx/MUy,$ that is, the relative price of good x to good y is proportional to the marginal utility of good x to the marginal utility of good y.

Thus, there arose another theoretical system for the determination of relative prices. Its focus is on the use value or utility of a good. As Schumpeter points out:

> Jevons, Menger, and Walras—Gossen too— . . . established what Adam Smith, Ricardo, and Marx had believed to be impossible, namely, that exchange value can be explained in terms of use value.[21]

Underlying this shift of attention from costs of production to utility, from the supply side to the demand side, from an "objective" to a "subjective" theory of value, seems to be a complete change in viewing the world.[22] Where the classical economists were primarily concerned with the production, reproduction, and expansion of the goods in society, the neoclassical economists were primarily concerned with a society of *given* resources. Thus, Robbins argued that

> In pure Economics we examine the implication of the existence of scarce means with alternative uses. As we have seen, the assumption of relative valuations is the foundation of all subsequent complications.[23]

This shift of focus from the reproducibility of goods, to the idea of a fixed supply of scarce resources, brought about other changes in economic theory. So, for example, P.H. Wicksteed, whom Sraffa has called "the purist of marginal theory,"[24] explicitly called for a shift of attention away from the field of production and to the domain of consumption:

> the differential theory of economics will never allow us to forget that organized "production," which is the proper economic field, is a means only, and derives its whole significance from its relation to "consumption" or "fruition" which is the vital field, and covers all the ends to which production is a means; and, moreover, the economic laws must not be sought and cannot be found on the properly economic field. It is on the vital field, then, that the laws of economics must be discovered and studied. . . . [25]

With the shift of focus from production to consumption, from "objective" to "subjective" theories of value, prices became indexes of scarcity.[26] In neoclassical theory, a good has a high price because it is relatively scarce. In classical theory, a good will have a high price because it is difficult to produce; this high price may then in turn cause only small quantities of that good to be produced, and hence it will be "scarce."[27] (For example, consider a Rolls Royce which is relatively scarce in our society largely because it is so expensive to make.) Hence, in classical theories goods may be scarce because they are relatively expensive, whereas in neoclassical theory goods are expensive because they are relatively scarce. Thus, with neoclassical economic theory there is a reversal of the causal factor explaining the relative scarcity and value of goods in society.

With the rise of neoclassical economics, the analysis of the determinants of demand came to occupy center stage. Generally speaking, first consumption, utility, and demand were analyzed; then that analysis was expanded to incorporate issues concerning the determinants of supply. A paradigmatic example of this can be found in Hicks' *Value and Capital,* defending this approach by arguing that

> It is useful to have spent so much time on the theory of exchange. . . . We shall find, when we go on to deal with production in the following chapters, and even when we come to study dynamic problems in Part IV, almost exactly the same questions coming up as those which we have examined here. They will appear at first slightly more complicated, but they can be thrown into familiar forms; and so it will turn out that we know the answers already. That is why the theory of exchange is an essential part of the study of the economic system in general.[28]

When neoclassical economists did turn their attention to production, they treated land, labor, and capital as various scarce factors of production, each of which contributed to the production process. Each factor of production was "rewarded" according to its marginal contribution to production. Just as in the "output" markets, goods were relatively priced in proportion to the marginal utility which consumers perceived they could obtain from their use, in the "input" markets each factor of production was rewarded according to the marginal contribution which it made to the production process. Thus, in equilibrium $Pa/Pb = MPa/MPb,$ that is, the relative price of factor input a to factor input b is proportional to the marginal product of factor input a to the marginal product of factor input $b.$

In neoclassical theory, land, labor, and capital became scarce factor inputs which were not conceptually distinct from each other. No longer was profit seen as a residual factor which remained after all other necessary costs of production were paid. Now profit (or interest—in this theory it was generally assumed that in the absence of various degrees of risk, the rate of profit would equal the rate of interest) became a return to the factor input known as capital, and its "price" was determined in the same way as the price of any other factor input. Again, Wicksteed is very clear on this point:

> I now turn to some of the most obvious consequences of the differential theory of distribution. They are all included in the one statement that

> when fully grasped this theory must destroy the very conception of separate laws of distribution such as the law of rent, the law of interest, or the law of wages. It is by determining the differential equivalence of all the factors of production, however heterogeneous, that we reduce them to a common measure and establish the theory of distribution; just as it is by determining the differential equivalence of all our pursuits and possessions that we attempt to place a shilling or an hour or an effort of the mind where it will tell best, and so distribute our money or time or mental energy well. There can no more be a law of rent than there can be a law of the price of shoes distinct from the general law of the market. The way in which the several factors render their service to production differs, but the differential service they render is in every case identical, and it is on this identity or equivalence of service that the possibility of co-ordinate distribution rests.[29]

Thus, conceptually there is no difference between any of the factors of production, and each and every factor of production is paid in proportion to its marginal contribution to the production process.[30]

In this theory the quantity of capital in society is largely determined by the price of capital. Just as in the output market, a fall in the price of a good will generally result in an increase in the quantity demanded of that good (except in the case of a so-called Giffen good), in the input market a fall in the price of capital (i.e., in the interest rate) will result in an increase in the quantity demanded of capital. So, to take just one example, Hicks held that

> How will the quantity of intermediate products—the quantity of capital—be determined?
> It turns out to be determined through the rate of interest. A fall in the rate of interest would encourage the adoption of longer processes, requiring the use (at any moment) of larger quantities of intermediate products.[31]

The difference in approach between the classical and neoclassical theories can perhaps be better appreciated by considering their respective handling of skilled labor, or so-called human capital theory. In modern human capital theory, which can be viewed as an extension of neoclassical theory,[32] workers can invest in themselves. This investment increases their marginal productivity. This in turn increases the demand for their labor, which will lead to an increase in the price of their labor. In equilibrium, the increase in the price of their labor will be proportional to the increase in their marginal productivity, so that again $Pa/Pb = MPa/MPb$ (where a and b are various factor inputs). Here, an increase in investment in human capital leads to an increase in productivity, which leads to an increase in the demand for the factor input, and hence to an increase in the price of this factor input.

In handling skilled workers, the classical economists generally looked at the cost of producing and reproducing skilled workers. If skilled workers are needed in the production process, then wages must be high enough to cover for the added costs of educating and training the worker. If the worker invests in his own education and training, then wages must be high enough to include the average or normal rate of profit on that investment. Thus, Adam Smith held that

> A man educated at the expense of much labour and time to any of those employments which require extraordinary dexterity and skill, may be compared to one of those expensive machines. The work which he learns to perform, it must be expected, over and above the usual wages of common labour, will replace to him the whole expense of his education, with at least the ordinary profits of an equally valuable capital. . . .
> The difference between the wages of skilled labour and those of common labour is founded upon this principle.[33]

Here, if skilled workers are needed in the production process, then the increase in the cost of producing and reproducing the workers will necessitate an increase in the price of skilled labor. In classical economics the increase in the price of skilled labor is largely felt on the supply side (the cost of producing and reproducing the skilled worker); in neoclassical economics the increase in the price of skilled labor is largely felt on the demand side (the marginal product of skilled labor going up, thus increasing the demand for that type of labor).

The great British economist, Alfred Marshall, denied that there were any major differences between the classical and neoclassical economists,[34] and attempted to work out a synthesis of the two approaches. Yet, in spite of his attempt, it does seem that there is a fundamental difference between the two approaches; the classical economists looked at the economy as one producing and reproducing itself through time; the neoclassical economists were largely concerned with *scarcity* and the allocation of scarce given resources among infinite wants.[35] This entailed a relative shift of emphasis from production to consumption, from emphasizing supply to emphasizing demand, and from objective theories of value (i.e., value being primarily determined in the production process) to subjective theories of value (i.e., value being primarily determined by the amount of utility which consumers *perceive* they may obtain from a good). Writing in 1914, and addressing himself "to those who already accept the marginal theory of Value and Distribution,"[36] Philip Wicksteed concluded that

> Here I must close these almost random indications of some of the directions in which I think that convinced apostles of the differential economics should revise the methods of economics exposition. For myself I cannot but believe that if this were accomplished, all serious opposition to the doctrine would cease, that there would once again be a

body of accepted economic doctrines, and that Jevon's dream would be accomplished and economic science re-established 'on a sensible basis.'[37]

Yet, neoclassical economics did not completely sweep away all remnants of the classical approach to the economy. Outside of academia, Marxists such as Lenin,[38] Rosa Luxemburg,[39] and Rudolf Hilferding[40] continued to do theoretical work using the Marxian labor theory of value, and their work was largely based on such classical themes as the production and reproduction of the economic system, with emphasis on supply and the determinants (or limits) to economic growth. Other work in the classical tradition included that of Vladimir Dmitriev,[41] L. von Bortkiewicz,[42] J. von Neumann,[43] and the input-output approach of Wassily Leontief.[44] Finally, of course, mention must be made of the pioneering work of John Maynard Keynes, with his emphasis on the determinants of aggregate output and employment.

Keynes' relationship to the neoclassical and classical schools of economic thought is an ambiguous one. On the one hand, as he is often taught in the United States, Keynes can be interpreted as being a special case of neoclassical economics. Through the use of IS-LM curves, it appears that Keynes' analysis of unemployment hinges on the assumptions of wage rigidity and imperfect information. Indeed, Hicks has argued that "Mr. Keynes goes so far as to make the rigidity of wage-rates the cornerstone of his system."[45] Also, it is true that Keynes did agree that the real wage rate is equal to the marginal product of labor.[46]

Thus, by this interpretation of Keynes, if there were complete wage and price flexibility and perfect information, then there would always be full employment and the neoclassical analysis would hold. The logical conclusion of this interpretation of Keynes can perhaps be found in the new rational expectations school. They frequently assume that there is perfect information (or at least very good information) and that wages and prices are flexible (or at least are relatively flexible), and then frequently end up back in a pre-Keynesian neoclassical world of allocating scarce resources among infinite wants.[47]

On the other hand, Keynes himself felt that he had created a general theory, which incorporated neoclassical economic theory as a relatively uninteresting (and misleading) special case:

> I shall argue that the postulates of the classical theory are applicable to a special case only and not to the general case, the situation which it assumes being a limiting point of the possible positions of equilibrium. Moreover, the characteristics of the special case assumed by the classical theory happen not to be those of the economic society in which we actually live.[48]

(It should be noted that by classical theory Keynes is referring to the *followers* of Ricardo, or what is now generally considered to be neoclassical theory.)

A long debate has developed as to whether Keynes is a special case of neoclassical economics or whether neoclassical economics is a special case of Keynesian economics. Underlying this debate seems to be the argument as to whether Keynes should be interpreted as part of the neoclassical tradition (through the use of the so-called neoclassical synthesis) or whether Keynes should be "more closely linked to Ricardo and Marx of the classical tradition" as argued by Jan Kregel in *The Reconstruction of Political Economy.*[49]

Although the debate at this time is perhaps inconclusive (no doubt partly owing to a certain ambiguity in Keynes' writing which lends itself to various contradictory interpretations), two points do stand out. One is that much of Keynes' analysis, and his concerns with the determinants of aggregate income and employment, can indeed be used in a classical-type analysis.[50] The other is that Michal Kalecki, whose analysis is in many ways very similar to that of Keynes and some of whose work actually predates that of the *General Theory,* is clearly working within the classical tradition. The Polish Kalecki drew his inspiration from the reproduction schemes of Volume II of Marx's *Capital* as well as from the work of the Marxist Rosa Luxemburg.[51] It is perhaps for this reason that some modern economists such as Joan Robinson and Amit Bhaduri, who want to return to the classical approach to economics (without Say's Law or the Marxian labor theory of value), call for an analysis within the tradition of Marx, Sraffa, and *Kalecki* (rather than within the tradition of Marx, Sraffa, and Keynes).[52] Indeed, as Harry and Elizabeth Johnson have pointed out, some of the economists currently working at Cambridge (England) and calling themselves post-Keynesians may very well be more indebted to the work and approach of Kalecki rather than to that of Keynes himself.[53]

NOTES

1. "Every commodity (product or instrument of production) is equal to the objectification of a given amount of labor time. Their value, the relation in which they are exchanged against other commodities, or other commodities against them is equal to the quantity of labor time realized in them." *Grundisse,* p. 140.

2. See Appendix A.

3. Cambridge University Press, 1960.

4. On the use of circularity in modern economic theory, see Andras Brody *Proportions, Prices and Planning: A Mathematical Restatement of the Labor Theory of Value,* (New York: American Elsevier, 1970), Chap. 2.2, pp. 84–94.

5. To some, the diagram may appear to be crude. However, it presents (at the risk of oversimplification) what I conceive to be the fundamental issue involved in this study.

6. Note also that the labor theory of value may be viewed as a subset of, or may be incorporated into, the commodity theory of value.

7. It largely follows the interpretation offered by Maurice Dobb, *Theories of Value and Distribution Since Adam Smith: Ideology and Economic Theory* (Cambridge University Press, 1973).

8. On the importance of value theory see, e.g., Lionel Robbins: "The most fundamental propositions of economic analysis are the propositions of the general theory of value. No matter what particular 'school' is in question, no matter what arrangement of subject-matter is adopted, the body of propositions explaining the nature and the determinations of the relation between given goods of the first order will be found to have a pivotal position in the whole system." *An Essay on the Nature and Significance of Economic Science*, 2nd edition (London: Macmillan, 1949), p. 73. For an opposing (minority) viewpoint on the futility of pursuing value theory, see the popular social theorist Daniel Bell, "Models and Reality in Economic Discourse," in *The Public Interest* Special Issue (1980): pp. 46–80.

9. Mill, *Principles*, 1848, Book III, chap. 1; quoted in Schumpeter, *History of Economic Analysis*, p. 603.

10. In this work Schumpeter is being followed in that "By theories of value we mean attempts at indicating the factors that account for a thing's having exchange value or—though this is not strictly the same—the factors that 'regulate' or 'govern' value." [History of Economic Analysis, p. 590.]

11. Ricardo, *The Principles of Political Economy and Taxation* (J. M. Dent and Sons 1973), p. 7.

12. See M. Hollis, and E. Nell, *Rational Economic Man* (Cambridge University Press, 1975); V. C. Walsh and H. N. Gram, *Classical and Neoclassical Theories of General Equilibrium* (Oxford University Press, 1980); and Luigi Pasinetti, *Structural Change and Economic Growth*, Cambridge University Press, 1982), Chap. 1.

13. See, e.g., Adam Smith, *The Wealth of Nations*, Book III.

14. Ricardo, *The Principles of Political Economy and Taxation*, p. 5.

15. Smith, *The Wealth of Nations*, p. 373

16. Ricardo, *The Principles of Political Economy and Taxation* p. 53.

17. See Vladimir Dmitriev, "The Theory of Value of David Ricardo: An Attempt at a Rigorous Analysis," reprinted in Dmitriev, *Economic Essays on Value, Competition and Utility* (Cambridge University Press, 1974); and Piero Sraffa, "Introduction" to David Ricardo, *On The Principles of Political Economy and Taxation*, Vol. I of *Works and Correspondence of Ricardo*, pp. xiii–lxii.

18. See Maurice Dobb, *Theories of Value and Distribution Since Adam Smith* (Cambridge University Press, 1973), Chaps. 3 and 4.

19. Although some might disagree—see, e.g., Frank Hahn, "General Equilibrium Theory," *The Public Interest* Special Issue (1980): 123–138.

20. Harvard University Press, 1947, p. 90.

21. *Schumpeter, History of Economic Analysis*, pp. 911–912.

22. See Note 12.

23. Robbins, *An Essay on the Nature and Significance of Economic Science*, p. 83.

24. Sraffa, *Commodities*, p. v.

25. Wicksteed, "The Scope and Method of Political Economy," *The Economic Journal* **XXIV** (1914): 1–23, reprinted in *A.E.A. Readings in Price Theory* **VI** 1952, pp. 3–26; the quote is from p. 14.

26. Robbins, *An Essay on the Nature and Significance of Economic Science*, pp. 55–56.

27. On this point see Luigi Pasinetti, *Lectures on the Theory of Production* (New York: Columbia University Press, 1977), p. 189.

28. 2nd edition, Oxford University Press, 1946, p. 77. See, also, Samuelson, *Foundations of Economic Analysis*, for the same type of approach.

29. Wicksteed, "The Scope and Method of Political Economy," pp. 19–20.

30. Compare this with, for example, a classical approach by Dmitriev, who argued that "following Ricardo, we take profit on capital to mean only one quite definite form of income *regulated by its own precisely defined laws* . . . the 'profit on capital' is obtained by virtue of

the mere possession of capital . . ." [Dmitriev, *Economic Essays on Value, Competitor and Utility*, p. 77; emphasis added].

31. Hicks, *Value and Capital*, p. 118.

32. See Gary Becker, *Human Capital* (Columbia University Press, 1964). For a useful introduction to human capital theory, see David Gordon, *Theories of Poverty and Underemployment* (D. C. Heath and Company, 1972).

33. Smith, *The Wealth of Nations*, pp. 203–204. See, also, p. 377: "The improved dexterity of a workman may be considered in the same light as a machine or instrument of trade which facilitates and abridges labour, and which, though it costs a certain expense, repays that expense with a profit."

34. Marshall, *Principles of Economics*, 8th edition, p. ix; for his view on the consistency of classical and neoclassical theories of capital, see p. 583.

35. Martin Bronfenbrenner, a self-professed theoretical eclectic, would like to keep *both* approaches: "Why, I wonder, must we remain impaled on the Either-Or? Messy though it seems, I cannot bring myself to discard either system root and branch, or pledge exclusive allegiance to either." ["Review of Walsh and Gram, *Classical and Neoclassical Theories of General Equilibrium*," *History of Political Economy* 12, No. 4 (1980): 621.

36. Wicksteed, "The Scope and Method of Political Economy," p. 3.

37. Ibid., pp. 25–26.

38. Lenin, *Imperialism, The Highest Stage of Capitalism* (Moscow: Progress Publishers, 1975).

39. Luxemburg, *The Accumulation of Capital* (London: Routledge and Kegan Paul, 1951).

40. Hilferding, *Das Finanzkapital*, (Vienna: Wiener Volksbuchhandlung, 1923).

41. Dmitriev, *Economic Essays on Value, Competition and Utility* (Cambridge University Press, 1974); especially the first essay.

42. von Bortkiewicz, "On the correction of Marx's fundamental Theoretical Construction in the Third Volume of Capital," 1907, reprinted in English in E. von Bohm-Bawerk, *Karl Marx and the Close of His System*, edited by Paul Sweezy (New York: Kelly, 1949); and "Value and Price in the Marxian System," *International Economic Papers*, No. 2 (1952).

43. von Neumann, "A Model of General Economic Equilibrium," *Review of Economic Studies* 13, (1945): 1–9.

44. Leontief, *The Structure of the American Economy* (New York: Oxford University Press, 1951).

45. Hicks, *Value and Capital*, p. 266.

46. Keynes, *The General Theory of Employment, Interest, and Money* (Harcourt, Brace and World, 1974), pp. 5 and 17.

47. See Rodney Maddock and Michael Carter, "A Child's Guide to Rational Expectations," *Journal of Economic Literature* **XX**, No. 1 (1982): 39–51; and Federal Reserve Bank of Minneapolis, 1978 *Annual Report*, "Eliminating Policy Surprises: An Inexpensive Way to Beat Inflation," reprinted in Puth, *Current Issues in the American Economy*, pp. 131–136.

48. Keynes, *The General Theory of Employment, Interest, and Money*, p. 1.

49. Macmillan, London, 1973, p. 33.

50. As Pasinetti does in his *Structural Change and Economic Growth*.

51. See Dobb, *Theories of Value and Distribution*, p. 221. For an introduction to the work of Kalecki, see George Feiwel, *The Intellectual Capital of Michal Kalecki* (University of Tennessee Press, 1975).

52. Joan Robinson and Amit Bhaduri, "Accumulation and Exploitation: An Analysis in the Tradition of Marx, Sraffa, and Kalecki," *Cambridge Journal of Economics* 4, No. 2 (1980).

53. Harry and Elizabeth Johnson, *The Shadow of Keynes: Understanding Keynes, Cambridge, and Keynesian Economics* (University of Chicago Press, 1978).

2

SRAFFA AND THE
COMMODITY THEORY OF VALUE

Joan Robinson and Amit Bhaduri have argued that

> Piero Sraffa was completely successful in his aim of providing a basis
> for the critique of neoclassical theory but the model in *Production of
> Commodities by Means of Commodities* provides a very narrow basis
> for constructive analysis.[1]

This chapter will present and interpret Sraffa's basic model, insofar as
it relates to value theory. Sraffa's work, though narrow, is essential, dealing
as it does with value theory. It will later be shown in this study how Marx's
work can then be constructed so as to rest upon Sraffa's theory of value. Of
course, one advantage to Marx's work is that it does provide a very broad
basis for constructive analysis.

Wassily Leontief has suggested that

> Although it rightly claims to be the most rigorous of social sciences,
> economics does not progress—as a typical natural science does—in a
> straight line. Like a broad river slowly winding its way across a flat
> plain, economic thought advances in curves and loops. It turns left and
> right and divides from time to time into separate branches, some of
> which end up in stagnant pools, while others unite again into a single
> stream.[2]

In connection with this view of economics, it is clear that Sraffa
himself has long been interested in and influenced by the classical approach
to economics. In an early 1926 article (which marked the beginning of
modern theoretical work on imperfect competition), Sraffa argued for the
importance of cost (or what may be termed conditions of supply) in the
determination of value:

> This first approximation, as far as it goes, is as important as it is useful: it emphasizes the fundamental factor, namely, the predominant influence of cost of production in the determination of the normal value of commodities. . . .[3]

Recall that by "value" economists mean that which enables a commodity to be exchanged in certain proportions with other commodities, so that when commodities are exchanged for money they may have a definite market price. As Jerome Rothenberg has pointed out,

> 'value theory' is one of the twin pillars supporting the edifice of economic analysis. (The other is income theory.) It is not a branch of normative economics, but of positive economics. It is that branch of pure theory which deals with the determination of market prices on all commodities and productive services (including intermediate goods-capital) and with the influence which these prices have on the allocation of the economy's limited productive resources.[4]

In 1960, Sraffa published the *Production of Commodities by Means of Commodities*. That book was meant to be the prelude to a critique of economic theory (indeed that is the subtitle of the book). In the first two chapters Sraffa develops what the present author has been calling a commodity theory of value.[5]

Sraffa initially assumes a commodity producing society, that is, a society which produces goods with the goal to be exchanged for other goods.[6] In Sraffa's model it takes commodities to produce commodities. Sraffa initially assumes that the system is in a self-reproducing state, with no economic growth. Each commodity is produced in a separate industry and needs other commodities in order to be produced. At the end of each production period (or "harvest," which may be taken to be a year), the commodities must be exchanged with each other in such a ratio that the system can reproduce itself. So, for example, if some of the output of industry *a* is needed as an input in industry *b*, then somehow or other that particular quantity of *a* must end up in industry *b* so that industry *b* can continue to produce in the future.

Sraffa assumes that the output of society is initially given. He does not inquire as to the determinants of the quantity of output produced; he simply takes this as a given. Hence, at this stage of his analysis, what is generally considered to be conditions of "demand" cannot determine value, since Sraffa excludes this from his model.

At this stage of his analysis, Sraffa also takes the production processes actually used in his model as given. There are no possible variations in the quantity of "factor inputs" used to produce the commodity outputs; hence there can be no possible marginal products of factor inputs. (As seen above, in neoclassical economic theory, it is the marginal product of a factor input which helps to determine the price of the factor input—yet here there are no marginal product curves.) As Sraffa points out in his preface,

> No changes in output and (at any rate in Parts I and II) no changes in the proportions in which different means of production are used by an industry are considered, so that no question arises as to the variation or constancy of returns. The investigation is concerned exclusively with such properties of an economic system as do not depend on changes in the scale of production or in the proportions of 'factors' . . . without change either in the scale of an industry or in the 'proportions of the factors of production' there can be neither marginal product nor marginal cost. In a system in which, day after day, production continued unchanged in those respects, the marginal product of a factor (or alternatively the marginal cost of a product) would not merely be hard to find—it just would not be there to be found.[7]

Note that in some ways Sraffa's prelude to a critique of neoclassical economic theory is an external one.[8] In Sraffa's world there are basically no "margins"—hence there can be no marginal cost curves, no marginal revenue curves, no marginal product curves, indeed, no marginal anything. Also, since he ignores the determinants of output, he is also ignoring questions of demand, utility, and consumer behavior in general. This is a major reason why Sraffa's work is so difficult for most economists to understand, since so many of the general ideas and concepts found in neoclassical price theory simply do not exist in Sraffa's world.

Sraffa is, however, concerned with production. As Sraffa points out in his preface, his standpoint "is that of the old classical economists from Adam Smith to Ricardo," a view of the world which "has been submerged and forgotten since the advent of the 'marginal' method."[9]

Sraffa initially considers a two-commodity world.[10] Assume that 280 quarters of wheat and 12 tons of iron are needed to make 400 quarters of wheat (in one production period). Assume that the iron industry needs 120 quarters of wheat and 8 tons of iron to make 20 tons of iron. Assume that there is no "fixed" capital, that is, in each production period, all the means of production are entirely used up. At the end of the production period, the wheat industry must somehow get 12 tons of iron so that it can begin production anew in the next production period. Similarly, at the end of the production period, the iron industry must somehow get 120 quarters of wheat in order to begin production anew. Thus, the requirement that commodities are used to make other commodities, and that the system be able to reproduce itself over time, necessitates that the commodities be traded with each other in certain exchange ratios.[11] In this simple case, 12 tons of iron must be traded for 120 quarters of wheat, so the exchange ratio between the two commodities to reproduce the economic system is 10 quarters of wheat equals 1 ton of iron.[12]

The system can be mathematically formalized. Let Pa be the price of wheat and Pb equal the price of iron.

Then we can say that

$$280Pa + 12Pa = 400Pa \qquad (1)$$

$$120Pa + 8Pb = 20Pb \qquad (2)$$

The first equation says that 280 units of wheat times the price of a unit of wheat plus 12 units of iron times the price of a unit of iron will create 400 units of wheat times the price of a unit of wheat. (The second equation can be interpreted analogously). Suppose this society was on a "wheat" standard, where 1 quarter of wheat was equal to $1 ($Pa = 1$). In that case we could find the price of iron from the first equation:

$$280 + 12Pb = 400$$

$$12Pb = 120$$

$$Pb = 10.$$

In this case the price of 1 one ton of iron would be $10. Thus, 1 ton of iron would be 10 times as expensive as 1 quarter of wheat, or 10 quarters of wheat will exchange for 1 ton of iron, the same as above.

The same idea can be expressed in tabular form:

TABLE 1

	Inputs		Outputs	
	Wheat	Iron	Wheat	Iron
Wheat industry	280	12	400	
Iron industry	120	8		20
TOTAL	400	20	400	20

Table 1 shows that in the wheat industry 280 quarters of wheat and 12 tons of iron make 400 quarters of wheat. At the end of the production period, the wheat industry will keep 280 quarters of wheat so that it can resume the production process in the next production period. It will then trade 120 quarters of wheat for 12 tons of iron, again so that it can resume the production process in the next production period. Similarly, the iron industry, in order to be able to produce the same output the next year (it is assumed that the technology and the level of production do not change) must keep 8 tons of iron and exchange 12 tons of iron with the wheat industry in return for 120 quarters of wheat.

Note that in this system output cannot expand because all of the output is used as inputs. The system produces 400 quarters of wheat and 20 tons of iron in a production period, and it uses up (or productively consumes) 400 quarters of wheat and 20 tons of iron in the same time period.

Next Sraffa gives an example of an economy with three industries.[13]

240 quarters wheat + 12 tons iron + 18 pigs = 450 quarters wheat

90 quarters wheat + 6 tons iron + 12 pigs = 21 tons iron

120 quarters wheat + 3 tons iron + 30 pigs = 60 pigs

Again this system has been constructed so that there is no surplus in the system, so that all outputs are used up as inputs. Again, if the system is to reproduce itself over time, then the various commodities must be traded with each other in very definite proportions.[14] In this case, 10 quarters of wheat must equal 1 ton of iron which must equal 2 pigs. It is commodity production itself, with each commodity being produced by definite quantities of other commodities, which gives the commodities "value" and which requires that the commodities be exchanged in definite ratios or "exchange values."

This system can be generalized. Let $a, b, \ldots, k$ be the various commodities produced. Let A be the quantity annually produced of commodity a, and B be the quantity annually produced of b, etc. Let $Aa, Ba, \ldots, Ka$ be the quantities of $a, b, \ldots, k$ annually used in the industry producing A. Let $Ab, Bb, \ldots, Kb$ be the corresponding quantities used to produce B, and so on. The above quantities represent the amount produced in each industry and the inputs needed in each industry. They are assumed to be known. The unknowns are $Pa, Pb, \ldots, Pk$ which represent the values of the units of commodities $a, b, \ldots, k$. The system can then be represented by a series of k equations

$$AaPa + BaPb + \ldots + KaPk = APa$$

$$AbPa + BbPb + \ldots + KbPk = BPb$$

$$\ldots$$

$$AkPa + BkPb + \ldots + KkPk = KPk$$

Since the system is assumed to be in a self-replacing state, $Aa + Ab + \ldots + Ak = A$; $Ba + Bb + \ldots + Bk = B$; $\ldots$; $Ka + Kb + \ldots + Kk = K$.

Sraffa tersely concludes his first chapter by arguing that

One commodity is taken as standard of value and its price made equal to unity. This leaves $k - 1$ unknowns. Since in the aggregate of the equations the same quantities occur on both sides, any one of the equations can be inferred from the sum of the others. This leaves $k - 1$ independent linear equations which uniquely determine the $k - 1$ prices.[15]

The interpretation offered here is that what Sraffa has indeed done in this first chapter is to set up a commodity theory of value. In his system, commodities have value because they are produced by other commodities. That is why they are able to be exchanged with other commodities. For the system to reproduce itself over time,[16] the commodities will be exchanged with each other in quite definite proportions; hence they will have definite exchange values. When one commodity is taken as a standard of value and its price made equal to unity, this commodity is in effect converted into money. (This is discussed in greater detail in Chapter 7.) When commodities express their value in terms of the one commodity used as the standard of value, they are merely expressing their price. (Again, this will be elaborated upon in Chapter 7.) Hence, Sraffa has elaborated a theory of prices resting upon what may be called a commodity theory of value.

Chapter 2 of Sraffa's work is entitled "Production with a Surplus."[17] Here Sraffa introduces the rate of profit. Profits themselves arise when commodities produce *more* commodities than are used up in production, so that at least one commodity is produced in excess of the quantity of it used up in the production process. Mathematical economists are familiar with this notion which has been given the name "the Hawkins–Simons condition."[18] When the Hawkins–Simons condition is met, that is, when commodities produce more commodities than are used up in the production process, commodities can be said to create surplus value. Surplus value is the value of the excess commodities produced by the production process.

This may be formalized as follows. Assume that there is an average rate of profit and call this rate r. Assume that all payments to commodity inputs are paid in advance. Then

$$(AaPa + BaPb + \ldots + KaPk)(1 + r) = APa$$

$$(AbPa + BbPb + \ldots + KbPk)(1 + r) = BPb$$

$$\ldots$$

$$(AkPa + BkPb + \ldots + KkPk)(1 + r) = KPk$$

and $Aa + Ab + \ldots + Ak$ is less than or equal to A; $Ba + Bb + \ldots + Bk$ is less than or equal to B; $\ldots$; $Ka + Kb + \ldots + Kk$ is less than or equal to K, that is, the quantity produced of each commodity is at least equal to the quantity of it which is used up in all branches of production.

In words, the above says that for each industry, the output of the industry times its price must equal the quantity of all the inputs used in the production process times their respective prices, times one plus the rate of profit. For example, suppose there was a production process which used 100 dollars worth of inputs. If the average rate of profit were 10%, and that industry were making the average rate of profit, then the value of the output of that industry must equal ($100) (1 + 0.10) = $110.

The above equational system contains K independent equations (one for each industry). This can determine the K-1 relative prices (since one commodity is again taken as standard of value and its price is made equal to one) and the rate of profit.[19]

Suppose there was an economy with only two commodities which could be characterized by Table 2:

TABLE 2

	Inputs		Outputs	
	Wheat	Iron	Wheat	Iron
Wheat industry	280	12	575	
Iron industry	120	8		20
TOTAL	400	20	575	20

Now, more commodities are produced as outputs than are consumed as inputs. Here, 20 tons of iron are produced as outputs and are used up as inputs; however, 575 quarters of wheat are produced as outputs, whereas only 400 quarters of wheat are used up as inputs. Thus, the system will have a surplus of 175 quarters of wheat which is not necessary for the reproduction of the system. This surplus is both a physical surplus (175 actual quarters of wheat) and a value surplus, since the wheat itself will have a value. In this model, commodities can be said to have created surplus value (as well as surplus commodities). This surplus will be distributed to the two industries in proportion to the *value* of the advanced commodities in such a way so that the *rate* of profit is the same in both industries.

Mathematically, this may be reformulated

$$(280Pa + 12Pb) (1 + r) = 575Pa$$

$$(120Pa + 8Pb) (1 + r) = 20Pb$$

If the economy were on the "wheat" standard, so that the price of 1 quarter of wheat equaled $1, then there would be two unknowns for which to solve: Pb, which is the price of one ton of iron, and the rate of profit. Solving for this one finds that the rate of profit is 25% and the price of 1 ton of iron equals $15, which means that 1 ton of iron will exchange for 15 quarters of wheat.[20]

Thus, if the level of output is known, and the commodity inputs needed to produce that level of output are also known, then solutions can be found for prices and the rate of profit, assuming that each industry gets the same rate of profit and that the system is reproducing itself over time. There is no need to rely upon "marginal productivities," or embodied labor time in commodities in order to determine relative prices and the rate of profit. The system itself will generate the relative prices and the rate of profit needed to reproduce itself over time. The system itself is simply one of commodities producing commodities by means of commodities. It is for this reason that Sraffa's theoretical system may be said to be based on a commodity theory of value.[21]

NOTES

1. Joan Robinson and Amit Bhaduri, "Accumulation and Exploitation: An Analysis in the Tradition of Marx, Sraffa, and Kalecki," p. 103.

2. "Preface," p. 7 to Brody, *Proportions, Prices and Planning: A Mathematical Restatement of the Labor Theory of Value.*

3. Piero Sraffa, "The Laws of Returns under Competitive Conditions," *The Economic Journal* **XXXVI** (1926): 535-550, reprinted in *A.E.A. Readings in Price Theory*, VI, pp. 180-197; the quote is from page 187.

4. Rothenberg, "Values and Value Theory in Economics" in Sherman Krupp, *The Structure of Economic Science: Essays on Methodology*, pp. 221-242; the quote is from p. 221.

5. I am not familiar with anyone else who has given Sraffa's theory of value that name. Indeed some economists have mistakenly assumed that Sraffa has no theory of value at all; see, e.g., Claudio Napoleoni, who suggests that "Sraffa's break with the subject-object relationship is a break with all the theories of value." ("Sraffa's 'Tabula Rosa'," *New Left Review* (Nov.-Dec. 1978): 77).

6. See Chapter 5 for some of the historical preconditions which are necessary before human societies can progress to the level of commodity production, that is, routinized production for exchange.

7. Sraffa, *Production of Commodities by Means of Commodities*, p. v.

8. See Alessandro Roncaglia, *Sraffa and the Theory of Prices* (New York: Wiley, 1978), pp. 98-99.

9. Sraffa, *Production of Commodities by Means of Commodities*, p. v.

10. Ibid., p. 3. Sraffa's opening sentence is "Let us consider an extremely simple society which produces just enough to maintain itself." This sentence has been the source of some confusion, since it is slightly misleading. Sraffa is assuming a commodity producing society, which is therefore a relatively complex one (not a simple one) and which can only arise at a certain stage of societal development. Thus, as Jesse Schwartz has entitled an article, "There is nothing simple about a commodity," (in Schwartz, ed., *The Subtle Anatomy of Capitalism*, pp. 474-500). For an elaboration of this point, see Chapters 5, 6, and 8 of this study. A

preliminary discussion by Sraffa on what he means by a commodity might have eliminated the source of much confusion. It may be noted here that this study will not go into the controversy of what a "service" is or how to handle the question of "services" in economic theory.

11. Alternatively, one may say that the above requirements determine the exchange ratios with which commodities must exchange.

12. Sraffa, *Production of Commodities by Means of Commodities*, p. 3.

13. Ibid., p. 4.

14. Alternatively, one may say that the requirement that the system reproduce itself over time, and the production conditions under which commodities are needed as inputs to produce commodities as outputs serve to *determine* the ratios with which the various commodities will exchange with each other.

15. Sraffa, *Production of Commodities by Means of Commodities*, p. 5.

16. This is an assumption of Sraffa's model. For a brief defense of Sraffa's approach, which, at this stage of his analysis, may be termed mechanistic, see Hawkins, *The Language of Nature* (San Francisco: 1964) pp. 333-335.

17. Sraffa, *Production of Commodities by Means of Commodities*, pp. 6-11.

18. This also implies that the Frobenius root of an input-output matrix must be less than one. For a discussion of some of the mathematical issues involved with this type of analysis (which deals primarily with the properties of non-negative square matrixes), see Akira Takayama, *Mathematical Economics* (Hinsdale, Ill.: The Dryden Press, 1974), pp. 360-409.

For the development of the Hawkins-Simons condition, see Hawkins, *Conditions of Macroeconomic Stability*, p. 312. This mathematical proof (which for economists is perhaps of relatively minor importance compared to the other issues discussed in the rest of that paper) contained an error which was spotted by Herbert Simon. (See David Hawkins and Herbert Simon, "Note: Some Conditions of Macroeconomic Stability," *Econometrica* **17** (July-October, 1949): 245-248 for the correct proof.

19. Sraffa, *Production of Commodities by Means of Commodities*, p. 7. Alternatively, one may say that relative prices and the rate of profit are *determined* by: (a) the requirement that the system reproduce itself over time; (b) the production conditions under which commodities are needed as inputs to produce commodities as outputs; and (c) the institutional requirement imposed upon this commodity producing system that each industry receive the same rate of profit.

20. If this is compared with the example given in Table 1, it will be found that productivity essentially increased in the wheat industry, which would cause the price of wheat to fall. Since in both cases the price of a unit of wheat has been set equal to one by definition, this fall in the price of wheat must manifest itself by a rise in the price of iron, which indeed is the case.

21. The ability of the system itself to generate values also rests upon the principle of duality. As Brody explains: "Very simply the economic principle of duality means that all intricate productive processes can be examined from two aspects: as physical processes creating use values and as processes simultaneously assigning values to them. . . . In the analysis of such complicated systems certain parts of the system (its physical parameters or—in economic systems—certain activities, types of labor and of product) may not be directly commensurable because of their naturally heterogeneous character. However, for a clearer description and understanding of the system's operation, and later, for the control of these processes, a common denominator, a homogeneous measure becomes necessary. This problem of order, measurement and control can be solved by taking into account those very interrelations that connect the parts of the system. *Thus the system provides its own measuring instrument based on its own intrinsic laws and interrelations.*" [Brody, *Proportions, Prices and Planning: A Mathematical Restatement of the Labor Theory of Value*, pp. 62-63 (emphasis added); for Brody's entire discussion on duality, see pp. 62-67.]

3

THEORETICAL IMPLICATIONS FROM THE COMMODITY THEORY OF VALUE

Sraffa originally put forth his work as a prelude to a critique of neoclassical economic theory. Hence, we will briefly discuss this critique and the resulting capital controversies and "reswitching controversies" which his work generated. Certain peculiarities arise from the fact that Sraffa presented his work primarily as a *critique* of neoclassical theory, rather than as an explicitly rival economic theory. These peculiarities are noted: they include the timing and amount of wage payments. Suggestions are offered on how these issues should be handled when using the Sraffian framework in a positive manner. References are also given to those fields of economic analysis where work is currently being done within a Sraffian framework, using a commodity theory of value.

The commodity theory of value, which Sraffa used, has also been used to criticize the Marxian labor theory of value. A brief explanation of Marx's labor theory of value, and the "transformation problem" which seems intrinsic to this theory of value, are given. Criticisms of the labor theory of value, criticisms which seem to be largely based upon a commodity theory of value, are presented. Please note: it is not the intention of this chapter to add to or critically evaluate these critiques of the labor theory of value.[1] However, two points are raised, points which seem to be insufficiently realized in the literature. One, it seems that criticisms of Marx's labor theory of value are largely based upon another theory of value, namely, a commodity theory of value. Two, it seems that if one wants to work within a Marxian framework without using the labor theory of value, then the labor theory of value must be replaced by another theory of value. Subsequent chapters of this study show how this can be done.

In his work, Sraffa treats labor inputs differently from other commodity inputs, being paid both at the end of the production period and being indeterminant, that is, Sraffa lets the wage rate vary. One of the reasons

Sraffa does this is to help develop the argument that capital, as an independent "factor of production," cannot be measured independently of the distribution of income among people. Sraffa, by letting the wage rate vary, finds that

> Reversals in the direction of the movement of relative prices, in the face of unchanged methods of production, cannot be reconciled with *any* notion of capital as a measurable quantity independent of distribution and prices.[2]

The measurability of capital is an important issue in neoclassical theory, and Sraffa's work has largely generated the so-called capital controversy.[3] Sraffa's work constitutes a critique of neoclassical price theory, since that theory uses the quantity of capital to help determine the rate of profit and hence to help determine all other relative prices in that theoretical model of the world.

As C. E. Ferguson, a defender of neoclassical theory, points out:

> But in the last analysis neo-classical theory, in its simple and not-so-simple forms, depends upon the basic nature of the 'thing' called capital.[4]

Ferguson goes on to assert that

> . . . we can say that the lower rate of interest, the greater the capital intensity of production. All other neoclassical results follow immediately from this simple relation.[5]

It is exactly this statement by Ferguson which Sraffa has called into question.

As a side issue, at first much of the controversy generated by Sraffa centered around the *empirical* question of the likelihood of "reswitching."[6] Reswitching occurs when there is a choice of production techniques, and the same technique becomes the most profitable one to use at *both* relatively low and relatively high rates of profit.[7] This way of looking at the capital controversy in general, and the reswitching problem in particular (i.e., that what is at question is an empirical issue), seems to be based upon a fundamental methodological confusion. One cannot answer a theoretical criticism of the neoclassical theory of price determination by testing the empirical likelihood of reswitching actually occurring in practice.[8]

Currently, the capital controversy seems to be centering around the vulnerability of neoclassical economics (to the Sraffian-based criticism) in its fully disaggregated general equilibrium version.[9] However slowly, the depths of the criticism of neoclassical economics is gradually being felt by the economics profession. So, for example, Christopher Bliss, in a recent textbook on capital and income distribution (which is more or less consciously seen as an alternative to the Marxian system),[10] rarely uses an aggregate production function and he minimizes the importance of marginal ideas.[11]

As pointed out in Chapter 2, Sraffa's work, although specifically designed to be a prelude to a critique of neoclassical economic theory, is also an alternative theory of prices [12] based upon a commodity theory of value. As an alternative theory of prices, it seems to me to be a mistake to treat labor power differently from any other commodity input, *insofar* as having wages paid at the end of the production process or having wages be indeterminant. For one thing, this has obscured the fact that Sraffa is indeed using a theory of value which is simply based on (literally) the production of commodities by means of commodities. Also, in capitalism, labor power, that is, a worker's capacity to labor, is in many (though not all) ways a commodity just as any other. At a given time, under given socio-economic conditions, the amount of work labor power does and its price[13] (i.e., the wage rate) is given. Hence, labor power may (in the above respects) be treated as any other commodity input and its price at any time may be taken as given.[14]

Currently, work based on Sraffian-type models is being done in such diverse fields as general economic theory,[15] international economics,[16] rent and urban economics,[17] the handling of fixed capital and joint production,[18] as well as in economic anthropology.[19]

As far as Marxist economics is concerned, Sraffa's work was warmly received by Marxist economists when it first appeared, insofar as it was perceived as a critique of neoclassical economic theory. Indeed, some Marxists felt it to be compatible with Marxist economic theory.[20] However, Sraffa's framework was also relatively quickly used to criticize Marx's labor theory of value.

It turns out that a major difficulty in attempting to criticize Marx's theory of value arises from the fact that Marx uses the labor theory of value not only to help determine relative prices but also to analyze the "laws of motion" of capitalist societies.[21] Heretofore criticisms of the labor theory of value have largely focussed on its usefulness as a form of price theory, whereas defenders of it have focussed on its usefulness in analyzing broader social issues. Thus, attackers and defenders of the labor theory of value have often been arguing past one another, each discussing separate questions. This can be clearly seen in the attack, at the beginning of the century, on Marxist economics by Bohm-Bawerk and the subsequent reply by Rudolf Hilferding.[22] This debate (or lack of one) was largely repeated in the *Journal of Economic Literature* in the early and mid 1970s. Here, Paul Samuelson, one of the giants of the economics profession, took the role of the attacker of the labor theory of value (as a theory of relative prices), while William Baumol, another giant in the economics profession, took the role of defender of the labor theory of value (as being particularly useful for getting beneath the surface manifestations of capitalist societies.)[23]

At this point, it is necessary *to attempt* a quick summary of the labor theory of value.[24] In Marxian economics, the value of a commodity is the amount of socially necessary labor time it takes to produce (or more accurately, to reproduce) that commodity.[25] The value of a worker's capacity to work, that is, of labor power, is the amount of socially necessary labor time it takes to reproduce that worker (and the worker's family).[26] This is also called the value of variable capital or v. The value of labor power ultimately reduces to the value of the commodities which the worker and the worker's family need to consume in order to live.[27] The value of the commodities which the worker produces over and above that needed to reproduce himself and his family is called surplus value (or s). The rate of surplus value (or the rate of "exploitation") is s/v. For example, if workers work an 8 hour day and it only takes 2 hours for the workers to produce commodities equal to the value of their social reproduction, then the rate of surplus value is $6/2 = 300\%$.

Marx divides the capital owned by the capitalists into variable capital (the amount of money invested in labor power) and constant capital, i.e., the value of the rest of the capital invested by the capitalist. It is held that constant capital cannot create surplus value — only variable capital can.[28] Thus, according to Marx,

> It is easy to form the notion that machinery as such posits value, because it acts as a productive power of labor. But if machinery required no labour, then it would be able to increase the use value; but the exchange value which it would create would never be greater than its own costs of production, its own value, the labour objectified in it.[29]

Since only labor power creates surplus value, more surplus value is created in those industries which are relatively labor intensive (or, as Marx says, have a low organic composition of capital) than are relatively capital intensive (or have what Marx calls a high organic composition of capital).[30] However, capitalists do not merely receive the surplus value created in their own industry. Instead, capitalists receive (in long-run equilibrium) income in proportion to the amount of money which they have invested in their own enterprise. Thus, in the process of the equalization of the monetary rate of profits, capitalists in industries with a high organic composition of capital will receive more surplus value than their workers actually produce, while those capitalists in industries with a low organic composition of capital will receive less surplus value than their own workers actually produce. Therefore, in the process of the equalization of the monetary rate of profit in all industries, there is a shift of surplus value from industries with a low organic composition of capital to those with a high organic composition. This shift of surplus value means that, in general, Marxian values will not equal Marxian prices of production. Marx himself uses value analysis in Volumes I and II of *Capital* (where value is the amount of labor time embodied in the commodity); it is only in Volume III of *Capital* that Marx discusses the transformation of values into prices of production, in which case surplus value is appropriated by the capitalist in proportion to the amount of money which he has invested in his total capital (i.e., in both variable and constant capital).

The need (and resulting perplexities) of going from Marx's value categories to price categories has been referred to in the literature as the "transformation problem." In spite of the transformation from values to prices of production, Marx held that

> . . . the sum of the profits in all spheres of production must equal the sum of the surplus-values, and the sum of the prices of production of the total social product equal the sum of its value.[31]

Marx felt that the mass of surplus value would equal the mass of profits (assuming no rent or interest)[32] and that the rate of profit in value terms $(s/(v + c))$ would equal the rate of profit in money terms.

Much of the criticism of the labor theory of value, which is based upon what is here being called the commodity theory of value, has centered upon the transformation problem. It was the obscure Russian economist, Vladimir Dmitriev, who first showed how to calculate labor values without having to "*historically trace back* the means of production (tools) used in each step to the original instance of producing a tool with free land and unaided labour."[33]

Largely inspired by Sraffa's *Production of Commodities by Means of Commodities,* many modern economists have calculated the values of commodities and compared them with those prices of production found by using what is here called a commodity theory of value.[34] They have found some paradoxes and have often used these paradoxes to argue against Marx's labor theory of value. For example, Abraham-Frois and Berrebi have concluded that

> Contrary to Marx's thesis, not all branches of production participate in the determination of the general rate of profit, which is determined exclusively by the conditions of production in the sectors producing production goods on one hand, and wage goods on the other. The general rate of profit is exclusively determined by the direct and indirect production of the commodities of these two sectors while the conditions

of production of luxury goods have no influence whatsoever on the determination of the general rate of profit. . . .

We have already seen that the scheme of 'transformation' of values into prices of production set out by Marx emphasizes on the one hand the equality between the sum of profits and the sum of surplus-value and the equality between the sum of prices and the sum of values on the other. Once the system of prices of production is written in a logically consistent manner and not in the approximate way that Marx suggested . . . there is no longer any logical reason why these equalities should be true in general. . . .

The system of prices (of production) is thus independent of the value system; this poses a fundamental challenge to Marxian theory since for Marx the 'transformation' problem gave at the same time an explanation and a causal relation of the following type: value - rate of profit - price of production.[35]

Steedman, in what is perhaps the most comprehensive set of criticisms of the labor theory of value derived from a Sraffian perspective, has drawn (among others) the following conclusions:

If there is only one available method for the production of each commodity, each method using only circulating capital and producing only one product then:

i) the physical quantities of commodities and of labour specifying the methods of production, together with the physical quantities of commodities specifying the given real wage rate, suffice to determine the rate of profit (and the associated prices of production);

ii) the labour-time required (directly or indirectly) to produce any commodity — and thus the value of any commodity — is determined by the physical data relating to the methods of production; it follows that value magnitudes are, at best, redundant in the determination of the rate of profit (and prices of production);. . .

If there are alternative methods of production then:

i) the profit maximizing choice of production methods will depend on the given real wage rate — but, for a given wage, the rate of profit and prices of production are still determined by the physical quantities representing the alternative production methods and that real wage;

ii) the amount of labour-time required for the production of commodities are only determined once the choice of production methods is known. But that choice is made in maximizing the rate of profit. The determination of the profit rate (and prices of production) is thus logically prior to the determination of the values of commodities. Clearly, then, values cannot determine the rate of profit (or the prices of production) . . .

and finally

> the rate of profit is not in general, equal to total surplus value divided by
> the sum of total constant capital and total variable capital ($s/c + v$).[36]

On the basis on this sort of criticism, some economists have called for
work to be done within a Marxist framework, but without the labor theory
of value.[37] Other economists have attempted to reformulate the labor
theory of value, cognizant of the criticism of it taken from a Sraffian
perspective,[38] while many others have attempted to defend the labor theory
of value.[39] Many Marxist economist contend that the Sraffian and Marxist
approaches are absolutely incompatible. So, for example, Paul Mattick, in
reference to Sraffa's work, has argued that

> The past 'decade of high criticism' . . . remained within the confines of
> bourgeois theory; thus, it could lead only to an ideologically more ade-
> quate theory of capitalist production than that provided by the now
> bankrupt neoclassical theory.[40]

Fine and Harris have argued that

> There is no way in which the neo-Ricardian propositions can be united
> with those of the Fundamentalists in one whole.[41]

Many Marxist economists insist that

> The importance of value analysis lies in the correct interpretation of the
> concept 'laws of motion'—here value analysis is indispensible.[42]

On the other hand, some work is being done using a Marxist
framework, but deliberately not using the labor theory of value.[43] The problem with this approach is (at least) twofold. On the one hand, it is still not
entirely clear what is left of Marx's work when the labor theory of value is
abandoned. Marx's theory of value runs throughout *Capital*. This is
because *Capital* is about the capitalist mode of production, and that mode
of production is based upon the production of value, and particularly
surplus value. This is why value is everywhere throughout Marx's work:
production based upon value guides the production and reproduction of
both the means of production as well as the social relations of production.[44]
Consequently, value for Marx refers to not only so-called quantitative
aspects (e.g., in some sense determining prices and profits) of capitalism,
but also to qualitative aspects of captialism (e.g., the actual social relations
of production, the development of various Marxist concepts, etc.).[45]

In light of this, it seems that abandoning the labor theory of value requires at the same time the use of another theory of value upon which Marx's theoretical apparatus can rest. This brings us to our second point: it is insufficiently realized that Sraffa and the Sraffian-based criticisms of the labor theory of value are essentially using another theory of value, namely, a commodity theory of value. It is one of the essential themes of the present work that the commodity theory of value is so close to the labor theory of value (indeed it can be viewed as a generalization of the labor theory of value) that it can be inserted into the Marxian framework in place of the labor theory of value. In so doing, very little of Marx's work needs to be changed.[46] To help dramatize the difference between the labor theory of value and the commodity theory of value (and to show that they are in fact two different theories of value) it may be interesting to consider a model of a fully automated society.

NOTES

1. To do so properly would require another study.
2. Sraffa, *Production of Commodities by Means of Commodities,* p. 38; emphasis in original.
3. For a review of this complex subject, see G. C. Harcourt, *Some Cambridge Controversies in the Theory of Capital* (Cambridge University Press, 1972).
4. C. E. Ferguson, *The Neoclassical Theory of Production and Distribution* (Cambridge University Press, 1969), p. 251.
5. Ibid., p. 252. In this regard, see also the quote by Hicks, discussed in Chapter 1.
6. See ibid., p. 258; William J. Baumol, *Economic Theory and Operations Analysis,* 4th edition, (Englewood Cliffs, N.J.: Prentice-Hall, 1977), p, 665; Paul Samuelson, *Economics,* 9th edition, (McGraw-Hill, 1973), p. 616.
7. See Sraffa, *Production of Commodities by Means of Commodities,* Chap. 12, pp. 81–87.
8. For further information on this point, see Roncaglia, *Sraffa and The Theory of Prices,* pp. 102–103.
9. See the essays in Murray Brown, Kazuo Sato, and Zarembka, eds., *Essays in Modern Capital Theory* (New York: American Elsevier, 1975).
10. Christopher Bliss, *Capital Theory and the Distribution of Income* (New York: American Elsevier, 1975), p. 352.
11. Ibid.
12. Indeed this is the theme of Roncaglia, *Sraffa and The Theory of Prices.*
13. As well as the prices of other inputs.
14. This is how Ian Steedman treats workers in *Marx After Sraffa,* a major work criticizing the labor theory of value from a Sraffian perspective. Mathematically, this reduces the number of equations by one (since labor power is not capitalistically produced; instead it is produced largely in the family). However, the number of unknowns is also reduced by one (the price of labor power, i.e., the wage rate, being given exogenously). Thus the system is still mathematically determined. On this point, see also Dmitriev, *Economic Essays on Value, Competition and Utility,* p. 74. For discussion of the assertion that it makes very little

difference in the nature of the system determining relative prices whether workers are paid at the beginning or the end of the production process, see Roncaglia, *Sraffa and The Theory of Prices*, pp. 29–31, and Steedman, *Marx After Sraffa*, pp. 103–105.

15. For two prominent examples, see Luigi Pasinetti, *Structural Change and Economic Growth*, 1981, and Michio Morishima, *The Economic Theory of Modern Society* (Cambridge University Press, 1976).

16. See the articles in Ian Steedman, ed., *Fundamental Issues in Trade Theory*, (New York: St. Martins Press, 1979), as well as Steedman's *Trade Amongst Growing Economies* (Cambridge University Press, 1980).

17. On this, see Pradeep Bandyopadhyay's "Neo-Ricardianism in Urban Analysis," *The International Journal of Urban and Regional Research*, 6(1) (1982), as well as his "Marxist Urban Analysis and the Economic Theory of Rent," *Science and Society* **XLIV** (1) (1982).

18. See the essays in Luigi Pasinetti, ed. *Essays on the Theory of Joint Production* (Columbia University Press, 1980), and A. van Schaik, *Reproduction and Fixed Capital* (Tilburg University Press, 1976).

19. Stephen Gudeman, "Anthropological Economics: The Question of Distribution," *Annual Review of Anthropology* **7** (1978): 347–379, and Gudeman, *The Demise of a Rural Economy*, 1978.

20. See, e.g., Ronald Meek, "Introduction to the Second Edition" in *Studies in the Labor Theory of Value*, and Maurice Dobb, *Theories of Value and Distribution Since Adam Smith*.

21. So, for example, Marx argues in Vol. III of *Capital*, when he is discussing prices of production, that "The value of the commodity remains important as a basis because the concept of money cannot be developed on any other foundation, and price, in its general meaning, is but value in the form of money." [p. 193] For a development of the concept of money based upon a commodity theory of value, see Chapter 7.

22. Bohm-Bawerk, *Karl Marx and the Close of His System*, edited by Paul Sweezy, and Rudolf Hilferding, "Bohm-Bawerk's Criticism of Marx," in the same work.

23. Paul Samuelson, "Understanding the Marxian Notion of Exploitation: A Summary of the So-Called Transformation Problem Between Marxian Values and Competitive Prices" *Journal of Economic Literature* **IX**, No. 2 (1971): 399–443; Samuelson, "The Economics of Marx: An Ecumenical Reply," *Journal of Economic Literature* **X**, (June 1972): 51–57; Samuelson, "Reply on Marxian Matters," *Journal of Economic Literature* **XI** (1973): 64–68; Samuelson, "Insight and Detour in the Theory of Exploitation: A Reply to Baumol," *Journal of Economic Literature* **XII** (March 1974): 62–70; Samuelson, "Rejoinder: Merlin Unclothed, A Final Word," *Journal of Economic Literature* **12** (March 1974): 75–77. For Baumol's point of view, see "The Transformation of Values: What Marx 'Really' Meant (An Interpretation)," *Journal of Economic Literature* **XII** (March 1974): 51–62, and "Comment," *Journal of Economic Literature* **XII** (March 1974): 74–75. The amount of heat engendered between the two is rather interesting in light of the fact that *neither* of the two economists can be considered to be a Marxist. Among economists more directly influenced by Marx's work, the amount of heat generated by issues concerning the usefulness and validity of the labor theory of value has been very great indeed. To cite just one example, in England, disagreements over this issue caused many economists to leave the Conference of Socialist Economists, which as a body generally defended the use of the labor theory of value. See Simon Clarke, "The Value of Value: Rereading 'Capital'," *Capital and Class* (Spring 1980): 1–18, and the book which the Conference of Socialist Economists put out on the labor theory of value, Diane Elson, ed., *Value, The Representation of Labour in Capitalism* (London: CSE Books, 1979).

24. The "correct" interpretation of the labor theory of value is itself a highly controversial issue. This is partly because, as Hodgson has pointed out, "Marx never made it clear what was meant by the labor theory of value. In fact, as far as I am aware, he never used the term. Sometimes, but rarely, he used the term 'law of value'. Hence it is very difficult to impute a precise meaning to the former phrase." [Marx Without the Labor Theory of Value, p. 60.]

25. "The value of every commodity . . . is determined not by the necessary labour-time contained in it, but by the *social* labour-time required for its reproduction." [*Capital*, Vol. III, p. 141; emphasis in original.]

26. "As in the case of every other commodity so in that of labour-power its value is determined by the amount of labour necessary for its reproduction; that the amount of this labour is determined by the value of the labourer's necessary means of subsistance, hence is equal to the labour required for the reproduction of the very conditions of his life, that is peculiar for this commodity (labour-power), but no more peculiar than the fact that the value of labouring cattle is determined by the value of the means of subsistence necessary for its maintenance, i.e., by the amount of human labour necessary to produce these means of subsistence." [*Capital*, Vol. II, p. 382.]

27. "The value of labour-power is determined by the value of the necessaries of life habitually required by the average labourer. The quantity of these necessaries is known at any given epoch of a given society, and can therefore be treated as a constant magnitude. What changes, is the value of this quantity." [*Capital*, Vol. I, p. 568.]

28. "But the creation of surplus-value . . . arises out of the exchange of value for value-creating power, out of the conversion of a constant into a variable magnitude." [*Capital*, Vol. II, p. 220.]

29. Marx, *Grundrisse*, p. 767, fn.

30. For present purposes, difficulty in measuring the labor intensity of an industry, or an industry's organic composition of capital, will be ignored. For a discussion of this issue, see Pradeep Bandyopadhyay, "The Renewal of Marx's Economics," *Catalyst*, No. 12 (1978).

31. Marx, *Capital*, Vol. III, p. 173.

32. "Surplus-value and profit are actually the same thing and numerically equal." [*Capital*, Vol. III, p. 48.]

33. Pradeep Bandyopadhyay, "The Renewal of Marx's Economics," *Catalyst*, No. 12 (1978) (emphasis in original). This article contains a good introduction to some of Dmitriev's theoretical work with reference to modern Marxist economics. For more on this point, see Appendix B.

34. This sort of comparison was also made earlier, see, e.g., Dmitriev and particularly Bortkiewicz's work. As Steedman in *Marx After Sraffa* has noted, "It might be wondered whether 'Marx after Dmitriev' or 'Marx after Bortkiewicz' might not be a proper title for the present work but Sraffa's work has proved to mark a turning point, by providing a rigorous framework of analysis within which the pioneering works of Dmitriev and Bortkiewicz become (important) special cases." [28 fn.]

35. Abraham-Frois and Berrebi, *Theory of Value, Prices and Accumulation: A Mathematical Integration of Marx, von Neumann and Sraffa* (Cambridge University Press, 1979), particularly Chap. 1, pp. 1–31; the above quotes are from pp. 24, 26, and 28, respectively.

36. Steedman, *Marx After Sraffa*, pp. 202–205.

37. Ibid., pp. 206–207; Joan Robinson and Amit Bhaduri, "Accumulation and Exploitation: An Analysis in the Tradition of Marx, Sraffa and Kalecki," *Cambridge Journal of Economics* 4, No. 2 (1980); Pierangelo Garegnani, "Sraffa's Revival of Marxist Economic Theory," *New Left Review*, No. 112, (Nov.-Dec. 1978): 71–75.

38. See, among others, Michio Morishima, *Marx's Economics: A Dual Theory of Value and Growth* (Cambridge University Press, 1973); Robert Paul Wolff, "A Critique and Reinterpretation of Marx's Labor Theory of Value," *Philosophy and Public Affairs* (Spring 1981): 89–120; and Sam Bowles and Herb Gintis, "Structure and Practice in the Labor Theory of Value," *Review of Radical Political Economy* 12, No. 4 (1981). In a sense, this last article may be viewed as the converse of the present study. In their attempt to save the labor theory of value (through its reformulation), Bowles and Gintis argue that much of Marx's work (particularly the early parts of *Capital*) must be discarded. The approach taken here is to discard the labor theory of value and yet salvage as much of Marx's work as possible.

39. See, among other defenses of the labor theory of value, B. Fine and L. Harris, "Controversial Issues in Marxist Economic Theory," *The Socialist Register,* London, 1976, pp. 141–178; the essays in Diane Elson, *Value, the Representations of Labour in Capitalism*; Anwar Shaikh, "Marx's Theory of Value and the 'Transformation Problem'," in *Schwartz*, pp. 106–139; Thomas Sekine, "The Necessity of the Law of Value," *Science and Society* **XLIV**, No. 3 (1980): 289–304; Erik Olin Wright, "The Value Controversy and Social Research," *New Left Review* (July–August, 1979): 53–82; and David Laibman, "Exploitation, Commodity Relations and Capitalism: A Defense of the Labor-Value Formulation," *Science and Society* **XLIV**, No. 3 (1980): 274–288.

40. Paul Mattick, "Review of Maurice Dobb, 'Theories of Value and Distribution Since Adam Smith," *Science and Society* **XXXVIII**, No. 2 (1974): 222–223.

41. Fine and Harris, "Controversial Issue in Marxist Economic Theory," p. 174.

42. David Laibman, "Values and Prices of Production: The Political Economy of the Transformation Problem," *Science and Society* **XXXVII** (Winter 1974): 436.

43. See, for example, Geoff Hodgson, "A Theory of Exploitation Without the Labor Theory of Value," *Science and Society* **XLIV**, No. 3 (1980): 257–273; G. A. Cohen, *Karl Marx's Theory of History: A Defense* (Princeton, N.J.: Princeton University Press, 1978); Marco Lippi, *Value and Naturalism in Marx* (London: N.L.B. 1979); and Arun Bose, *Marxian and Post-Marxian Political Economy* (Penguin Books, 1975) and *Marx on Exploitation and Inequality* (Oxford University Press, 1980).

44. "Capitalist production, therefore, under its aspect of continuous connected process, of a process of reproduction, produces not only commodities, not only surplus-value, but it also produces and reproduces the capitalist relation; on the one side the capitalist, on the other the wage-labourer." [*Capital*, Vol. I, p. 633.]

45. See, for example, Martin Nicolaus, who argues that "The determination of value is the major question to which the work [i.e., the *Grundrisse*] as a whole addresses itself. . . . The bulk of the content is the examination of this question in its various aspects, at various levels of abstraction and with different degrees of simplicity or complexity." [Nicolaus, "Forward" to *Grundrisse*, p. 16.]

46. This is particularly true with what have come to be called the qualitative aspects of Marx's analysis. Quantitatively, certain discrepancies arise depending upon whether Marx's labor theory of value is used, to determine such things as the rate of profit, or whether the commodity theory of value is so used. Most importantly, using a commodity theory of value, there is no reason to suppose a falling rate of profit with technological change. (See Marx, *Capital*, Vol. III, Part III, pp. 211–266.) Indeed, using a commodity theory of value, with technological change (assuming it does not take place solely in those industries producing luxury goods) and wages being constant, profits will *rise*, not *fall*. (This was first pointed out by Bortkiewicz, "Value and Price in the Marxian System," pp. 47–48.) Also, there is no reason to suppose that those countries which have a "low organic composition of capital" (i.e., are relatively backward in the development of their technology) should have a higher average rate of profit than those countries which have a "high organic composition of capital" (i.e., are more technologically advanced). Indeed, ceteris paribus, the more developed country (in terms of technology) will have a higher rate of profit than the relatively backward country. (See Spencer Pack, "Cambridge Theories of Underdevelopment," Presentation to International Workshop, University of New Hampshire, Spring 1981.)

4

A MODEL OF A
FULLY AUTOMATED SOCIETY

Here we will consider a model of a fully automated society. This model will show how equilibrium relative prices and profits may be calculated in such a society. This raises issues which, although first put forward by the Russian economist, Vladimir Dmitriev, in 1898,[1] have been inappropriately neglected in recent studies of Marxist political economy. Thus, this model will be used to

(a) present another criticism or paradox facing the labor theory of value;[2] and

(b) further illustrate that the Sraffian Marxists or neo-Ricardians are using a commodity theory of value, a theory of value which, though in many ways very similar to Marx's labor theory of value, is yet nonetheless distinctly different from it.

It is sometimes felt by Marxists that the capitalist mode of production is historically limited for strictly economic reasons. The ultimate end of capitalism (assuming it is not previously overthrown) would be when there is a fully automated society. In a fully automated society, there would be no productive workers. Without productive workers, there could be no surplus value. Without surplus value, there could be no profits. Furthermore, in a fully automated society, the machines themselves would have no value. Thus even though the machines were in the past constructed by human labor, the fact that they would be currently reproducing themselves would mean that they would have zero value, since, according to Marx,

> the value of every commodity—thus also of the commodities making up the capital—is determined not by the necessary labour-time contained in it, but by the *social* labour-time required for its reproduction.[3]

43

Since no social labor-time would be required to reproduce anything in a fully automated society, there would be no value, no surplus value, and no rate of surplus value.[4] Furthermore, there would be no profits. It would appear that the ultimate catastrophe had befallen the capitalist class—in their drive to increase productivity they had expelled all productive labor; since, according to the labor theory of value, only labor, and not machines, can produce surplus value, profits, and the rate of profit, in a fully automated society, these would have all disappeared, and production (which in this society is production for profit) would necessarily cease.

Thus, Ernest Mandel argues that

> We have here arrived at the absolute inner limit of the capitalist mode of production. This absolute limit lies neither in the complete capitalist penetration of the world market (i.e., the elimination of non-capitalist realms of production)—as Rosa Luxemburg believed—nor in the ultimate impossibility of valorizing total accumulated capital . . . it lies in the fact that the mass of surplus-value itself necessarily diminishes as a result of the elimination of living labour from the production process in the course of the final stage of mechanization—automation. Capitalism is incompatible with fully automated production in the whole of industry and agriculture because this no longer allows the creation of surplus-value or valorization of capital. It is hence impossible for automation to spread to the entire realm of production in the age of late capitalism.[5]

This conclusion of Mandel appears to follow logically from the labor theory of value. Yet, according to the commodity theory of value, this analysis seems to be misleading and erroneous. Using the commodity theory of value, it turns out that there conceivably could be a fully automated society based upon commodity production and ownership of the means of production by one social class, with a positive rate of profit, as well as positive relative prices among commodities.[6]

To take a specific example, imagine a fully automated society which produces only three commodities: computers, gold, and wheat. Suppose that for the economy as a whole there are 56 computers. Suppose 28 of those computers are in the computer making industry. Suppose that in 1 year they can make 56 new computers, and in so doing they are completely used up. Suppose that in the gold industry 16 computers can make 48 units of gold in 1 year, and in the wheat industry 12 computers can grow 8 units of wheat in 1 year, and that in both of these industries at the end of 1 year the original computers are entirely used up. (See Table 3.)

In 1 year 56 computers can make 56 new computers, 48 units of gold, and 8 units of wheat; at the end of that year the original 56 computers are all used up. This is a commodity producing society. At the end of the year, the entire social product is owned by one social class, the social class that owns

TABLE 3

| | Inputs | Outputs | | |
	Computers	Computers	Gold	Wheat
Computer industry	28	56	–	–
Gold industry	16	–	48	–
Wheat industry	12	–	–	8
TOTAL	56	56	48	8

the means of production. Any social classes that do not own the means of production are getting on the best they can: through "charity" from the class that owns the means of production, theft, or whatever. Assume the free mobility of capital, so that there is an equal rate of profit, and that each member of the social class which owns the means of production is entitled to a share of the social product, depending upon how much of the means of production that person owns.[7]

Note that even for the class which owns the means of production (and the resulting social product), we are still in an era of "scarcity." (Of course, social classes which do not own the means of production may very well be in really dire straits.) One computer, in a given time period, can only produce so much of a commodity, be it more computers, gold, or wheat. Since the owners of each industry must trade their products with the owners of the other industries, definite relative prices will emerge.

In this society there is no fixed capital or joint production of commodities. The owners of the computer industry as a whole will keep 28 of the computers that their industry makes in 1 year; and, they will sell 16 of the computers to the gold industry and 12 computers to the wheat industry. With that money, they will buy a definite amount of gold and wheat. Meanwhile, the owners of the gold industry will keep some of their gold and exchange the rest to the owners of the wheat and computer industries. They will buy 16 computers, as well as a given amount of wheat. The owners of the wheat industry will keep some of the wheat for their own use and sell the rest to the owners of the gold and computer industries; they will purchase some gold from the gold industry and 12 computers. At the end of the year, the owners of each industry will have the necessary number of new computers to resume production for the next year. The property owning class as a whole will own the 48 units of gold and 8 units of wheat produced in that year. Notice that since the number of computers used up is the same as the number of computers made in one year (and computers are the only means of production), this economy cannot expand, i.e., it is in a state of simple reproduction.

Suppose this society is on the "gold standard" and one unit of gold is equal to $1. The variables to be determined are the price of one computer, the price of one unit of wheat, and the rate of profit in money terms (remember there is no rate of profit in Marxian value terms). Following the procedure used before,[8] there are three equations to solve three unknowns:

$(1 + r) (28pc) = 56\ pc,$
$(1 + r) (16pc) = 48,$
$(1 + r) (12pc) = 8\ pw;$ where
r = rate of profit,
pc = price of one computer,
pw = price of one unit of wheat (and the price of one unit of gold, by assumption, equals \$1).

The first equation says (1 plus the rate of profit) times (28 times the price of one computer) must equal the price of one computer times the number of computers produced (56). This equation alone is enough to determine the rate of profit which turns out to be 100%.[9] Thus, the rate of profit for all industries in this society is determined solely by the production conditions in the computer industry; this is because only computers are needed as an input in the production of all the other commodities in the society.[10] Through substitution, the price of one computer is determined to be \$1.50, and one unit of wheat \$4.50.

Thus, contrary to what one would expect from the labor theory of value, there can, in fact, be a positive rate of profit and relative prices in a fully automated society. Actually, once one frees oneself from the idea that only productive social labor can produce the mass of surplus value, and that the mass of (Marxian) surplus value determines the mass of monetary profits in a society, this result is not really surprising. The rate of profit is just the mass of profits in money terms divided by the amount of capital advanced in money terms. With increasing productivity, everything else remaining the same, naturally the rate of profit will increase, even as (or if) the number of productive workers decreases.

This example of a fully automated commodity producing society has been used to dramatize some of the paradoxical conclusions which will result when the labor theory of value is used to try to determine relative prices and the rate of profit in monetary terms. Contrary to what one would expect from the labor theory of value, there (theoretically) can be profits and relative prices in a commodity producing society which uses no human workers. Moreover, the fact that there is no Marxian rate of surplus value and yet, even in this simple model with no joint production, there is a positive monetary rate of profit seems to cast further doubt on the usefulness of the Marxian concept "rate of surplus value" and of the labor theory of value when used to help determine such things as relative prices and the monetary rate of profit.[11]

Admittedly, it is easy to ridicule models of this sort which envision a fully automated society with no workers. It turns out that a model of this type was first put forth by Vladimir Dmitriev in 1898 as a criticism of the Marxist labor theory of value.[12] One modern reviewer of Dmitriev has made fun of Dmitriev's model and said that the assumption of a society without human workers is equivalent to the hypothesis "if chicken had teeth."[13]

Yet models of this sort should not be ridiculed,[14] because the point is not whether there actually will ever be a society which is fully automated; that is, this is not an *empirical* issue.[15] Rather, models of fully automated societies should be conceived of as thought experiments. They are theoretical experiments which can serve to cast light on current theories.[16] Actually, thought experiments are well known in the field of physics.[17] For example, in modern physics there is a famous example of a poor cat which

> is placed in a steel chamber, together with the following hellish contraption (which must be protected against direct interference by the cat): A Geiger counter contains a tiny amount of radioactive substance, so tiny that within an hour one of the atoms may decay, but it is equally probable that none will decay. If one decays the counter will trigger, and via a relay activate a little hammer which will break a container of cyanide. If at the end of an hour the cat is still living one would say that no atom has decayed. An indication of the first decay would be the presence of equal parts of the living and the dead cat.
>
> The typical feature in these cases is that indeterminacy is transferred from the atomic to the crude macroscopic level, which then can be decided by direct observation. This prevents us from accepting a 'blurred model' too naively as a picture of reality. By itself it is not all unclear or contradictory. There is a difference between a blurred or poorly focused photograph and a picture of clouds or patches of fog.[18]

The theoretical point in the above example does not depend upon the empirical likelihood of a cat actually wandering into such a contraption. Hence, no amount of econometric-type work (e.g., measuring the statistical probability of a cat entering into a trap of this sort) could shed light on the theoretical issues raised by the above thought experiment.[19] Similarly, the theoretical puzzles which a model of a perfectly automated society casts upon Marx's labor theory of value do not depend upon the empirical likelihood that such a society will ever actually come into existence.

In any event, the above model of a fully automated society does pose additional theoretical paradoxes for Marx's labor theory of value. Moreover, it serves to highlight that there are indeed differences between a commodity and Marx's labor theory of value. They are two different theories of value which will often yield different results.

Nonetheless, the rest of this work will show that the two different theories of value are so similar that much of Marx's work can indeed be based upon a commodity theory of value. After reviewing some of the theoretical and historical assumptions underlying Marx's *Capital*, Marx's theoretical development of the concept of capital will be reworked using a commodity theory of value rather than the labor theory of value. In this reworking of the theoretical genesis of capital, it will first be seen that a commodity has both a use value and an exchange value. From this basic dichotomy, Marx showed how exchange value generates money, which in turn generates capital which is self-expanding value. What Marx did not develop is the fact that as a use value a commodity can be put to two different uses. It can either be consumed or used to make more commodities. When commodities are used to create more commodities they can be said to create value. It is the second crucial aspect of a commodity, that it can be used to create more commodities, upon which the commodity theory of value is largely based and upon which Marx's theoretical development of capital can also be securely anchored.

NOTES

1. Dmitriev, *Economic Essays on Values, Competition and Utility*; for more on this, see Appendix C.

2. However, this is not necessarily a fatal criticism of the labor theory of value. For a possible answer from an orthodox Marxian position, see Note 6.

3. Marx, *Capital*, Vol. III, p. 141; emphasis in original.

4. "If production could proceed altogether without labour, then neither value, nor capital, nor value-creation would exist." [*Grundrisse*, p. 539.]

5. Mandel, *Late Capitalism* (London: N.L.B., 1975), p. 207.

6. As noted in the Introduction, there is no one satisfactory definition of what Marx meant by a mode of production. In this instance, this lack of specification of what is meant by a mode of production can lead to serious theoretical difficulties. The model about to be presented assumes a commodity producing society with private ownership of the means of production. This would suggest that it is a capitalist society. On the other hand, since it is a model of a fully automated society, there is no market for labor power, since it assumes that there are no workers. Can a society with no workers be considered capitalist? Note further: if, as argued below (see Chapters 5 and 6), that value is a concept which Marx used only with reference to a capitalist mode of production, and if the model about to be presented is not a model of a capitalist mode of production, then does that mean that this model cannot be used to criticize Marx's labor theory of value? This seems to me to be an unwarranted interpretation. Nonetheless, this entire issue does (at the very least) serve to indicate some of the difficulties which followers and interpreters of Marxian theory face due to Marx's lack of specification of some of the key concepts which he uses.

7. Notice that what is crucial to the distribution of income in this society is the distribution and ownership of private property. A concern with various types of property relations is evident in the work of C. B. Macpherson, who at one point correctly points out that "If one envisages the extreme of an automated society in which nobody has to labour in order to

produce the material means of life, the property in the massed productive resources of the whole society becomes of utmost importance. The property that would then be most important to the individual would no longer be the right to access to the means of labour; it would be instead, the right to a share in the control of the massed productive resources." [*The Real World of Democracy* (Canadian Broadcasting Corporation, 1965), p. 137.]

8. It is assumed that this society is in a state of simple reproduction.

9. This equation also has a solution of $pc = 0$; however, this solution is ruled out by the second equation.

10. For an elaboration of this point, see Sraffa, *Production of Commodities by Means of Commodities*, pp. 7–8.

11. As an aside, the results of this model are mathematically equivalent to those when workers are used in the production process, but they receive no wages, i.e., they "live on air." Compare the results here with Steedman's results on p. 96 in *Marx After Sraffa*.

12. Dmitriev, Economic Essays on Value, Competition and Utility, pp. 61, fn.; (see Appendix C).

13. "Cette proposition est stupide, dira-t-on. Et c'est tout à fait vrai. Mais sa stupidité tient seulement au caractère parfaitement irréel de l'hypothèse que nous avons bien été obligé d'adopter pour suivre notre auteur. Peut-on imaginer une production sans travail humain? Non, puisque la production implique l'organisation *consciente et intelligente* de moyens en vue de fins déterminées. L'hopothèse de Dmitriev est donc du type 'si les poules avaient des dents.'" [Henri Denis, "Postface: V. K. Dmitriev ou les Malheurs de la Sagesse Mathématique," p. 265.] Denis goes on to conclude that although Dmitriev was a good mathematician, he was a poor dialectician, and hence could not understand Marx's theory of value: "Pour comprendre la valeur, il faut donc être dialecticien en même temps que mathématicien.

"Or, si Dmitriev sait compter, il est un pauvre dialecticien. Le résultat est celui que nous avons eu. Puisse-t-il servir d'exemple aujourd'hui!"

For a more respectful discussion of Dmitriev's model, see Maurice Dobb, "The Sraffa System and Critique of the Neo-Classical Theory of Distribution," *De Economist* **118** (1970); reprinted in Hunt and Schwartz, *A Critique of Economic Theory*, p. 217.

14. Actually, the presence of ridicule in these discussions should serve as a flag of warning that we may be dealing with an issue of the utmost importance. See, for example, Schumpeter, who noted that "Nicolas Copernicus (1473–1543) completed his manuscript in or about 1530. For decades his idea spread quietly without let or hindrance. It met indeed with opposition and even *ridicule* from professors who continued to hold onto the Ptolemaic system, but this is only what we should expect in the case of a new departure of such importance." [*History of Economic Analysis*, p. 81, fn,; emphasis added.]

15. This type of reaction is reminiscent of the original reaction to the reswitching controversy (see Chapter 3).

16. This is not to deny that there may possibly be historical tendencies leading to a fully automated society, as argued by some. (See, e.g., the article by Susan Chace, on page 1 of *The Wall Street Journal*, January 6, 1983, "Tomorrow's Computer May Reproduce Itself, Some Visionaries Think.") However, the validity (or lack of validity) of this point is not germane to the immediate issue at hand.

17. For Albert Einstein's use of thought experiments, see Gerald Holton's "Einstein, Michelson, and the 'Crucial' Experiment" in Holton, *Thematic Origins of Scientific Thought: Kepler to Einstein* (Cambridge, Mass.: Harvard University Press, 1973), pp. 261–352.

18. Schrödinger, *Naturwiss* **23**, 807 (1935), quoted from J. M. Jauch, *Are Quanta Real?* (Bloomington, Ind.: Indiana University Press, 1973), p. 106 fn. This fascinating little book also discusses the use of thought experiments in the chapter entitled "Fourth Day," pp. 67–97.

19. Also, whether one could practically or physically perform the experiment is not at issue.

5

THEORETICAL AND HISTORICAL ASSUMPTIONS CONCERNING THE CAPITALIST MODE OF PRODUCTION

We have been asserting that the Sraffian commodity theory of value is so similar to Marx's theory of value that it can be substituted for the labor theory of value, and that Marx's analysis of capitalism can then be built upon that theory of value. However, before this is actually done, this chapter presents a viewpoint on the scope and basic features of Marx's analysis of capitalism.[1] It argues that Marx presents an analysis of capitalism as a historically specific mode of production with certain invariant properties which require a separate historical-institutional analysis. Without this separate analysis, one is liable to mistake the limits of any theory of commodity production. After this chapter on Marx's methodology, we will continue with the actual reconstruction of Marx's analysis based upon a commodity theory of value.

The subject matter of Marx's lengthy work, *Capital*, is the capitalist mode of production:

> In this work I have to examine the capitalist mode of production, and the conditions of production and exchange corresponding to that mode.[2]

Marx felt that this mode of production, and the corresponding social relations associated with it, was a historically specific type of production which only arose (and only could arise) at a definite stage of social development. Marx's economic analysis is therefore also a historically specific one in that it only purports to analyze the capitalist mode of production.[3]

This may be contrasted with current textbook definitions of the subject matter of the science of economics. These definitions tend to follow Lionel Robbins' argument that "Economics is the science which studies human behaviour as a relationship between ends and scarce means which have alternative uses."[4] This conception of the subject matter of economics does not restrict the use of economic analysis to any particular type of society, since, in the words of one textbook writer:

> *any* society is constrained in its production by the quantities of land, labor, and capital it has on hand . . . economics is the study of the ways in which a society makes choices. Not only does a society as a whole make choices about the allocation of its resources, but the individuals in that society must also make a wide variety of choices.[5]

In contrast, Marx's *Capital* is meant to be the study of a historically specific mode of production, which arose at a certain period of history, and will no doubt also some day be replaced by a new system of production.[6] It is *not* meant to be some kind of abstract history of capitalism (although it is designed to give insights into the past).[7] It is supposed to "lay bare the economic laws of motion of modern society."[8] To do this, Marx does not start with, e.g., feudalism, even though Marx felt that capitalism historically grew out of the dissolution of feudal society.[9] Instead, Marx begins his analysis with the commodity.[10]

It must be stressed that in beginning his analysis with the commodity, Marx is already *presupposing* the existence of the capitalist mode of production. Marx does not start with the commodity because capitalist production historically grew out of simple commodity production.[11] The *historical* appearance of various economic categories, such as the category commodity, does not determine the order in which they appear in Marx's work.[12] Rather, the order of their appearance in Marx's work depends upon their interrelations with each other as part of a capitalist system. In the capitalist system, everything depends upon everything else, or, as Marx put it:

> in the completed bourgeois system every economic relation presupposes every other in its bourgeois economic form, and everything posited is thus also presupposition . . . [13]

If Marx begins his analysis with commodities (which of course he does), it is because he theorizes that commodities generate money which in turn generates capital, which, after all, is the name of Marx's work, and (more importantly) is considered by Marx to be the fundamental concept of modern economics:

> The exact development of the concept of capital is necessary, since it is the fundamental concept of modern economics, just as capital itself, whose abstract, reflected image is its concept, is the foundation of bourgeois society.[14]

Therefore, at the very beginning of *Capital,* as everywhere else in it, the pre-existence of the capitalist mode of production must be assumed.[15]

Thus, for example, it is a mistake to see the labor theory of value as something Marx meant to hold true only in simple commodity production. He meant for it to hold true in capitalist society, which is the object of his analysis;[16] as a matter of fact, he felt that the labor theory of value *only* held true in capitalist societies since

> the determination of value by pure labour time takes place only on the foundation of the production of capital, hence the separation of the two classes.[17]

Thus, at the very beginning of *Capital,* as elsewhere in that work, the theoretical existence of the capitalist mode of production must be taken as given.

Although the capitalist mode of production is assumed to already exist at the beginning of *Capital,* capitalism can arise *historically* only at a certain stage in the history of humanity. Some of the basic historic requirements for the existence of the capitalist mode of production are as follows.

Capitalism involves the exchange of commodities. This in itself assumes that there is a division of labor.[18] Futhermore, capitalism assumes that most products are produced as commodities, that is, that they are produced for *other* people to use. This assumes a society where producers create things not directly for themselves, but to be used by others.[19] Moreover in capitalist society, commodities are exchanged, but they are not exchanged directly for each other, as in a barter economy;[20] instead, they are exchanged for money. The production of commodities in exchange for money assumes that people largely relate to each other through the mediation of a "thing" known as money;[21] this thing (money) represents a matrix of social relations which can only arise at a certain stage in history.

The production of commodities which are to be exchanged for money implies that people become dependent upon other people (through the mediation of exchange and money) to supply them with the necessities of life. This implies a society where people do not produce their own means of subsistence; instead, they produce a commodity which they exchange for money, with which they buy the things they need in order to live.[22] Thus, a developed system of money and monetary exchange is a necessary historical prerequisite for the capitalist mode of production:

> Money and money circulation—what we called simple circulation—is the presupposition, condition, of capital itself, as well as of the circulation of capital . . . . When we speak of capital and of its circulation, we stand on a stage of social development where the introduction of money does not enter as a discovery, etc., but is rather a presupposition.[23]

A further prerequisite for capitalist production is wage laborers. A wage laborer is one who sells a particular type of commodity, her/his labor power or her/his capacity to work. A wage laborer sell her/his labor power to a capitalist in exchange for money; the capitalist then sets the worker to work producing other commodities.[24]

In order for a worker to be able to work for a capitalist, that worker must be free to do so. That is, the worker cannot be a slave or a serf or in some other extraeconomic way hampered from working for a capitalist. This freedom for the worker to work for any capitalist can only come about at a certain stage in history, and is an historical assumption of the capitalist mode of production.[25]

Another historical prerequisite for the existence of wage laborers is that they be separated from the means of production,[26] because a person who can support a family from tilling the soil, or who has access to the means of production, will not generally go to work for a capitalist and become a wage laborer. Therefore, a wage laborer must not only be free to work for capitalists, but must be economically forced to do so in order to acquire the money with which to purchase the commodities needed to support herself/himself. It is in this sense that the worker must be "free" from the means of production.[27] This double freeing of the worker, free to work for any capitalist, yet also free from access to the means of production, is also a product of history and a historical assumption for the existence of the capitalist mode of production:

> The positing of the individual as a *worker*, in this nakedness, is itself a product of *history*.[28]

Finally (at the risk of being obvious), it may be pointed out that the capitalist mode of production presupposes the existence of capitalists and of capital. This in turn presupposes not only the existence of money and circulating commodities,[29] but the existence of a group of people who act as merchants:

> the formation of the merchant estate, which presupposes that of money, . . . is likewise a presupposition for capital . . . since commerce is both historically as well as conceptually a presupposition for the rise of capital.[30]

These merchants are people who buy and sell (but do not produce) commodities for a profit.[31]

Capital also presupposes not only the existence of money, but of a certain private *accumulation* of money.[32] This accumulation of money is necessary to circulate commodities. Capitalist production presupposes that a certain quantity of money already exists since:

> The capitalist mode of production—its basis being wage-labour, the payment of the labourer in money, and in general the transformation of payments in kind into money payments—can assume greater dimensions and achieve greater perfection only where there is available in the country a quantity of money sufficient for circulation and the formation of a hoard (reserve fund, etc.) promoted by it. This is the historical premise. . . . Hence the increased supply of precious metals since the sixteenth century is an essential element in the history of the development of capitalist production.[33]

Capital also presupposes that a certain quantity of goods already exist in the form of commodities. Various commodities are needed so that capitalists can purchase raw material, equipment, etc., with which the workers can work;[34] and commodities are needed so that workers can take their wage, which they receive in the form of money, and purchase things to support themselves and their families.[35]

This concludes the discussion of the theoretical and historical assumptions concerning the capitalist mode of production. It is important to keep in mind that the subject of Marx's analysis is the capitalist mode of production. This mode of production is historically specific in that it can only arise at a given point in time. Some of the key historical presuppositions for the existence of capitalism have been outlined above. These include the existence of commodity production, of money, wage laborers, capitalists, etc. It should be stressed that while these are the given historical presuppositions of capitalism, once capitalism exists, capitalism continually reproduces these presuppositions.[36] What are originally the historical preconditions of the capitalist mode of production become the result of the capitalist mode of production as this system continually reproduces itself in time. Therefore,

> once developed historically, capital itself creates the conditions of its existence (not as conditions for its arising, but as results of its being).[37]

NOTES

1. For a similar interpretation of Marx's methodology, see the recent article by Richard Nordahl, "Marx on the Use of History in the Analysis of Capitalism," *History of Political Economy* **14**, No. 3, (1982): 342–365, and Robert Albritton, "The Theoretical and Historical in Marxian Political Economy," unpublished.

2. Marx, "Preface to First Edition," *Capital*, Vol. I.

3. "Whenever we speak of production, then, what is meant is always production at a definite stage of social development—production by social individuals. It might seem, therefore, that in order to talk about production at all we must either pursue the process of historical development through its different phases, or declare beforehand that we are dealing with a specific historic epoch such as, e.g., modern bourgeois production, which is indeed our particular theme." [*Grundrisse*, p. 85.]

4. Robbins, *An Essay on the Nature and Significance of Economic Science*, p. 16; see, also, e.g., Ferguson and Gould, *Microeconomic Theory*, "Economics is a social science that is concerned with the means by which scarce resources are used to satisfy competing ends," [p.1]; or Mansfield, *Microeconomics*: "Economics is concerned with the way in which resources are allocated among alternative uses to satisfy human wants" [p. 2].

5. Nicholson, *Intermediate Microeconomics*, p. 3; emphasis added. See also, Gary Becker, *The Economics of Human Behavior* for creative analyses using economics as an ahistorical theory of social choice.

6. "Analysis of the capitalist mode of production demonstrates . . . that it is a mode of production of a special kind, with specific historical features; that, like any other specific mode of production, it presupposes a given level of the social productive forces and their forms of development as its historical precondition: a precondition which is itself the historical result and product of a preceding process, and from which the new mode of production proceeds as its given basis; that the production relations corresponding to this specific, historically determined mode of production—relations which human beings enter into during the process of social life, in the creation of their social life—possess a specific, historical and transitory character; and finally, that the distribution relations are their opposite side, so that both share the same historically transitory character." [*Capital*, Vol. III, p. 878.]

7. "Our method indicates the points where historical investigation must enter in, or where bourgeois economy as a merely historical form of the production process points beyond itself to earlier historical modes of production. In order to develop the laws of bourgeois economy, therefore, it is not necessary to write the real history of the relations of production. But the correct observations and deduction of these laws, as having themselves become in history always leads to primary equations . . . which point towards a past lying behind this system. These indications, together with a correct grasp of the present, then also offer the key to the understanding of the past—a work in its own right. . . ." [*Grundrisse*, pp. 460–461.]

8. Marx, Preface to First Edition," *Capital*, Vol. I, p. 14.

9. "The economic structure of capitalist society has grown out of the economic structure of feudal society. The dissolution of the latter set free the elements of the former." [*Capital*, Vol. I, p. 786.]

10. "The wealth of those societies in which the capitalist mode of production prevails, presents itself as 'an immense accumulation of commodities,' its unit being a single commodity. Our investigation must therefore begin with the analysis of a commodity." [*Capital*, Vol. I, p. 41.] Marx is here quoting himself, from the opening sentence of the *Critique*.

11. Actually, according to Marx, "the production of commodities does not become the normal, dominant type of production until capitalist production serves as its basis." [*Capital*, Vol. II, p. 31; see also *Capital*, Vol. I, p. 639.]

12. "It would therefore be unfeasible and wrong to let the economic categories follow one another in the same sequence as that in which they were historically decisive. Their sequence is determined, rather by their relation to one another in modern bourgeois society. . . ." [*Grundrisse*, p. 107.]

13. Marx, *Grundrisse*, p. 278.

14. Ibid., p. 331; alternatively, one may say that Marx starts with the commodity because it is the conceptual center of the capitalist mode of production, from which the forces and relations of production can be derived. (See *Grundrisse*, pp. 100–101.)

15. "In the succession of the economic categories, as in any other historical, social science, it must not be forgotten that their subject, here, modern bourgeois society, is always what is given, in the head as well as in reality. . . ." [*Grundrisse*, p. 106.]

16. "As in the theory the concept of value precedes that of capital, but requires for its pure development a mode of production founded on capital, so the same thing takes place in practice. . . . The existence of value in its purity and generality presupposes a mode of production in which the individual product has ceased to exist for the producer in general and even

more for the individual worker, and where nothing exists unless it is realized through circulation. . . . This determination of value, then, presupposes a given historic stage of the mode of social production and is itself something given with that mode, hence a historic relation." [*Grundrisse*, p. 252.]

17. Marx, *Grundrisse*, p. 817.

18. ". . . [T]here is no exchange without division of labour, whether the latter is spontaneous, natural, or already a product of historic development." [*Grundrisse*, p. 99.]

19. "To have *circulation*, what is essential is that exchange appear as a process, a fluid whole of purchases and sales. Its first presupposition is the circulation of commodities themselves, as a natural, many-sided circulation of those commodities. The precondition of commodity circulation is that they be produced as exchange values, not as immediate use values, but as mediated through exchange value. . . . Circulation as the realization of exchange values implies: (1) that my product is a product only in so far as it is for others; hence suspended singularity, generality; (2) that it is a product for me only in so far as it has been alienated, become for others; (3) that it is for the other only in so far as he himself alienates his product; which already implies (4) that production is not an end in itself for me but a means." [*Grundrisse*, p. 196.]

20. "The form of barter in which the overflow of one's own production is exchanged by chance for that of others' is only the *first occurrence* of the product as exchange value in general, and is determined by accidental needs, whims, etc. But if it should happen to continue, to become a continuing act which contains within itself the means of its renewal, then little by little, from the outside and likewise by chance, regulation of reciprocal exchange arises by means of regulation of reciprocal production, and the costs of production, which ultimately resolve into labour time, would thus become the measure of exchange. This shows how exchange comes about, and the exchange value of the commodity." [*Grundrisse*, p. 205; emphasis in original.]

21. "Exchange, when mediated by exchange value and money, presupposes the all-round dependence of the producers on one another, together with the total isolation of their private interests from one another, as well as a division of social labour whose unity and mutual complementarity exist in the form of a natural relation, as it were, external to the individuals and independent of them. The pressure of general demand and supply on one another mediates the connection of mutually indifferent persons." [*Grundrisse*, p. 158.]

22. "A developed determination of prices presupposes that the individual does not directly produce his means of subsistence, but that his direct product is an *exchange value*, and hence must first be mediated by a social process, in order to become the *means of life* for the individual. Between the full development of this foundation of industrial society and the patriarchal condition, many intermediate stages, endless nuances." [*Grundrisse*, p. 193; emphasis in original.]

23. Marx, *Grundrisse*, p. 670.

24. "It is the elementary precondition of bourgeois society that labour should directly produce exchange value, i.e., money; and similarly, that money should directly purchase labour, and therefore the labourer, but only in so far as he alienates his acitivity in the exchange. Wage labour on one side, capital on the other, are therefore only other forms of developed exchange value and of money (as the incarnation of exchange value)." [*Grundrisse*, p. 225.]

25. "On one side, historic processes are presupposed . . . dissolution of the landed property relations . . . dissolution of the guild relations . . . dissolution of the client-relations in the various forms in which non-proprietors appear in the retinue of their lord as co-consumers of the surplus product . . . all these processes of dissolution means the dissolution of relations of production in which: use value predominates, production for direct consumption; in which exchange value and its production presupposes the predominance of the other form: and hence that, in all these relations, payments in kind and services predominate over payment in money

... all the dissolved relations were possible only with a definite degree of development of the material (and hence also the intellectual) forces of production." [*Grundrisse*, p. 502]

26. "A presupposition of wage . . . is free labour and the exchange of this free labour for money. . . . Another presupposition is the separation of free labour from the objective conditions of its realization." [*Grundrisse*, p. 471.]

27. "The separation of labour from its product, of subjective labour-power from the objective conditions of labour, was therefore the real foundation in fact, and the starting point of capitalist production." [*Capital*, Vol. I, pp. 624–625.]

28. Marx, *Grundrisse*, p. 472; emphasis in original.

29. "Circulation and exchange value deriving from circulation, the presupposition of capital." [*Grundrisse*, p. 259.]

30. Marx, *Grundrisse*, p. 672.

31. ". . . [M]erchant's capital appears as the historical form of capital long before capital established its own domination over production. Its existence and development to a certain level are in themselves historical premises for the development of capitalist production (1) as premises for the concentration of money wealth, and (2) because the capitalist mode of production presupposes production for trade, selling on a large scale, and not to the individual customer, hence also a merchant who does not buy to satisfy his personal wants but concentrates the purchases of many buyers in his one purchase. . . ." [*Capital*, Vol. III, p. 327.]

32. "In order to come into being, capital presupposes a certain accumulation; . . . this accumulation, necessary for capital to come into being, which is therefore already included in its concept as presupposition—as a moment—is to be distinguished essentially from the accumulation of capital which has already become capital." [*Grundrisse*, p. 320.]

33. Marx, *Capital*, Vol. II, p. 334.

34. "Various conditions appear which have to have arisen, or been given historically, for money to become capital and labour to become capital-positing, capital-creating labour, wage labour. . . . The essential conditions are . . . (1) on the one side the presence of living labour . . . separated from the conditions of living labour as well as from the means of existence . . . (2) objectified labour found on the other side, must be an accumulation of use values sufficiently large to furnish the objective conditions not only for the production . . . but also for the absorption of surplus labour . . . (3) a free exchange relation—money circulation between both sides." [*Grundrisse*, p. 463.]

35. Since, for example, "formerly the peasant family produced the means of subsistence and the raw materials, which they themselves, for the most part consumed. These raw materials and means of subsistence have now become commodities; the large farmer sells them, he finds his market in manufactures. Yard, linen, coarse woolen stuffs—things whose raw materials had been within the reach of every peasant family had been spun and woven by it for its own use—were now transformed into articles of manufacture. . . ." [*Capital*, Vol. I, pp. 819–820.]

36. ". . . [I]ts historic presuppositions, which precisely as such historic presuppositions, are past and gone, and hence belong to the history of its formation, but in no way to its contemporary history, i.e., not to the real system of the mode of production ruled by it . . . while the presuppositions under which money becomes capital appear as given, external presuppositions for the arising of capital—as soon as capital has become capital as such, it creates its own presuppositions, . . . by means of its own production process. These presuppositions which originally appeared as conditions of its becoming . . . now appear as results of its own realization . . . not as conditions of its arising but as results of its presence." [*Grundrisse*, pp. 459–460.]

37. Marx, *Grundrisse*, p. 459.

6

COMMODITIES

Volume I of Marx's *Capital* is divided into eight parts. Part I is entitled "Commodities and Money" and is approximately 120 pages long. This part is composed of three chapters of very unequal length. Chapter I is entitled "Commodities" and is approximately 55 pages long. It is broken down into four sections. Section I is entitled "The Two Factors of a Commodity; Use Value and Value (the Substance of Value and the Magnitude of Value)." This section establishes the dual nature of a commodity, being both a use value and an exchange value. As a use value, a commodity has a qualitative aspect (its various uses) and a quantitative aspect (a definite amount of the commodity being always assumed).

Marx develops the concept that commodities also have an exchange value. The exchange value of a commodity is quantitative in that a definite amount of one commodity can be exchanged for definite amounts of other commodities. Marx also argues that there is a qualitative side to exchange value, so that there is an intrinsic value, that is, an exchange value which is inseparably connected with and inherent in commodities. For Marx, the qualitative side to exchange value is that all commodities are products of labor; not particular labor, but human labor in the abstract. For Marx, value is the congelation of homogeneous human labor and is the common substance which manifests itself in the exchange of commodities.[1] The quantity of value which a commodity contains is measured by the amount of the value creating substance, i.e., the socially necessary labor time, which is contained in the article. Hence, the value of a commodity varies directly with the quantity of labor incorporated in it.

Here, we will discuss the importance of commodities in Marx's analysis,[2] and then we will rework section I of Chapter I of Marx's *Capital* using a commodity theory of value rather than Marx's labor theory of value. This reworking of this section of Marx results in the following major changes:

1. The common substance to all commodities which enables them to be compared with one another is that they are produced by other commodities, not that they are all products of human labor.

2. A thing can be a use value without having value, not because it contains no human labor as Marx argued[3] but because it is not produced by other commodities

3. The use value to which commodities are put is of vital importance. Marx argues in the fifth sentence of *Capital* that we are not "concerned to know how the object satisfies . . . wants, whether directly as means of subsistence, or indirectly as means of production."[4] On the contrary, the reworking of Marx based upon a commodity theory of value suggests that it is vitally important to know the use value to which commodities are put, since when commodities are used to create other commodities, they may be said to create value.

In spite of these changes (or, alternatively, with these changes) Section I of Chapter I of *Capital* may be reconstructed upon the basis of a commodity theory of value rather than upon Marx's theory of value.

THE CENTRAL IMPORTANCE OF COMMODITIES IN MARX'S ANALYSIS

Marx begins his analysis with a discussion of commodities. This is true not only in *Capital*, but in the 1859 *Critique* as well.[5] The reason which Marx gives for starting his analysis with a commodity is rather ambiguous: this is how the wealth of bourgeois societies, or those societies in which the capitalist mode of production prevails, "presents" itself.[6] Therefore, this is where Marx begins his analysis; or so Marx says. Actually things are not so simple, as the publication in 1904 of a planned Introduction to the *Critique of Political Economy* makes clear.[7] In that work, Marx wrestles for over 25 pages with the question of where to begin his analysis. Yet, at the end of this unfinished manuscript, it is still not very clear why Marx started his analysis with a discussion of commodities.

The interpretation offered here is as follows.[8] As pointed out in the previous chapter, the subject matter of Marx's work is the capitalist mode of production. Before Marx can get to this subject, he needs to establish why there is capital in the first place. Marx felt that at a certain point in history products become commodities; commodities in turn generate money,[9] which in turn generates capital.[10] Capital is not something which arises by convention or by social consent. Rather it is a relation which arises more or less spontaneously under given social historical conditions.[11]

Here, it may be helpful to refer to Marx's theory of the state. Marx does not believe that the political state came into being simply because of the common consent of individuals.[12] For Marx, any theory of the state must explain why there is a state at all, and under what historical and social conditions a state arises.[13] Explanations that at some point in time people simply consciously decided to have a state[14] are viewed by Marx as being inadequate.

Similarly, in conducting his economic analysis, Marx wants to analyze and explain why certain economic categories exist. For example, in dealing with money Marx argues that

> Every one knows, if he knows nothing else, that commodities have a value form common to them all, and presenting a marked contrast with the varied bodily forms of their use-value. I mean their money form. Here, however, a task is set us, the performance of which has never yet even been attempted by *bourgeois* economy, the task of tracing the genesis of this money form, of developing the expression of value implied in the value relation of commodities, from its simplest almost imperceptible outline, to the dazzling money form.[15]

Marx felt he was the first economist to even attempt to analyze why there is money, or, as he puts it, to trace the "genesis of this money form." He needs to do this so that he can then go on to explain why there is capital, or in his own colorful words, why it comes about that

> He, who before was the money owner, now strides, in front as capitalist; the possessor of labour-power follows as his labourer. The one with an air of importance, smirking, intent on business; the other, timid and holding back, like one who is bringing his own hide to market and has nothing to expect but—a hiding.[16]

Thus, the objective of the first two sections of *Capital*, Part I, "Commodities and Money" and Part II, "The Transformation of Money into Capital," is to establish why there is capital in the first place.[17] Just as for Marx, the state does not simply arise out of common consent, but only arises out of certain material conditions and at a certain time in history, so too with capital. The function of the first two sections of *Capital* is to explain why capital exists at all.[18]

Again, Marx is not giving a historical account of the rise of capitalism.[19] He is explaining theoretically why capital comes into existence. At a certain point in time, products become commodities. As will be seen in detail, commodities generate money which in turn generates capital. Marx could have begun his analysis with products in general. However, as argued above, Marx was specifically concerned with the capitalist mode of production and with how that mode of production differed from other modes of production. Products as such appear in all human societies. Yet, the *distinguishing* feature of bourgeois societies is that there most products take on the form of commodities.[20] Hence, Marx begins his analysis not with products in general, but with commodities.

WHAT IS A COMMODITY?

A commodity[21] is a thing which has both a use value and an exchange value.[22] The use value of a commodity is similar to what modern economists would call the utility given off by the commodity. In the theory of value under consideration, the use value of a commodity is not quantifiable; or rather, following Marx, the ability to measure use value is rejected. Hence, questions of ordinal versus cardinal measurements of utility, interpersonal comparisons of utility, etc., are not considered.[23] Although the use value of a commodity is not quantifiable,[24] it is essential that a commodity have a use value—otherwise, the thing is not a commodity.[25]

As a use value, a commodity can be put to one of two uses: it may be consumed or it may be used to create other commodities.[26] When a commodity is used to create other commodities, it may be said to create value.

A commodity is also an exchange value. The exchange value of a commodity is its ability to exchange itself for another commodity.[27] Although the exchange value of a commodity depends upon that commodity having a use value,[28] the magnitude of a commodity's exchange value is not determined by its use value. Rather, the magnitude of a commodity's exchange value depends upon its conditions of production.[29]

Why is it that commodities have an exchange value, that is, why is it that commodities may be exchanged for other commodities? Marx answers this by asserting that commodities may be exchanged for each other because they all have a common substance—embodied labor. For Marx, the exchange of commodities is possible because all commodities are, in the final analysis, nothing but congealed labor, and because of this they may be compared and exchanged.[30]

Using a commodity theory of value, it may be proposed that commodities have value because they are produced by other commodities. Commodities manifest their value by their ability to be exchanged for other commodities; this manifestation is called exchange value.

Now, if a carpenter makes a chair for personal use or to give away to a friend, that chair is not a commodity; rather, it is merely a product or a gift. If, on the other hand, a carpenter makes a chair with a goal of exchanging it for another type of good, then that chair is a commodity. A commodity is a product which is produced with the intention of exchanging it with another product. From this example, it is evident that not all things which have use value are commodities.[31] Furthermore, it is only under specific historic and social circumstances that a product becomes a commodity.[32] Commodities do not arise spontaneously in nature. A chair or an ounce of gold is not naturally a commodity; commodities are products of society.[33]

An apple growing in the wild does not have any value. However, this is not because, as Marx thought, there is no human labor embodied in the apple.[34] Rather, according to the commodity theory of value being proposed here, that apple has no value because it is not produced by other commodities. However much use value that apple may possess (if use value could be quantified), that apple would possess no value because it would not have been produced by another commodity.

The value of a commodity manifests itself as that commodity's exchange value.[35] The commodity, when considered as an exchange value, necessarily generates money. Attempts by early socialists to abolish money while retaining commodities were Utopian, and would necessarily fail, since money cannot be abolished so long as products take the form of commodities.[36] The question then arises, why and how do commodities necessarily generate money? Marx's answer to this question, which may be based on commodity theory of value, constitutes what is perhaps the most difficult section of *Capital*.[37]

NOTES

1. Marx, *Capital*, p. 45.

2. A discussion of commodities is appropriate for several reasons. Among others, it seems that any theory of value which holds that the key to why commodities have value in the type of society now under consideration is that they are produced by other commodities ought to commence with a clear discussion of the definition of a commodity. Unfortunately, this has not been done in the past, giving rise to some misunderstandings, such as the ones discussed in Chapter 8. Also, this is where Marx begins his analysis in *Capital*. (What are we to make of this coincidence?)

3. Marx, *Capital*, p. 47.

4. Ibid., p. 42.

5. The opening lines of that work are, "The wealth of bourgeois society, at first sight, presents itself as an immense accumulation of commodities. Every commodity, however, . . ." [*Critique*, p. 27.]

6. Marx, *Critique*, also, *Capital*, p. 41.

7. "Introduction" reprinted in Marx, *Critique* and *Grundrisse*. This work was never published in Marx's lifetime and was discarded by him as an "anticipation of results that are still not proven." [Dobb, "Introduction" to Marx, *A Contribution to the Critique of Political Economy*, p. 5.]

8. This interpretation largely follows Uno, *Principles of Political Economy: Theory of a Purely Capitalist Society*.

9. "The product becomes a commodity; the commodity becomes exchange value; the exchange value of the commodity is its immanent money-property; this, its money-property,

separates itself from it in the form of money, and achieves a general social existence separated from all particular commodities and their natural mode of existence; the relation of the product to itself as exchange value becomes its relation to money, existing alongside it. . . ." [*Grundrisse*, pp. 146–147.]

10. "Money—here taken as the independent expression of a certain amount of value existing either actually as money or as commodities—may be converted into capital on the basis of capitalist production, and may thereby be transformed from a given value to a self-expanding, or increasing value. . . . In this way, aside from its use-value as money, it acquires an additional use-value, namely that of serving as capital. Its use-value then consists precisely in the profit it produces when converted into capital." [*Capital*, Vol. III, pp. 338–339.] In order to anticipate objections as to the present indeterminancy of the concept "capital," it may be here noted that the precise meaning of capital, and how capital arises out of the commodity form, will be developed in the course of this work.

11. Thus, Marx is concerned that "it will be necessary later, before this question is dropped, to correct the idealist manner of presentation which makes it seem as if it were merely a matter of conceptual determinations and of the dialectic of these concepts. Above all in the case of the phrase: product (or activity) becomes commodity; commodity, exchange value; exchange value, money." [*Grundrisse*, p. 151.] This is because, at a certain point in time, products do indeed become commodities which then in turn generate money and capital.

12. "Money does not arise by convention, any more than the state does." [*Grundrisse*, p. 165.]

13. See, e.g., Engels' attempt to do this in *The Origin of the Family, Private Property and the State*.

14. See, e.g., Locke: "Where-ever therefore any number of men are so united into one Society, as to quit every one his Executive Power of the Law of Nature, and to resign it to the public, there and there only is a Political, or Civil Society. And this is done where-ever any number of Men, in the state of Nature, enter into Society to make one People, one Body Politic under one Supreme Government, or else when any one joins himself to, and incorporates with any Government already made. For hereby he authorizes the Society, or which is all one, the Legislative, thereof to make Laws for him as the publick good of the Society shall require; to the Execution whereof, his own assistance (as to his own Decrees) is due. And this *puts Men* out of a State of Nature *Into* that of a *Commonwealth*, . . . [Locke, "Of Political or Civil Society" in *Second Treatise*, Chap. 7, paragraph 89; emphasis in original.]

15. Marx, *Capital*, Vol. I, p. 55; emphasis in original.

16. Ibid., Vol. I, p. 196.

17. The above quote is in fact the final two sentences of Part II.

18. This apparently is not understood by, e.g., Paul Samuelson. After giving Sraffian-based arguments against the labor theory of value, he jumps to the conclusion that therefore Volume I of *Capital* should be ignored by modern economists. Instead, according to Samuelson, modern economists should only read Volume III of *Capital*. Yet, nowhere in Volume III of *Capital* does Marx attempt to give an explanation of why money and capital do in fact exist; this is only done in Volume I of *Capital*. Admittedly, this is done on the basis of the labor theory of value which Samuelson and many other economists do not subscribe to. It is a primary objective of this work to show how this theoretical genesis of capital can be based upon a Sraffian commodity theory of value. (See Samuelson, "Understanding the Marxian Notion of Exploitation.")

19. See, e.g., in Marx, *Grundrisse*: "The history of landed property, which would demonstrate the gradual transformation of the feudal landlord into the landowner, of the hereditary, semi-tributary and often unfree tenant for life into the modern farmer, and of the resident serfs, bondsmen and villeins who belonged to the property into agricultural day-labourers, would indeed be the history of the formation of modern capital. It would include within it the connection with urban capital, trade, etc. *But we are dealing here with developed*

bourgeois society, which is already moving on its own foundation." [pp. 252-253; emphasis added.]

20. "Capitalist production is distinguished from the outset. . . . It produces its products as commodities. The fact that it produces commodities does not differentiate it from other modes of production; but rather the fact that being a commodity is the dominant and determining characteristic of its products." [*Capital*, Vol. III, p. 879.] This clarifies the ambiguity in Marx noted at the beginning of this chapter. Marx starts with the commodity not simply because this is how the wealth of bourgeois societies presents itself; but, also because the historical fact that most products in bourgeois societies take on the form of a commodity distinguishes bourgeois from "prebourgeois" societies.

21. This section presents an analysis of what a commodity is, based upon a commodity theory of value.

22. This work will not go into the controversy over whether a service is a commodity.

23. For seminal discussions of these issues in neoclassic economic thought, see, e.g., Hicks, *Value and Capital*, Chap. 1, pp. 11-25, and Robbins, *An Essay on the Nature and Significance of Economic Science*, Chap. 4 pp. 72-103.

24. Schumpeter has argued that the classical economists did not know how to quantify utility and that "A. Smith or Ricardo or J. S. Mill . . . did not see how 'value in use' could possibly be made to explain 'value in exchange.' They saw no further than that the former was a condition of the latter." Schumpeter, *History of Economic Analysis*, fn. p. 912.

25. "The use value of the commodity is presupposed, not for its owner, but rather for the society generally." [*Grundrisse*, p. 882]; "In fact, however, the use value of the commodity is a given presupposition, the material basis in which a specific economic relation presents itself. It is only this specific relation which stamps the use value as a commodity." [*Grundrisse*, p. 881.]

26. "A commodity is, in the first place, an object outside us, a thing that by its properties satisfies human wants of some sort or another. The nature of such wants, whether, for instance, they spring from the stomach or from fancy, makes no difference. Neither are we here concerned to know how the object satisfies these wants, whether directly as means of subsistence or indirectly as means of production." [*Capital*, pp. 41-42.] Here, right at the very beginning of *Capital*, Marx alludes to the fact that a commodity can be used either to be consumed or to create other commodities; however, he does not follow up the implications of this point.

27. "Exchange-value seems at first to be a *quantitative relation*, the proportion in which use-values are exchanged for one another." [*Critique* p. 28; emphasis in original.]

28. "For something to become an object of exchange, to have exchange value, it must not be available to everyone without the mediation of exchange; it must not appear in such an elemental form as to be common property. To this extent, rarity is an element of exchange value. . . ." [*Grundrisse*, p. 176.]

29. This point will be further discussed in the next chapter. For examples of how to *determine* the magnitude of a commodity's exchange value, when using a commodity theory of value, see Chapters 2 and 4.

30. "Two things are only commensurable if they are of the same nature. Products can be measured with the measure of labour—labour time—only because they are, by their nature, labour. They are objectified labour. . . . Only because products *are* labour can they be measured by the measure of labour, by labour time, the amount of labour consumed in them." [*Grundrisse*, p. 613; emphasis in original.]

31. "A thing can be useful, and the product of human labour, without being a commodity. Whoever directly satisfied his wants with the produce of his own labour, creates, indeed, use-values, but not commodities." [*Capital*, p. 48.]

32. "No producer, whether industrial or agricultural, when considered by himself alone, produces value or commodities. His product becomes a value and a commodity only in the context of definite social interrelations." [*Capital*, Vol. III, pp. 638-639.]

33. "A product posited as exchange value is in its essence no longer a simple thing; it is posited in a quality differing from its natural quality; it is posited as a relation, more precisely as a relation in general, not to one commodity but to every commodity, to every possible product." [*Grundrisse,* p. 205.]

34. "The purely natural material in which no human labour is objectified, to the extent that it is merely a material that exists independently of labour, has no value, since only objectified labour is value." [*Grundrisse,* p. 366; see, also, *Capital,* p. 47.]

35. ". . . exchange value is the only form in which the value of commodities can manifest itself or be expressed." [*Capital,* p. 45.]

36. Marx discusses this point at length in his criticism of Proudhon in *The Poverty of Philosophy*.

37. See Marx, "Preface to the First Edition" in *Capital,* Vol. I, pp. 11-12.

7

THE THEORETICAL GENESIS OF MONEY

Section III of Chapter I of *Capital* is entitled "The Form of Value, or Exchange Value."[1] This section, and Chapter II which follows it,[2] traces the theoretical genesis of money. Here, Marx elaborates on the fact/contradiction that a commodity is *both* a use value and an exchange value to show how money arises. Marx argues that value only manifests itself in the social relation of commodity to commodity. His task here is to trace the genesis of the money form, which is the value form common to all commodities. Marx traces the simplest value relation, or the elementary form of value, where one commodity is compared to some other individual commodity. Marx finds that, in this value relation, the value of commodity *a* comes to be expressed in the *physical* presence of commodity *b*. In this relation, *a* comes to appear as only a use value, and *b* as only exchange value. Marx then expands the simple value relation into a series of the elementary forms of value; this Marx calls the total or expanded form of value. Marx then develops the implications of this form of value. The series of the elementary relative expressions which constitute the total or expanded form of value may then be reversed, giving what Marx calls the general form of value. This further enhances the value form of the commodity and further separates the two aspects of a commodity (use and exchange value) in such a way that only one commodity becomes directly exchangeable for all others. From this general form of value, one particular commodity becomes the universal equivalent and becomes directly exchangeable for all other commodities. This particular commodity becomes the money-commodity, or serves as money, or is (originally) *simply* the money form of the commodity. This money form was theoretically derived by Marx from the simple commodity form. Thus, for Marx, money is something which arises out of the contradictions inherent in a commodity, and money comes to represent value in general.

Chapter II, simply entitled "Exchange," elaborates on the fact that since commodities are nonuse values for their owners and use values for their nonowners, they must be exchanged. Marx discusses how, out of the actual exchange of commodities, money, the universal equivalent, emerges, and why certain commodities (namely, the precious metals) become selected (due to their physical characteristics) to function as money. For Marx, the development of the exchange of commodities will necessarily generate money.

The rest of this chapter (of this work) will present an account of Marx's theoretical genesis of money, based upon a commodity rather than Marx's labor theory of value. This reworking of this section of Marx results in one major change. For Marx, the magnitude of a commodity's value is determined by the amount of socially necessary labor time embodied in that commodity. Alternatively, using a commodity theory of value, the quantitative relations between commodities are *not determined* solely by the amount of labor required to produce the various commodities. Consequently, one cannot *determine* the value of a commodity simply by looking at the amount of labor embodied in that commodity. Instead, the quantitative relations between commodities are determined by the amount of all commodity inputs required to produce commodity outputs (where labor power is also a commodity). Consequently, the magnitude of exchange value is not determined *simply* by embodied labor, but by the production process in general. This important point bears repetition. For Marx, using the labor theory of value, one may determine the value of a commodity without specific reference to any other commodity; one need only know the amount of socially necessary labor needed to produce that commodity. On the other hand, using the commodity theory of value, one cannot determine the value of a commodity in isolation from the production conditions of all the other commodities which are needed either directly or indirectly for the production of the commodity in question.[3]

In spite of these changes (or, alternatively, with these changes), Marx's analysis of the theoretical genesis of money may be reconstructed upon the basis of a commodity theory of value rather than upon his labor theory of value.

THE GENESIS OF THE MONEY FORM

The value of a commodity cannot be ascertained merely by looking at the commodity. This is because a commodity can *express* its value only by coming into a relationship with another commodity.[4] The ability of a commodity to be exchanged with another commodity is called its exchange value.

The simplest expression of a commodity's exchange value occurs when one commodity equals another, for example, in the equation, one shirt equals one case of beer, or one shirt is worth one case of beer.

It turns out that the theoretical development of the money form can be traced from this simple equation.[5] Here the shirt is worth one case of beer. The *value* of the shirt is expressed in the *physical body* of the beer.[6] The shirt can express its value only because it is in a relationship to the beer;[7] hence, it can express its value *relatively* to the beer. The shirt in this equation assumes what Marx calls the relative form of value.

The value of the shirt is expressed in the beer; or, the beer may be said to be the equivalent of the shirt. The value of the shirt is, clearly, one case of beer. Yet, it is not clear what the value of the beer is. By being the equivalent of the shirt, the beer in this equation assumes what Marx calls the equivalent form of value. Unfortunately, it is not possible to ascertain the value of a commodity when it acts as the equivalent of another.[8]

Now, this distinction between the relative and equivalent forms of value seems to "turn upon minutiae."[9] In a sense it does, yet the distinction is crucial toward understanding how and why money necessarily develops from a commodity. Eventually, the commodity which serves as the equivalent form of value will turn into money.[10] In its money form, the distinction made above becomes clearer. For example, in saying that one shirt equals $10, or that one shirt is worth $10, it is evident how much the shirt is worth. The shirt is worth $10. The shirt expresses its value as so much money. The shirt has value because it can be exchanged for a certain quantity of money. Yet, it is not clear what the value of money is in the above equation. (Surely the value of a dollar is not simply one-tenth of a shirt.) The value of the commodity which assumes the equivalent form is not deducible from any simple equation.

The equation one shirt equals one case of beer can be reversed to one case of beer equals one shirt. This would not affect the value form. In this situation the beer would assume the relative form and the shirt would have the equivalent form. In any one equation, one commodity must be at one or the other of the poles of the equation, the pole of relative value or that of equivalent value.

In the equation one shirt equals one case of beer, the value of the shirt, by expressing itself in the actual physical body of the beer, converts the beer into a *representative* of value. The actual commodity, beer, represents the value of the shirt.[11] Moreover, the value of the shirt may be separated from the shirt. This can be done by actually exchanging the shirt for the beer. Note that, according to this argument, value may take on an objective existence independent of the commodity in which it is embodied.[12] In this equation, the value of the shirt assumes an independent existence in the actual physical body of the beer. The physical body of the beer comes to represent value; it thus *seems* as if beer is value itself.

Beer, when considered simply as beer, may be wanted merely for its clear refreshing taste. However, beer, a commodity, when put in the above *relationship* with the shirt, comes to represent the value of the shirt. Beer becomes the equivalent of the shirt not (according to this theory of value) of the shirt's use-value or utility, but the equivalent of the shirt's value. Since beer is the equivalent of the shirt's value, it comes to appear that beer itself is value.

This argument may become clearer by considering the commodity which generally has served as the equivalent form of value—gold. Gold itself is a commodity. It has value because it is produced by other commodities. Other commodities express their value in gold. Gold comes to represent value, because commodities express their value in gold. Hence it comes to appear that gold itself is value: it appears that gold is intrinsically, inherently, naturally valuable. Actually, gold is *only* valuable because it is a commodity produced by other commodities. Yet, by coming to represent all value, it appears that gold is valuable because of some inherent natural property, and not because of certain definite social relationships.[13]

To return to the problem at hand: how and why does some definite commodity become money?[14] In the equation one shirt equals one case of beer, the value of the shirt is *qualitatively* expressed as equal to the beer by the fact that the commodity beer is directly exchangeable with it. The value of the shirt is quantitatively expressed by the fact that a definite quantity of beer (in this situation, one case) is exchangeable with a definite quantity of shirts.

The expression of value in the relationship of exchange originates in the nature of value. Value begins in the production process and the exchange relation merely brings it out. Yet, the simple equation one shirt equals one case of beer suffers from several defects. The commodity shirt is actually *qualitatively* equal to all commodities insofar as all commodities may be considered as values. Yet, in the above equation, it appears as if the commodity shirt is qualitatively equal only to the commodity beer. Also, the commodity shirt is *quantitatively* proportional to a given amount of all other commodities; in the above equation, this, too, is omitted.[15]

This shirt may be placed in a relation with any commodity. Instead of just the one shirt equals one case of beer, there is also one shirt equals *a* pounds of coffee, one shirt equals *b* loaves of bread, one shirt equals *c* records, one shirt equals *d* ounces of gold, etc. This may be called the total or expanded form of value. Here the *value* of the shirt may be expressed as so much of any other commodity as being worth so much beer, or so much coffee, or so much gold, etc. Thus, one may speak of the beer value of the shirt, or the football value of the shirt, or the gold value of the shirt.[16]

This series of equations may be expanded to infinity. The value of the shirt may be expressed in the *physical* substance of any other commodity. From this form of value, it is now evident that as a value, the shirt is equal to every other commodity, and may be exchanged in a definite proportion with any and every other commodity. Unfortunately, there are now an infinite number of commodities acting as the equivalent. Each commodity, when it is in the role of the equivalent, expresses the value of the commodity in the relative position of the equation (in this case, the shirt) but cannot express its own value.[17]

The whole series of equations may be inverted as follows:

$$\left.\begin{array}{l} a \text{ pounds of coffee} \\ b \text{ loaves of bread} \\ c \text{ records} \\ d \text{ ounces of gold} \end{array}\right\} = \text{one shirt}$$

Now it is the shirt which assumes the position of equivalent value. All other commodities express their value in the commodity shirt. This may be called the general form of value. The shirt, in its physical concreteness, comes to represent the value of each and every other commodity. Thus, to find out the value of, say, a record, one must merely find its value in shirts. All commodities express their value in the commodity shirt; the shirt, now being in the equivalent form of value, cannot express its own value.

The shirt thus becomes a universal equivalent which is directly exchangeable with all other commodities.[18] Now, all other commodities express themselves as being worth so many shirts. Thus, the commodity shirt has been tranferred from a simple commodity with a use value and an exchange value to a commodity which represents value itself.[19] Yet, there is nothing innate about a shirt or about the production process which goes into making a shirt which enables the shirt to perform the task of representing value. Rather, it is the development of the commodity form itself which comes to select one commodity (in our example, the commodity shirt) to act as a universal equivalent. In its function as a universal equivalent, the shirt comes to represent value itself and becomes *directly exchangeable* with all other commodities. In order to find the value of shirts, one must consider the above-mentioned expanded form of value. That is, the value of the shirt, which is the universal equivalent, must be found by comparing it to each and every particular commodity.[20]

So, for example, one shirt equals *a* pounds of coffee, one shirt equals *b* loaves of bread, etc. Again, this concept may be made more familiar to modern readers by thinking of the value of the dollar, the modern day universal equivalent. The value of every commodity may be expressed as being worth so many dollars, for example, one (bargain-based) shirt may be worth $10. Yet, what is the value of a dollar? The value of a dollar is not simply, say, one-tenth of a shirt, *or* one-thirtieth of an economics textbook, *or* one-ten thousandth of a new car. The value of a dollar can only be found by creating some kind of index, or by comparing it to each *and* every other commodity.

In the general form of value, one commodity stands apart from all other commodities and acts to represent the value of all other commodities. The universal equivalent can be any commodity whatsoever. At the time Marx wrote, one commodity had become the universal equivalent of all others—gold. That commodity which acts as the universal equivalent is called money.[21] Money develops out of the commodity form itself.[22] Every commodity comes to express its value in a certain quantity of gold, which acts as the universal equivalent. The expression of the value of a commodity in terms of the universal equivalent is called the price of that commodity.[23]

To recapitulate: every commodity is a use value and a value. The value of a commodity is determined in the process of production. The value of a commodity manifests itself as an exchange value, that is, as its abilty to be exchanged with other commodities. The value of a commodity cannot be determined in isolation, but only manifests itself when placed in relation to other commodities. In the course of relating to each other, one commodity develops into the function of universal equivalent and represents the value of all the other commodities. This commodity becomes the money commodity, or simply money.[24] When other commodities express their exchange value in terms of money, they are expressing their price.

MONEY AND EXCHANGE

Although a commodity is both a use value and an exchange value, the owner of a commodity is primarily concerned with the exchange value of that commodity.[25] The commodity owner wants to exchange the commodity in order to acquire another commodity. The seller of a commodity is always interested in the exchange value of the commodity;[26] the buyer of the commodity is always interested in the use value of the commodity. Thus, the use value of a commodity is not something which directly concerns the commodity owner. True, the commodity must have some kind of use value; otherwise the commodity would not have any exchange value. Yet, the exact type of use value of the commodity is not the concern of the commodity owner.[27]

In seeking to exchange their commodities,[28] commodity owners must meet each other as equals. They must not appropriate each other's commodities by force. Rather, they must recognize each other as private owners of commodities who have the power to exchange their commodities. Therefore, the exchange of commodities must take place by mutual consent.[29]

When commodity owners meet, they are not interested in each other as *people*. Rather, they are interested in each other as owners of commodities. Actually, what they are really interested in is the commodity owned by the other person. For example, when I go into a butcher shop, I am not interested in the butcher but interested in the meat; or, when I buy gas at Exxon, I am not interested in the well-being of the Rockefeller family but in the gas. Thus, in the exchange of commodities, people relate to each other through their commodities. Social relations are mediated through the commodities owned by people; humans relate to each other as commodity owners or as mere representatives of their commodity.[30]

The ability for commodity owners to meet and exchange their commodities is dependent upon certain agreed upon powers, social relations, laws, conceptions of property, etc. The exchange of commodities does not arise spontaneously out of nature.[31] Rather, it arises only at a certain level of social development

As pointed out above, through the exchange of commodities, one commodity inevitably develops as the universal equivalent, i.e., as money.[32] Thus, the individual commodity owner does not exchange a particular commodity for another arbitrary particular commodity.[33] Instead, the individual commodity owner exchanges a commodity for the universal equivalent, for that commodity which represents value itself, which is therefore directly exchangeable for other commodities.

Thus, commodities have value. They show this by being exchanged themselves for money, the universal equivalent. With money, the commodity owner can then buy any other commodity, since money represents value. The exchange of commodities is basically the exchange of values. The individual commodity owner exchanges a commodity, which contains a particular use value, for money which represents value itself.[34]

When a commodity is exchanged for money (or its value takes on the form of universal equivalent), the particular use value of the commodity, as well as the particular production process which went into making that commodity, is abstracted. Money represents value in general; hence it does not represent any particular production process or particular concrete labor.[35] The particular production process and the particular commodity is extinguished, so far as other commodity owners are concerned, once the particular commodity is exchanged for money. Thus, for example, when the butcher eyes my money on his cash register, he does not know (and probably does not care) that the money may have been obtained by my (say) owning a heroin factory. In that case, he would not realize that the money represented the value from producing heroin from opium. He would only know that the money represents value itself, and he would want it.

In time, the precious metals, particularly gold and silver, become the money expression of the general form of value. Although theoretically any commodity may become the universal equivalent, the precious metals in fact serve as the universal equivalent because of their physical characteristics, or use values (or utilities). Among their physical characteristics which are conducive to their serving as money are the following:

1. They exhibit uniform qualities in every sample. Hence, one piece of gold is as desirable as another.
2. They are easily divided or reunited. Hence they can represent smaller or larger quantities of value.
3. They are extremely maleable, making them serviceable for jewelry.
4. They are extremely durable so they do not wear out.
5. They have a heavy specific gravity, which means that a great deal of weight is contained in a small space; this is especially important for its use as a means of circulation.[36]

In time, gold and silver become money. They conveniently and durably serve as the universal equivalent. They serve as the universal equivalent because all other commodities express their value in them. All other commodities become the particular equivalents of money. It appears that all other commodities express their value in gold because gold is money. Actually gold is just a commodity which has become money in consequence of all other commodities expressing their values in it.[37]

Money, therefore, is only a commodity delegated to do a certain job, that of representing value. It is not a mere symbol,[38] nor a mere convention.[39] Rather, money represents value, and it contains value itself. With the development of money, value obtains a material existence separate from the commodity itself. Hence, it develops that

> The historical progress and extension of exchanges develops the contrast, latent in commodities, between use-value and value. The necessity for giving an external expression to this contrast for the purposes of commercial intercourse, finds no rest until it is once for all satisfied by the differentiation of commodities into commodities and money. At the same rate then, as the conversion of products into commodities is being accomplished, so also is the conversion of one special commodity into money.[40]

NOTES

1. Section II of Chapter I of *Capital* discusses the twofold character of the labor embodied in commodities. This short section argues that labor is both concrete, in that it produces particular use values, and that it is abstract, insofar as it produces values. Actually, one can say that *any* commodity when used to make other commodities is concrete, insofar as a particular type of commodity is making another particular type of commodity; furthermore, one can view this process (of making commodities making other commodities) as abstract, insofar as commodities are producing other values. Hence, this section does not seem to be too important in a reworking of Marx's development of capital using a commodity theory of value. For more on this, see page 72.

2. In between Section III of Chapter I and Chapter II is a digression on commodity fetishism ("The Fetishism of Commodities and the Secret Thereof"). For more on this, see the following chapter of this work. The order of presentation of Marx's ideas has been slightly rearranged in this reworking of Marx.

3. Some implications which arise from this important point are discussed in Appendix E. Here, it will merely be noted that the point mentioned in the text above opens up a range of questions which are outside the scope of this work. Once one makes the distinction between the creation and the determination of value, then one seems to be led to the conclusion that the determination of the magnitude of a commodity's value requires the investigation of the production process as a whole. This then seems to imply the use of some sort of theory of general equilibrium (or system of simultaneous equations, as used in Chapters 2 and 4); but this then raises the questions of how Marx can be viewed to be a "general equilibrium" theorist, and whether his work is compatible with any notion of general equilibrium. Moreover, once questions of general equilibrium theory are brought up, this then raises questions of how monetary phenomena will effect the real variables within the Sraffian and Marxist framework. Furthermore, once these questions have arisen the imaginative reader should have no trouble in bringing up other troubling issues (e.g., the handling of nonrenewable resources; the role of demand; the integration of theories of imperfect competition; instances where output prices are different from input prices; etc.). Some of these issues are briefly discussed in Appendix E. These issues, although very important in their own right, seem to be relatively tangential to the main theme of the present work. This theme is that one may reconstruct Marx's argument of the theoretical genesis of capital based upon a commodity rather than the labor theory of value.

4. "Value can only manifest itself in the social relation of commodity to commodity." [*Capital*, Vol. I, p. 55]; "A commodity is a use-value or object of utility, and a value. It manifests itself as this two-fold thing, that is, as soon as its value assumes an independent form—viz., the form exchange-value. It never assumes this form when isolated, but only when placed in a value or exchange-relation with another commodity of a different kind." [*Capital*, Vol. I, p. 70.]

5. "The principal difficulty in the analysis of money is surmounted as soon as it is understood that the commodity is the origin of money. After that it is only a question of clearly comprehending the specific form peculiar to it. This is not easy because all bourgeois relations appear to be gilded, i.e., they appear to be money relations, and the money form, therefore, seems to possess an infinitely varied content which is quite alien to this form." [*Critique*, p. 64.]

6. "If one says, for instance, one yard of linen is worth two pounds of coffee, then the exchange-value of linen is expressed in the use-value of coffee, and it is moreover expressed in a definite quantity of this use-value." [*Critique*, p. 38.]

7. "Every commodity is compelled to choose some other commodity for its equivalent, and to accept the use-value, that is to say, the bodily shape of that other commodity as the form of its value." [*Capital*, Vol. I, p. 65.]

8. "When a commodity acts as equivalent, no quantitative determination of its value is expressed." [*Capital*, Vol. I, p. 65.]

9. Marx, "Preface" to *Capital*, Vol. I, p. 12.

10. "The particular commodity which thus represents the exchange-value of all commodities, that is to say, the exchange-value of commodities regarded as a particular, exclusive commodity, constitutes *money*. It is a crystallisation of the exchange-value of commodities and is formed in the exchange process." [*Critique*, p. 48; emphasis in original.]

11. "In this (equivalent) position it is a thing in which we see nothing but value, or whose palpably bodily form represents value." [*Capital*, Vol. I, p. 59.]

12. "The definition of a product as exchange-value thus necessarily implies that exchange-value obtain a separate existence, in isolation from the product. The exchange value which is separated from commodities and exists alongside them is itself a commodity, that is—*money*." [*Grundrisse*, p. 145; emphasis in original.]

13. This was the famous mistake Adam Smith attributed (probably somewhat unfairly) to the mercantalists. For discussions of this point, see Gray, *The Development of Economic Doctrine*, pp. 66–67; Schumpeter, *History of Economic Analysis*, pp. 360–362.

14. "The real question is: does not the bourgeois system of exchange itself necessitate a specific instrument of exchange? Does it not necessarily create a specific equivalent for all values?" [*Grundrisse*, p. 127.]

15. Marx, *Capital*, Vol. I, pp. 71–72.

16. This point was emphatically made by Bailey in an attack on Ricardo's theory of value. (See *Capital*, Vol. I, p. 72 fn.)

17. Marx, *Capital*, Vol. I, pp. 73–74.

18. "When we say that a commodity is in the equivalent form we express the fact that it is directly exchangeable with other commodities." [*Capital*, Vol. I, p. 64.]

19. "The commodity which has been set apart as the universal equivalent is now an object which satisfies a universal need arising from the exchange process itself, and has the same use-value for everybody—that of being carrier of exchange-value or a universal medium of exchange." [*Critique*, p. 48.]

20. "Since all commodities are merely particular equivalents of money, the latter being their universal equivalent, they, with regard to the latter as the universal commodity, play the parts of particular commodities." [*Capital*, Vol. I, p. 102.]

21. "The exchange value of a commodity, as a separate form of existence accompanying the commodity is *money*; the form in which all commodities equate, compare, measure themselves; that which dissolves into all commodities; the universal equivalent." [*Grundrisse*, p. 142; emphasis in original.]

22. "Thus the exchange value of a product creates money alongside the product." [*Grundrisse*, p. 145.]

23. "The elementary expression of the relative value of a single commodity, such as linen, in terms of the commodity, such as gold, that plays the part of money, is the price form of that commodity." [*Capital*, Vol. I, p. 81.]

24. "The money-form of an object . . . is simply the form under which certain social relations manifest themselves." [*Capital*, Vol. I, p. 103.]

25. "His commodity possesses for himself no immediate use-value. Otherwise, he would not bring it to market." [*Capital*, Vol. I, p. 97.]

26. "For its owner it is on the contrary a *non-use value* . . . the commodity is a use-value for its owner only so far as it is an exchange-value." [*Critique*, p. 42; emphasis in original.]

27. Marx is not concerned with the case where a commodity owner can either consume the product himself, in which case the product is not a commodity, or bring the product to market. Marx generally assumes that the product contains no use value for the owner. Thus, Marx has no parables of, e.g., the farmer trying to decide whether to market his output or eat it. This is in contrast to neoclassical economic theory; see, e.g., Hicks *Value and Capital*, pp. 35–37.

28. "To become use-values commodities must be altogether alienated; they must enter into the exchange process." [*Critique*, pp. 42–43.]

29. Marx, *Capital*, Vol. I, p. 96.

30. "The commodity, however, is the direct *unity* of use-value and exchange-value, and at the same time it is a commodity only in relation to other commodities. The *exchange process* of commodities is the *real* relation that exists between them. This is a social process which is carried on by individuals independently of one another, but they take part in it only as commodity-owners; they exist for one another only in so far as their commodities exist, they thus appear to be in fact the conscious representatives of the exchange process." [*Critique*, p. 41; emphasis in original.]

31. For a contrasting view, see, e.g., Adam Smith, *The Wealth of Nations*, pp. 117–118.

32. "To the degree that production is shaped in such a way that every producer becomes dependent on the exchange-value of his commodity . . . to the same degree must *money relations* develop." [*Grundrisse,* p. 146, emphasis in original.]

33. Anyway, the individual commodity owner is not interested in exchanging a commodity for just any other particular commodity; rather, the owner has many wants, and desires many different commodities.

34. "Although directly united in the commodity, use value and exchange value just as directly split apart . . . the commodity only becomes a commodity, only realize itself as exchange-value, in so far as its owner does not relate to it as use value. He appropriates use values only through their sale, their exchange for other commodities." [*Grundrisse,* p. 881.]

35. Some people feel that the distinction made by Marx between abstract and concrete labor is crucial. See, for example, *Colletti,* "Some Comments on Marx's Theory of Value"; also, Marx himself, *Capital,* Vol. I, p. 92 fn. Actually once it is clearly recognized that money itself represents value *in general,* then the distinction between abstract and concrete labor, or between abstract and concrete production, seems to become relatively insignificant. On this point, see, also, Steedman, *Marx After Sraffa,* p. 19.

36. See Marx, *Grundrisse,* pp. 174–180.

37. ". . . the commodity which has been set apart as universal equivalent acquires a dual use-value. In addition to its particular use-value as an individual commodity it acquires a universal use-value. This later use-value is itself a determinate form, i.e., it arises from the specific role which this commodity plays as a result of the universal action exerted on it by the other commodities in the exchange process." [*Critique,* p. 47.]

38. Occasionally in the *Grundrisse,* Marx refers to money as a symbol, see, e.g., p. 145. This apparently is a mistake on Marx's part which was corrected later in the *Critique* and in *Capital.* See Rosdolsky, *The Making of Marx's "Capital,"* Chapter 5; especially pp. 113–114.

39. Now, of course, paper money is not convertible to gold, and paper money is not representative of value; that is, paper money itself contains no (or very, very little) value. In light of the world-wide inflation since the United States went off the gold standard in 1971, as well as in view of the analysis of money contained herein, it may be worthwhile to consider going back to some sort of commodity standard on which to base the value of money. See, for example, the articles by Mundell, "Gold Would Serve into the 21st Century," *Wall Street Journal* (September 30, 1981), p. 29, and "The Debt Crisis: Causes and Solutions" (January 31, 1983).

40. Marx, *Capital,* Vol. I, p. 99.

8

COMMODITY FETISHISM

Section IV of Chapter I of *Capital* contains the famous digression on commodity fetishism.[1] In this section Marx develops the theory that in commodity producing societies the social character of people's labor appears as an objective character of the commodity. People relate to each other through the commodities they own, and commodities seem to acquire a life of their own; hence, a social relation between people assumes the form of a relation amongst things. That is to say, according to Marx, value is a relation between persons which comes to be expressed as a relation between things.[2] In commodity producing societies, labor assumes the form of a commodity, so that the social relations between individuals in the performance of their labor is disguised in the shape of social relations between the products of labor. The products of labor are treated as commodities and values, and labor is represented by the value of its product.

Here, we will rework Marx's theory of commodity fetishism based upon a commodity theory of value rather than Marx's labor theory of value.[3] We will show, contrary to what some feel,[4] that Marx's theory of commodity fetishism can be developed by using a properly specified commodity theory of value rather than Marx's labor theory of value. Indeed, in so doing, it will be shown that no major changes occur in the analysis of commodity fetishism when the commodity theory of value is inserted in place of the labor theory of value. The key to this reworking of this section of Marx's *Capital* lies in the clear understanding that, although a commodity is a thing, it is not a mere thing. More importantly, a commodity represents a form of property; property in turn is a relationship between people, and behind the property relationship between people are real powers between people.[5]

I will further expand on what is meant by commodity fetishism, and how the theory of commodity fetishism can be based upon a commodity theory of value, through a discussion and reply to a stimulating article by Frank Roosevelt.[6] The final part of this chapter is a defense against Roosevelt's argument that the work of such people as Sraffa and Joan Robinson is an example of commodity fetishism. It is argued that this is not true, and it is suggested that the root of the misunderstanding lies in an inadequate appreciation of the fact that Sraffa is dealing with commodities and not things. The implications of this distinction are further drawn out in the course of answering some of Roosevelt's criticisms.[7]

When it is said that a commodity possesses value, or that money comes to represent all value, it must be kept in mind that a commodity represents a social relationship. A commodity, considered *only* as a physical thing, does not have value. Commodities do not come forth from nature imbued with value. Commodities only have value because they are produced by other commodities. Furthermore, commodities can be produced by other commodities only in *human* societies, and only in human societies at a certain level of historical development. Commodities, considered as commodities, are not mere products of nature; *they are products of human societies.* Hence, commodities only have value because they reflect certain social relationships.

The attribution of social relationships to commodities as being inherent in the physical substance of commodities themselves is what Marx calls commodity fetishism.[8] Marx draws an analogy between commodity fetishism and religion.

According to Marx, the human mind invents various gods. These gods then seem to have various powers as they interact with each other and with people.[9] The gods themselves, as gods, seem to have power, and "in that world the productions of the human brain appear as independent beings endowed with life."[10]

So it is with the world of commodities. Commodities seem to have power (the ability to be exchanged with other commodities in certain given proportions) in and of themselves, as something due to their own physical characteristics, rather than as a result of given (human) social relations.

Thus, a commodity is (or reflects, embodies) a social relation. Furthermore, commodities can only exist if society rests upon certain types of *property relations.* Also, and most important, *all forms of property are social relations.* Things in themselves are not property; things only become property in society. Thus, whether things are private property, state property, common property, or whatever form of property, these things, when they are viewed as property, are expressing definite types of social relationships.[11]

Later it will be shown that capital is a certain type of commodity, basically a commodity which is used to create more commodities, or self-expanding value. Hence capital, being a certain type of commodity (i.e., capital is a subset within the set of commodities), also represents certain social relationships. Capital, *as with all forms of property*, is a social relationship.[12]

In commodity producing societies, people do indeed relate to each other through their commodities, and as commodity owners. Thus, if it appears that commodities have certain powers, that is because they do![13] However, they only have powers because of social institutions, because they reflect certain property and power relationships between people. Their powers are not natural, but arise only in human society, and only at a certain historical stage in the development of society.

For example, over time, with relatively stable prices, it will seem that, e.g., a slice of filet mignon naturally has more value than a cup of tea. Actually, neither a slice of filet mignon nor a cup of tea has any natural value; they only acquire value as commodities, as a form of property, hence as representing social relations.

Commodity fetishism is particularly striking with reference to the commodity which serves as the universal equivalent, i.e., gold.[14] Gold, when it comes out of the ground, is directly exchangeable for any other commodity; gold can buy anything which is for sale.[15] Hence, gold itself, as gold, seems to have strange magical properties.[16] Truly, gold can only buy anything because it serves as the universal equivalent; however, it appears that the universal equivalent is gold because of gold's innate physical properties. Thus:

> a social relation, a definite relation between individuals, here appears as a metal, a stone, as a purely physical, external thing which can be found, as such, in nature, and which is indistinguishable in form from its natural existence. Gold and silver, in and of themselves, are not money. Nature does not produce money, any more than it produces a rate of exchange or a banker. . . . To be money is not a natural attribute of gold and silver, and is therefore quite unknown to the physicist, chemist, etc., as such. But money is directly gold and silver.[17]

The precise relationship between Marx's use of the concept commodity fetishism and other schools of economic thought is poorly understood. Philip Armstrong, Andrew Glyn, and John Harrison, for example, feel that the concept commodity fetishism "would seem to" rest upon the labor theory of value.[18] Actually that is not true.

Almost every modern school of economic thought is aware (however dimly) of commodity fetishism. Take, for example, neoclassical economic theory. There, relative prices are ultimately determined by the marginal utility given off by commodity, so that $P_x/P_y = MU_x/MU_y$. Yet, the marginal utility of a good is not an inherent physical property of the commodity. The marginal utility given off by the commodity is entirely subjective

and depends upon people's tastes. The commodity as a physical thing has
no value; it only has value as people *perceive* that they can acquire utility
from it. In Lionel Robbins' words:

> It follows from what has just been said that the conception of an
> economic good is necessarily purely formal. There is no quality in things
> taken out of their relation to men which can make them economic
> goods. There is no quality in services taken out of relation to the end
> served which makes them economic. Whether a particular thing or a
> particular service is an economic good depends entirely on its relation to
> valuations.[19]

In the neoclassical theory of value, the value of a commodity is basically
subjective, depending upon what people perceive as the commodity's
marginal utility. In contrast to this, using either the Marxian labor theory of
value or the commodity theory of value proposed here, the commodity itself
does have an objective value. However, the commodity has that value only
as a commodity, hence as a social relation, and not because of its *physical*
nature.

Marx's advantage over other modern economists is not in his assertion
that commodities do not have value in and of themselves as physical objects. This is trivial. Rather, his contribution is that he shows how commodity fetishism necessarily arises under commodity production. People do
indeed relate to each other through their commodities. In commodity producing societies, commodities do have value. These are societies where
"production has the mastery over man, instead of being controlled by
him."[20] Here, social relations are indeed mediated through commodities.
So, for example, a commodity owner does wish to know how much of some
other product she or he will receive in exchange for her or his own.[21] Ordinary experience will indeed produce the (false) appearance that value is inherent to that commodity as a natural property, just as size or weight does.

It may be helpful here to recall that in one sense Marx's conception of
his subject matter is much broader than that of most modern non-Marxist
economists. In *Capital*, Marx is not only concerned with the production and
reproduction of goods and services in a capitalist society; he is also concerned with what may be called the reproduction of the social relations of
production. Marx is concerned with how the capitalist system, including the
social relations of production, reproduces itself. For this reason he is vitally
concerned with the appearances arising from capitalist production, and how
these appearances are perceived by people.[22] Indeed, *Capital* can be read as
a work which continually oscillates between the appearances which are
manifest on the surface of capitalist society and the so-called underlying
reality which generates these appearances.[23] On the basis of this

type of reading, it has been claimed that *Capital* is a work which "burns away illusion and discloses reality."[24]

Marx asserts that commodity and capitalist production will necessarily give off certain appearances. These appearances are not entirely false; they are simply only a part of the truth.[25] These appearances are *not* similar to vacuous hallucinations, for the appearances do not result from faulty perception.[26] Instead, in the case of commodity fetishism, they arise from the nature of the commodity itself, and from commodity production itself.

An example may be taken from chemistry to help clarify this point.[27] It appears (in the absence of gross pollution) that the air we breathe is of one homogeneous substance which may be called air. Actually, we know that air is made up of various component gases; nonetheless, in spite of this knowledge, air still appears to be one homogeneous substance.

The same holds true for commodities. It appears that commodities have value as one of their natural physical characteristics. However, it is commodity production itself, that is, the production of commodities by means of commodities, which necessarily gives rise to these appearances. Hence, Marx's major contribution to this area is to explain why commodity fetishism is indeed generated when products take on the commodity form.[28]

Recently, some writers have criticized Sraffa's work as being an example of commodity fetishism. For example, Frank Roosevelt has written an article entitled "Cambridge Economics as Commodity Fetishism."[29] The analysis presented above shows that a properly constructed commodity theory of value need not fall into the error of asserting that commodities contain value as part of their natural physical substance.

Nonetheless, in spite of this demonstration, it might be worthwhile to consider some of the points which Roosevelt makes. Unlike the present writer, Roosevelt feels very strongly that "it is fundamentally incorrect to link together the approaches of Marx and the Cantabrigians."[30] He further argues that "Sraffa's surplus is a physical rather than a value phenomenon."[31]

This point is not quite correct. Actually, Sraffa's surplus is a surplus of *commodities*. Commodities have both a use value and an exchange value, which, when expressed in money, is the price of the commodity. Hence, Sraffa's surplus, being a surplus of commodities (of outputs over inputs) is really *both* a physical and a value phenomenon.

Roosevelt states:

Because Sraffa fails to distinguish surplus from necessary labor, on the one hand, and treats the surplus as a physical phenomenon, on the other, he leads us to believe that the surplus we produce is a surplus of *things* rather than of labor.[32]

Actually, Sraffa's surplus is neither a surplus of (mere) things nor of labor. Sraffa's surplus is one of commodities.

Roosevelt also states:

> The Cantabrigians do not see capitalist production as something which involves specific social relations.[33]

Sraffa is dealing with the production of commodities by means of commodities. The second sentence of Chapter I states that "Commodities are produced by separate industries and are exchanged for one another at a market held after the harvest."[34] A commodity is not a thing; it is (as argued above) a social relationship. Hence, although Sraffa does not elaborate on the nature of the social relationships involved in commodity production,[35] he is dealing with specific social relations.

Roosevelt states:

> [Sraffa] obscures the historical significance of the fact that all the products of a capitalist economy come into being as values.[36]

Actually, in Sraffa's system all products come into being as commodities; hence, as values. By the way, in a capitalist economy many products are produced at and for use in the home; hence, they are not produced as values.[37]

Roosevelt also states:

> Sraffa has constructed an imaginary wold in which things produce things (by means of magic).[38]

Actually, Sraffa has constructed a world in which commodities produce commodities (by means of commodities). This bears a striking resemblance to the behavior of firms in capitalist societies. These firms purchase commodities in the various commodity markets. The firms then set the commodities to work to produce more commodities. The commodities which the firms produce are then sold in the market.

Roosevelt says:

> The Cantabrigians . . . in their view, *production consists of those interactions between people and nature which can be portrayed as technical relations*. . . . As a result they end up thinking of production not as a social affair but, rather, as a purely technical process. . . .[39]

Actually, for Sraffa production takes place by commodities. This already implies certain social relations. Sraffa assumes that at any given time the production process is given, and certain commodity inputs will be transformed into other outputs, via the production process. However, this is not a crucial assumption, and it can be relaxed to investigate the production process itself.[40]

It is true that some of the commodities the capitalists purchase may be more difficult to handle and control than others. For example, a production process which uses horses as a commodity input might be particularly messy, and the horses may at certain times of the day or year become particularly hard to handle. Perhaps the firm would need to hire special horse trainers or specialists in horse psychology to increase the output of the horses. Yet, at any given time the price of the horses, the work produced by the horses, and the horses' role in the production process may be taken as given.

The same argument holds for human workers. Workers sell their labor power, their capacity to work, to the capitalists. Labor power is a commodity. The capitalist purchases the commodity labor power and sets the worker to work producing other commodities. The commodity labor power has certain peculiarities, most notably a human will of its own. The workers may at certain times be particularly hard to handle. The firm may hire special personnel officers or specialists in industrial psychology to increase the output of the workers. Conversely, the workers may have recourse to their own devices to decrease their output and/or make their working conditions more pleasant. Yet, at any given time, the wage rate, the work produced by the workers, and the workers' role in the production process may be taken as given. This, by the way, is the approach taken not only by Sraffa and his followers, but by Marx as well.[41]

To sum up, the crux of the problem with Roosevelt's misdirected criticisms seems to be that he fails to realize that a commodity itself is a social relation. While Roosevelt does note that capital itself is a social relation,[42] he makes the mistake of thinking that Sraffa is talking about things rather than commodities. Yet, commodities are not mere things; commodities are owned by people, they are a form of property, and

> As soon as any society, by custom or convention or law, makes a distinction between property and mere physical possession it has in effect defined property as a right. And even primitive societies make this distinction. This holds both for land or flocks or the produce of the hunt which were held in common, and for such individual property as there was. In both cases, to have a property is to have a right in the sense of an enforceable claim to some use or benefit of something, whether it is a right to a share in some common resource or an individual right in some particular things. What distinguishes property from mere momentary possession is that property is a claim that will be enforced by society or the state, by custom or convention or law . . . philosophers, jurists, and political and social theorists have always treated property as a right, not a thing; a right in the sense of an enforceable claim to some use or benefit of something.[43]

Thus, commodities are a form of property and hence entail certain mutual rights between people as commodity owners. Moreover, underneath these property *rights* are *real powers* and social relations.[44]

Social relations are embedded in Sraffa's work, even though he nowhere clearly spells them out. The fact that Sraffa deals with commodity production, that there is a rate of profit, that one group of people receives income because they are involved in the production process and receive that income in the form of wages, while another group of people receives income in the form of profits — all this suggests that Sraffa has built a model which bears a striking resemblance to capitalist society, and which does take into account social relationships. In conclusion, neither Sraffa's work nor a properly specified commodity theory of value necessarily falls into the mistake of fetishizing commodities; moreover, one may develop Marx's theory of commodity fetishism based upon a commodity rather than Marx's labor theory of value.[45]

NOTES

1. "The Fetishism of Commodities and the Secret Thereof," pp. 81–96.

2. Marx, *Capital*, p. 85 fn.

3. G. A. Cohen's fine exposition of commodity fetishism in *Karl Marx's Theory of History: A Defense,* Chap. V, pp. 115–133, contains the assertion that most of Marx's "fetishism doctrine may be stated within a . . . material theory, such as Sraffa's" [p. 116 fn.]; however, he does not do so. Peculiarly, that is the only chapter in his main text which uses the labor theory of value. (See his "Foreword", particularly p. xii.)

4. See, e.g., Philip Armstrong, Andrew Glyn, and John Harrison, In Defense of Value: A Reply to Ian Stedman," *Capital and Class* No. 6, (1978): 1–31.

5. The interpretation offered in this chapter relies heavily upon the work of the political theorist C. B. MacPherson. On the importance of the specification of property rights and forms of property in economic theory, see Roemer, *A General Theory of Exploitation and Class* and " New Directions in the Marxian Theory of Exploitation and Class."

6. Roosevelt, "Cambridge Economics as Commodity Fetishism," *Review of Radical Political Economics* 7, No. 4 (1975); reprinted in Schwartz, *The Subtle Anatomy of Capitalism,* pp. 412–457

7. As a general rule, the present author has chosen not to directly criticize other writers. Among writers working more or less within a Marxist framework, there seems to be a relative superfluity of criticisms of each other and rather a lack of what may be termed positive analysis. Much of the criticism of others is rather hostile and pointed. This is no doubt at least partly due to the rather precarious position in which left-leaning academicians generally find themselves in advanced capitalist societies, and may be an example of displaced aggression. An exception is made here for Roosevelt due to the importance of his criticisms and the questions he raises.

8. "The crude materialism of the economists who regard as the natural properties of things what are social relations of production among people, and qualities which things obtain because they are subsumed under these relations, is at the same time just as crude an idealism, even fetishism, since it imputes social relations to things as inherent characteristics, and thus mystifies them." [*Grundrisse*, p. 687.]

9. Marx, *Capital*, Vol. I, p. 83.

10. Ibid.

11. See Macpherson, *Property: Mainstream and Critical Positions* (University of Toronto Press, 1978), Chap. 1.

12. Hence the emphasis by some followers of Marx (see, e.g., Bose, *Marx on Exploitation and Inequality*) that capital is a social relation is not wrong; however, it is vague, since capital is a type of commodity, and all commodities represent social relations. On this point, see Cohen, who argues that "capital is not a relationship between purchaser and vendor of labour power. Rather, it promotes that relationship and is reproduced by it." [*Karl Marx's Theory of History*, p. 352.]

13. "The social character of activity, as well as the social form of the product, and the share of individuals in production here appear as something alien and objective, confronting the individuals, not as their relation to one another, but as their subordination to relations which subsist independently of them and which arise out of collisions between mutually indifferent individuals. The general exchange of activities and products, which has become a vital condition for each individual — their mutual interconnection — here appears as something alien to them, autonomous, as a thing. In exchange value, the social connection between persons is transformed into a social relation between things; personal capacity into objective wealth." [*Grundisse*, p. 157.]

14. Marx, *Critique*, p. 49.

15. Thus, Christopher Columbus felt that "Gold is a wonderful thing! Whoever possesses it is master of everything he desires. With gold, one can even get souls into heaven." (Quoted in *Capital*, Vol. I, p. 148.)

16. On the perceived virtues of gold, see Jack Kemp, the Republican Congressman from New York State, who quotes approvingly that "Gold is just; it deals equally between one man and another, between past, present and future; it does not take from the weak and give to the strong; it should appeal to the seeker of social justice, to the social democrat." ("The Renewal of Western Monetary Standards," *Wall Street Journal* (April 7, 1982); Kemp is quoting William Rees-Mogg, the former editor of the *London Times*.)

17. Marx, *Grundisse*, p. 239.

18. Armstrong, Glynn and Harrison, "In Defense of Value: A Reply to Ian Steedman," p. 19.

19. Robbins, *An Essay on the Nature and Significance of Economic Science*, pp. 46–47.

20. Marx, *Capital*, Vol. I, p. 93; moreover, ". . . competition is nothing more than the way in which the many capitals force the inherent determinants of capital upon one another and upon themselves . . . the insipidity of the view that free competition is the ultimate development of human freedom; and that the negation of free competition equals negation of individual freedom. . . . This kind of individual freedom is therefore at the same time the most complete suspension of all individual freedom, and the most complete subjugation of individuality under social conditions which assume the form of objective powers, even of overpowering objects — of things independent of the relations among individuals themselves." [*Grundrisse*, p. 651–652.]

21. Marx, *Capital*, Vol. I, p. 86.

22. So Marx, at one point, warns the reader that "if, as the reader will have realized to his great dismay, the analysis of the actual intrinsic relations of the capitalist process of production is a very complicated matter and very extensive; if it is a work of science to resolve the visible, merely external movement into the true intrinsic movement, it is self-evident that conceptions which arise about the laws of production in the minds of agents of capitalist production and circulation will diverge drastically from these real laws and will merely be the conscious expression of the visible movements. The conceptions of the merchant, stockbroker, and banker, are necessarily quite distorted . . ." [*Capital,* Vol. III pp. 312–313.]

23. Cohen, "Karl Marx and the Withering Away of Social Science," *Philosophy and Public Affairs* **1**, No. 2, (1972); 183; see, also Marx: ". . . phenomena and their hidden

substratum. The former appear directly and spontaneously as current modes of thought; the latter must first be discovered by science. Classical political economy nearly touches the true relation of things, without, however, consciously formulating it." [*Capital*, Vol. I, p. 594.]

24. Goldway, "Appearance and Reality in Marx's *Capital*," p. 447.

25. Ibid., pp. 442–443.

26. "A social relation of production appears as something existing apart from individual human beings, and the distinctive relations into which they enter in the course of production in society appear as the specific properties of a thing — *it is this perverted appearance, this prosaically real, and by no means imaginary mystification* that is characteristic of all social forms of labour positing exchange-value." [*Critique*, p. 49; emphasis added.]

27. This is Marx's example. (See *Capital*, p. 86.)

28. "It is a characteristic feature of labour which posits exchange-value that it causes the social relations of individuals to appear in the perverted form of a social relation between things. . . . Although it is thus correct to say that exchange-value is a relation between persons, it is however necessary to add that it is a relation hidden by a material veil. . . . Exchange-value thus appears to be a social determination of use values, a determination which is proper to them as things and in consequence of which they are able in definite proportions to take one another's place in the exchange process, i.e., they are equivalents. . . . Only the conventions of our everyday life make it appear commonplace and ordinary that social relations into which people enter in the course of their work appear as the relations of things to one another and of things to people." [*Critique*, p. 34.]

29. In Schwartz, *The Subtle Anatomy of Capitalism.*

30. Ibid., p. 413.

31. Ibid., p. 442.

32. Ibid., p. 443; emphasis in original.

33. Ibid., p. 439.

34. Sraffa, *Production of Commodities by Means of Commodities*, p. 3.

35. As Marx does; see, e.g., his comment: "A negro is a negro. In certain circumstances he becomes a slave. A mule is a machine for spinning cotton. Only under certain circumstances does it become capital. Outside these circumstances, it is no more capital than gold is intrinsically money, or sugar is the price of sugar. . . . Capital is a social relation of production. It is a historical relation of production." [Karl Marx, "Lohnarbeit und Kapital," *Neue Rheinische Zeitung*, No. 266 (April 7, 1849), quoted in *Capital*, Vol. I, p. 839 fn.]

36. Roosevelt, "Cambridge Economics as Commodity Fetishism," p. 443.

37. On the importance of home production see, e.g., Scott Burns, *The Household Economy.*

38. *Roosevelt*, "Cambridge Economics as Commodity Fetishism," pp. 438–439.

39. Ibid., pp. 421–422; emphasis in original.

40. See, e.g., Steedman, *Marx After Sraffa*, Chap. 6, pp. 77–87.

41. "For the time being, necessary labour supposed as such; i.e., that the worker always obtains only the minimum of wages. This supposition is necessary, of course, so as to establish the laws of profit in so far as they are not determined by the rise and fall of wages or by the influence of landed property. All of these fixed suppositions themselves become fluid in the further course of development. But only by holding them at the beginning is their development possible without confounding everything. Besides, it is practically sure that, for instance, however the standard of necessary labor may differ at various epochs and in various countries, or how much, in consequence of the demand and supply of labour, its amount and ratio may change, at any given epoch the standard is to be considered and acted upon as a fixed one by capital. To consider these changes themselves belongs altogether to the chapter treating of wage labour." [*Grundrisse*, p. 817.]

42. Roosevelt, "Cambridge Economics as Commodity Fetishism," pp. 445–446.

43. Macpherson, *Property: Mainstream and Critical Positions*, p. 3.

44. See Cohen, *Karl Marx's Theory of History,* pp. 219–225, for an elaboration of this point.

45. The following analogy may prove helpful in illuminating some of the issues discussed in this chapter and in the work in general. One may say that things are to commodities as people are to labor power. Under certain social conditions, in certain societies, things take on the form of commodities, that is, things become commodities. Also, under certain social conditions, in certain societies, people take on the form of labor power, that is, people become labor power. The set of people may be construed to be a subset of the set of things; similarly, the set of labor power may be seen to be a subset of the set of commodities. This is true whether one is using either a commodity or a labor theory of value. (This analogy was suggested by Michael Federow.)

9

THE FUNCTIONS OF MONEY IN THE SIMPLE CIRCULATION OF COMMODITIES

Chapter III, the last chapter of Part I of *Capital*, is entitled "Money, or the Circulation of Commodities."[1] Marx's goal in this chapter is a rather limited though important one. Having previously argued that money will of necessity arise out of the circulation of commodities, and that money is (originally) merely the physical incarnation of the exchange value of commodities, or the universal equivalent, Marx argues that money will eventually generate the desire/need for money itself, and for *more* money (principally through its functions as a hoard and as a means of payment). Money, which is originally simply the reflex or the representation of the value inherent in all commodities, and which crystallizes out of the circulation of commodities, comes to be desired as an end in itself, as the representation of all value. Thus, money is desired in the place of the particular use values of particular commodities. Chapter III of *Capital* forms an important link to Part II of *Capital*, "The Transformation of Money into Capital," where Marx elaborates on the definition of capital and on how money (given the proper institutional framework, most notably a market for labor power) will generate capital.

Unless viewed in its proper perspective, this chapter of *Capital* may be disappointing to modern economists. In his presentation, Marx has not yet developed the notion of credit; hence, the idea of a liquidity preference, or of the shifting of assets in and out of various financial markets, is not and cannot yet be addressed in this chapter of *Capital*. Credit, which is the link between the future and the present, as well as the role of expectations in the face of uncertainty and the differences between equilibria with or without active money are all issues which are not and cannot yet be raised at this point in his analysis. Marx cannot yet deal with these issues because, according to him, "money based upon credit implies . . . conditions, which from our standpoint of the simple circulation of commodities, are as yet totally unknown to us."[2]

Thus, at this stage in his analysis, Marx is still only dealing with the simple circulation of commodities;[3] hence, he is unable to develop the full implications of a monetarized capitalist economy. For Marx, money does have other functions which are not addressed in this chapter; perhaps most notably, money may be used as credit. Yet, it is not until Volume III of *Capital* that Marx more fully elaborates upon this. There he argues that credit-money does *not* arise out of the circulation of money; instead, this form of money arises out of the circulation of bills of exchange. As Marx explains:

> I have shown earlier . . . how the function of money as a means of payment, and therewith a relation of creditor and debtor between the producer and trader of commodities, develop from the simple circulation of commodities. With the development of commerce and of the capitalist mode of production, which produces solely with an eye to circulation, this natural basis of the credit system is extended, generalised, and worked out. . . . Just as these mutual advances of producers and merchants make up the real foundation of credit, so does the instrument of their circulation, the bill of exchange, form the basis of credit-money proper, of bank-notes, etc. These do not rest upon the circulation of money, be it metallic or government-issued paper money, but rather upon the circulation of bills of exchange.[4]

However, in Chapter III of Volume I of *Capital*, that is, at the stage of his presentation with which we are now dealing, Marx is only concerned with developing the functions which money assumes during the course of the simple circulation of commodities. Marx is not yet dealing with capitalist production. He has not yet even introduced the notion of capitalist production.

In Volume I of *Capital*, Marx argues that the first chief function of money in the simple circulation of commodities is to act as a universal measure of value. For Marx, commodities are commensurable only because they are realized human labor, and money becomes the socially recognized incarnation of human labor.

Money comes to be used as a standard of price and as money of account. In the circulation of commodities, commodities change their form, from the commodity form, to the money form, and back to the commodity form. According to Marx, no value is created in this circulation of commodities. Money comes to be used as a means of purchase by actually realizing the price of other commodities. Here money is the medium of circulation; Marx determines the amount of money required to circulate commodities. Money takes the form of coins, which, when worn away, become a symbol of value. Marx argues that this is the basis upon which the commodities money may be replaced by paper money which is issued by the State.

Money may also be hoarded; in fact there develops the need to do so when money comes to be used as a means of payment. This occurs when, according to Marx, "with the development of circulation, conditions arise under which the alienation of commodities becomes separated, by an interval of time, from the realisation of their prices."[5] Some of the implications of this development are explored by Marx; this paves the way to Part II of *Capital*, where Marx presents his account of the theoretical genesis of capital.[6]

Here, we will present a reworking of Chapter III of *Capital*, "Money, or the Circulation of Commodities," based upon a commodity rather than upon Marx's labor theory of value. The reworking of this section of Marx results in the following major changes:

1. Commodities are not commensurable because they are realized human labor (as Marx held); rather they are commensurable simply because they are produced by other commodities.[7]

2. Commodities have value not because they are produced by human labor; instead they have value because they are produced by other commodities.

In spite of these changes (or, alternatively, with these changes), Chapter III of *Capital* may be reconstructed upon the basis of a commodity theory of value rather than upon Marx's labor theory of value.

Now, commodities themselves generate money. One commodity is set apart from all the others to represent value. Following Marx, it will be assumed that the commodity which functions as money is gold.

Money represents the value inherent in commodities. Value is an objective characteristic of commodities which they possess by virtue of being produced by other commodities. The first chief function of money is thus to act as a measure of value, "and only by virtue of this function does gold, the equivalent commodity par excellence, become money."[8]

The expression of a commodity's value in gold is that commodity's price. All commodities (except for the commodity which functions as money) come to express their value in money, that is, they come to have a price. Money itself has no price. Its value can only be expressed through the use of the expanded form of relative value, by comparing it with a given quantity of each and every other commodity.

With the development of money, all commodities may be compared with each other. Yet, the commodities are not compared directly with each other; the comparison is mediated by money. Thus, for example, a dozen eggs is not compared directly with so many cups of tea. Rather, both a dozen eggs and a cup of tea have a price, each being worth so much gold. By expressing their value in terms of gold, they may be (indirectly) equated with each other. Therefore, each commodity comes to express its value as a price, as being worth a certain quantity of gold. Furthermore, a certain quantity of gold comes to act as a *standard of price* by means of which different commodities may be compared.[9] That is, a definite physical quantity of gold functions as a standard of price.

Gold comes to function as a standard of price, so, for example, 1 ounce of gold equals $35. Once gold serves as a standard of price, commodities come to express themselves as so many dollars rather than as so much gold. This is because gold itself becomes coined. When this happens, a one dollar coin represents a certain quantity of gold, say 1/35 ounce of gold. The coins themselves are given names, e.g., 1/35 ounce of gold is a dollar. Commodities then come to express their values not in the gold itself, but in the names of the coins. For example, rather than saying that a football equals 1 ounce of gold, a football has a price of $35. A certain quantity of gold acts as a standard of price; and gold is able to do this only because it itself has value.

Thus it develops that a given unit of gold, say 1/35 ounce, is given a name, say, a dollar. That dollar then comes to represent both the value of all other commodities, and a certain quantity of gold.[10]

The price of a commodity shows that the universal equivalent, gold, is directly exchangeable for the commodity at the given price. Yet, it does not mean that the particular commodity is in fact exchangeable for gold. In order for a commodity to realize its price, it must actually be exchanged for gold. The asymmetry in the relationship arises out of the earlier discussed forms of value, which arises out of contradictions within the commodity itself. This asymmetry simply means that while money, the universal equivalent, can buy any commodity offered for sale, a commodity cannot always be readily sold into money.[11] This of course becomes painfully evident during recessionary periods of the business cycle.[12]

A commodity is originally a nonuse value to its owner. In order for it to become a use value, it must go through a circulation process. A commodity is first exchanged for gold. When commodities express their prices in gold, the gold is but the money form (i.e., it represents the value) of those commodities themselves. The gold, acting as money, is then exchanged for another commodity which is purchased for its use value. Thus the commodity realized its own value by being exchanged for the universal equivalent. This universal equivalent, money, represents all use values. The universal equivalent is then exchanged for another commodity, that is, for a particular form of its use value. This new commodity is purchased for its use value. It falls out of the sphere of exchange and into that of consumption.[13]

Money is the metamorphosed shape of all other commodities. It is the result of their general alienation.[14] Although gold can qualitatively purchase anything, the prices of other commodities define the limits of money's convertibility into other commodities by pointing to its quantity. Thus, although money can buy anything, its quantity is limited. Hence, it can only buy so much of other commodities.[15]

The circuit made by one commodity may be shown as C-M-C, where C stands for commodity and M for money. A commodity is exchanged for money which is exchanged for another commodity. The total of all the different circuits of the form C-M-C may be called the circulation of commodities.[16]

It is true that no one can sell a commodity unless someone else purchases a commodity. Yet, no one must purchase a commodity just because that person has just sold another commodity. If the interval in time between the two complementary phases of the complete metamorphosis becomes too great (i.e., from C-M, and then from M-C), then there could be an economic crisis. Thus, the simple circulation of commodities implies the possibility of an economic crisis.[17]

The circulation of commodities is not the same as the direct barter of products. Attempts to reduce the former to the later will obscure the differences between the circulation of commodities and the direct barter of products. Moreover, Marx argues that it is incorrect to

> explain away the contradictions of capitalist production, by reducing the relations between the persons engaged in that mode of production, to the simple relations arising out of the circulation of commodities. The production and circulation of commodities are . . . phenomena that occur to a greater or less extent in modes of production the most diverse. If we are acquainted with nothing but the abstract categories of circulation, which are common to all these modes of production, we cannot possibly know anything of the specific points of difference of those modes, nor pronounce any judgement upon them.[18]

With the formula C-M-C, a commodity begins the process of circulation. Another commodity ends the process. The movement of the commodity is therefore a circuit, with one commodity leaving and another commodity returning. However, in the circulation of commodities, a circuit is not made by the money. Money moves farther and farther away from its starting point. Money functions as a *means of purchase* when it realizes the price of a commodity. It transfers the commodity from the seller to the buyer, and removes the money from the buyer to the seller. Later, that seller will become a buyer, and the money will move farther away from the original money holder.[19]

The circulation of commodities is really nothing more than the change of form of commodities. The movement of money is the expression of the circulation of commodities. Yet, it may appear as if the circulation of commodities is the *result* of the movement of money. This would be a confusion of cause and effect. Money moves because commodities are changing their form (from nonuse value, to exchange value, to a use value). Yet, it appears that commodities circulate because of the movement of money:

> Money functions as a means of circulation, only because in it the values of commodities have independent reality. Hence its movement, as the medium of circulation, is, in fact, merely the movement of commodities while changing their forms.[20]

Money, when functioning as the medium of circulation, remains continually within the sphere of circulation. Yet, the sphere of circulation can absorb only so much money. So long as money is itself a commodity, gold, the price level is determined by the value of money. In the familiar equation of exchange, $MV = PQ$, the price level is determined by the value of money. For example, suppose V and Q are constant, and the value of gold declines (that is, fewer commodity inputs are needed to produce one unit output of gold). In this case the price level will rise.[21] Thus, the price level varies inversely with the value of gold. Ceteris paribus, an increase in the value per unit of gold will cause prices to fall, and a decrease in the value of gold will cause prices to rise. Given the price level, velocity, and the quantity of commodities circulating, the amount of money in circulation will be determined residually. Thus, in the circulation of commodities, the amount of money in circulation is determined by the value of the money (which is determined in the production process), the velocity of money, and the number of commodities circulating.

So, for example, a decline in the value of gold, will, ceteris paribus, cause an increase in the price level which will cause an increase in the amount of money in circulation. That is to say, prices go up, which cause the supply of money to go up.

The more familiar monetarist theory is that an increase in the supply of money causes an increase in the level of prices. This is not true (holds Marx) so long as money itself has value. Money has value as long as it is a commodity which is produced by other commodities.[22]

Therefore, commodities have prices. These prices are expressed by indicating that they are worth so much gold. In order for commodities to actually realize their prices, they must be exchanged for a definite amount of gold:

> The weight of gold represented in imagination by the prices or money-names of commodities, must confront those commodities, within the circulation, in the shape of coins or pieces of gold of a given denomination.[23]

Coining is the business of the State. The only difference between coin and bullion is one of shape. The gold can at any time pass from one form to the other. However, it happens that during the actual process of circulation, the coins wear away. In this manner,

> Name and substance, nominal weight and real weight, begin their process of separation. Coins of the same denomination become different in value, because they are different in weight.[24]

There is a natural tendency of circulation to change the coins into a semblance of what they claim to be. Coins become a symbol of the weight of the metal which they are supposed to contain. A distinction is created between the coins as mere pieces of metal, which contain a certain amount of value, and their function of symbolizing a certain amount of value. This creates the latent possibility of replacing metallic coins by tokens of some other material, including paper. Paper money does not represent value, that is, it contains no value itself. Rather it symbolizes value; it is a token of a certain amount of value. In this manner, the function of gold as coin becomes independent of the metallic value of that gold; paper notes can then serve as coins.[25]

Insofar as paper money merely replaces gold coins, the quantity of money in circulation is determined by the above-mentioned rules. If convertible paper money is issued by the state and if it exceeds its "proper limit," that is, excess money is forced into circulation, then the monetary theory of inflation comes into its own. In that case, assuming, that the velocity and quantity of commodities circulating are held constant, an increase in the (paper) money supplied will result in a rise in the general price level.[26]

In the formula C-M-C, money functions only as a medium of exchange. Its appearance is transitory, and its function is to transform one commodity into another. However, money is also a store of value (indeed, it originally functions as a medium of exchange only because it has value). As a store of value it is capable of being accumulated.

Money can be stored up and kept in the form of a *hoard*. With the development of the circulation of commodities there develops the desire and the necessity of storing up money. With hoarding, a new motive enters the scene.[27] Commodities are now sold not for the aim of later buying a new commodity. Instead, commodities are sold with the goal of replacing commodities with money.[28] Money, instead of appearing briefly in the metamorphosis of commodities, now becomes solidified into a hoard.[29]

Commodity owners attempt to sell commodities without buying new commodities, so that they can build up a hoard of gold. Commodity owners can, as a group, make sales without purchases and thus accumulate money because there is one group of commodity owners who are able to make purchases without making sales—these are the owners of the gold mines. The ability of these particular commodity owners to make purchases without making sales allows other commodity owners to make sales without purchases. Thus, "in this way, all along the line of exchange, hoards of gold and silver of varied extent are accumulated."[30]

Since gold can buy anything, it is qualitatively infinite. However, each hoarder has only so much gold, and can hence buy only so much. Thus arises the greed for gold. As it is put in the Bible:

> A feast is made for laughter,
> And wine maketh merry:
> But money answerth all things.
> —Ecclesiastes 10:19

Therefore, as explained above (see Chapter 7), commodities themselves generate money, the universal equivalent.[31] Since this money, precisely because it is the universal equivalent, can buy anything, it becomes a source of desire in and of itself (rather than just to aid in the transformation of one commodity into another). Since money is not just a medium of circulation but also a store of value, it may be kept in the form of a hoard. Although the value of money may itself vary (due either to changes in the production of gold or in the production of the other commodities), this does not change the fact that more gold is preferable to less gold:

> This antagonism between the quantitative limits of money and its qualitative boundlessness continually acts as a spur to the hoarder in his Sisyphus-like labour of accumulating. It is with him as it is with a conqueror who sees in every new country annexed, only a new boundary.[32]

Hoards themselves also serve as a latent supply of currency. With, for example, changes in the quantity of commodities circulating, or in the price level, the demand for money as currency will change. As the demand for money increases, hoards are transformed into currency and the supply of currency increases. As the demand for money decreases, part of the money returns to the form of a hoard.[33]

With the development of circulation, conditions arise under which the alienation of commodities becomes separated by an interval of time from the realization of their prices. First commodities are sold, but they are not *paid* for until later. The commodity changes hands, but the purchaser buys as the representative of money or of future money. Now the seller becomes a creditor and the purchaser becomes a debtor. In these circumstances, money now functions as a *means of payment*.[34]

With the use of money as a means of payment, the appearance of the two equivalents, commodities and money, ceases to be simultaneous. Here, money first serves to measure the value of the commodity to be sold. Then it functions as an ideal means of purchase; this causes the commodity to actually change hands. Finally, on the day fixed for payment, the money enters circulation, changes hands, and functions as a means of payment.

This is a further development in the importance of money. With the simple circulation of commodities, money comes into the scene only briefly as a means of circulation.[35] There the seller turns a commodity into money in order to satisfy some want. With hoarding, money as the expression of independent exchange value is stored up. Money is desired in and of itself.[36] With the development of money as a means of payment, the seller now sells in order to be able to pay a *previously* incurred debt. The goal of the sale by the debtor is thus to get money. Money functioning as means of payment thus furthers the desire and necessity for money.

With money functioning as a means of payment, the buyer can convert money into commodities before turning the commodities into money. The buyer is thus able to complete the second metamorphosis of commodities (M-C) before completing the first (C-M). Meanwhile, the seller's commodity circulates and has been converted into a use value before it has been converted into money.

With the development of money as a means of payment, a long chain of debts among different commodity owners develops. To a certain extent these lines of mutual debts can cancel each other out. In this situation money functions only ideally as a measure of value. Insofar as these payments actually have to be made, money does not function as a circulating medium (since the commodities are already circulating without money coming into circulation). Rather, money functions as the independent existence of exchange value, as value itself.[37]

This becomes evident if there is a financial crisis. In this case money becomes suddenly and immediately transformed from its ideal shape of money of account into hard cash as creditors insist on calling in their debts. In these circumstances the antithesis between commodities and their value form, money, becomes exacerbated.[38]

In summary, money grows out of the circulation of commodities. Money's first chief function is simply to represent the value of other commodities. As the universal equivalent of all other commodities, money acts to further the circulation of commodities. Money appears in circulation briefly in the metamorphosis of the value form of commodities (from being nonuse values to use values). However, money is also capable of being stored up or hoarded. Hoarding is a method of acquiring riches, since the hoard of money can potentially be used to purchase any other commodity. With the development of money as a means of payment, the pursuit of money as an end in itself (rather than just to assist in the circulation of commodities and the satisfaction of use values) develops further. Now the buyer of commodities becomes a debtor, and the buyer needs the money in order to pay off past debts. The buyer now needs not just other commodities, but money, exchange value itself. Furthermore, the development of money into a means of payment makes it necessary for the buyer to accumulate money in preparation for the dates fixed for the payment of these past debts.[39]

NOTES

1. Marx, *Capital*, Vol. I, pp. 106–162.
2. Ibid., p. 143.
3. For more on this, see Appendix D.
4. Marx, *Capital*, Vol. III, pp. 400–401.
5. Marx, *Capital*, Vol. I, p. 151.
6. Marx's account of the *historical* genesis of capital is given at the end of Volume I of *Capital*; see Part VIII, pp. 784–848.
7. For more on this, see Hawkins, *The Language of Nature*, pp. 333–341. This important point was also noted in Chapter 6. It bears repetition here because of its importance in fully comprehending the nature of the commodity theory of value.
8. Marx, *Capital*, Vol. I, p. 106.
9. "Gold . . . as a piece of metal of definite weight . . . is the standard of price. Gold becomes the measure of value because as an exchange-value it is compared with the exchange-values of other commodities; in its aspect as a standard of price a definite quantity of gold serves as a unit for other quantities of gold." [*Critique*, p. 71.]
10. Marx, *Capital*, Vol. I, p. 113.
11. Ibid., pp. 115–116.
12. ". . . [T]his contradiction between the commodity's particular natural qualities and its general social qualities contains from the beginning the possibility that these two separated forms in which the commodity exists are not convertible into one another. . . . There thus arises the possibility that the commodity, in its specific form as product, can no longer be exchanged for, equated with, its general form as money." [*Grundrisse*, p. 147–148.]
13. Marx, *Capital*, Vol. I, pp. 116–120.
14. So, as the sociologist Simmel puts it: "By being the equivalent to all the manifold things in one and the same way, money becomes the most frightful leveler. For money expresses all qualitative differences of things in terms of 'how much'? Money, with all its colorlessness and indifference, becomes the common denominator of all values; irreparably it hollows out the core of things, their individuality, their specific value, and their incomparability. All things float with equal specific gravity in the constantly moving stream of money. All things lie on the same level and differ from one another only in the size of the area which they cover." "The Metropolis and Mental Life" in *The Sociology of Georg Simmel*, p. 414.
15. Marx, *Capital*, Vol. I, pp. 123–124.
16. Ibid., p. 126.
17. Ibid., pp. 127–128.
18. Ibid., p. 128 fn.
19. Ibid., p. 129.
20. Ibid., p. 131.
21. However, *relative* prices are unaffected by changes in the value of the money commodity alone.
22. Ibid., pp. 132–139.
23. Ibid., p. 140.
24. Ibid., p. 141.
25. Ibid., pp. 141–142.

26. Ibid., pp. 143–144.

27. Not all approved of this new motive;

> Cursed be he above all others
> Who's enslaved by love of money.
> Money takes the place of brothers,
> Money takes the place of parents,
> Money brings us war and slaughter.
> —Anacreon, *Odes*, XXIX 8

28. Thus, "All else is nonsense in compare with gold." Artiphanes, *Fabulae Incertai*, Fragment No. 60.

29. Marx, *Capital*, Vol. I, p. 146.

30. Ibid., p. 148.

31. "The properties of money as (1) measure of commodity exchange; (2) medium of exchange; (3) representative of commodities (hence object of contracts); (4) general commodity alongside the particular commodities, all simply follow from its character as exchange value separated from commodities themselves and objectified." [*Grundrisse*, p. 146.]

32. Marx, *Capital*, Vol. I, p. 150.

33. Ibid., pp. 150–151.

34. Ibid., pp. 151–152.

35. "Since money as *universal material representative of wealth* emerges from circulation, and is as such itself a product of circulation. . . ." [*Grundrisse*, pp. 216–217; emphasis in original.]

36. "In the particular commodity, in so far as it is a price, wealth is posited only as an ideal form, not yet realized; and in so far as it has a particular use value, it represents merely a quite singular facet of wealth. In money, by contrast, the price is realized; and its substance is wealth itself . . . money is the general form of wealth, while the totality of these particularities form its substance. . . . Money is therefore the god among commodities. . . . From its servile role, in which it appears as mere medium of circulation, it suddenly changes into the lord and god of the world of commodities. It represents the divine existence of commodities, while they represent its earthly form." [*Grundrisse*, p. 221.]

37. Marx, *Capital*, Vol. I, pp. 154–156.

38. Ibid., p. 155.

39. This section has followed Marx in discussing money, or the circulation of commodities. It does not deal with simple commodity production, or, indeed, with production at all. This point, which has been insufficiently grasped by most followers and interpretators of Marx, is further elaborated in Appendix D.

10

THE TRANSFORMATION OF
MONEY INTO CAPITAL

Part II of *Capital* is entitled "The Transformation of Money into Capital."
Just over 30 pages long, this part of *Capital* is divided into three chapters of
approximately even length. Chapter IV, "The General Formula for Capital,"
argues that all new capital begins as money which by a definite process is
transformed into capital. Marx argues that the first distinction between money
used as money and money used as capital lies in their form of circulation.
Money used as money takes the form of circulation of C-M-C, where C stands
for commodity and M stands for money. On the other hand, money used as
capital takes the form of M-C-M', where M' is greater than M. This is buying commodities with money in order to sell those commodities for *more*
money. M' is an increase or excess over the original value M. The difference
between M' and M is called surplus value. Here money and commodities are
used to create more money; this is self-expanding value, which is capital.

Chapter V, "Contradictions in the General Formula of Capital," asks
the question, what permits the expansion of value and the creation of this
surplus value? How can one account for the origin of capital? Marx argues
that value does not grow in circulation, since according to his theory, in circulation there is only a change in the form of value, but there is no growth
in value. To find how value can grow, Marx argues that one must look to
the conditions of production.

Chapter VI, "The Buying and Selling of Labour-Power," answers the
question posed in the previous chapter. Marx argues that the change in
value originates in the use value of the commodity, that is, in how it is used.
Marx argues that "Mr. Moneybags," i.e., the owner of money, who is not
yet a capitalist, must find a peculiar commodity whose use value is itself a
source of value and whose consumption is an embodiment of labor, and
hence a creator of value. This Mr. Moneybags finds in the peculiar commodity labor power, that is, the worker's capacity to work.

Marx argues that labor power has a value. This is the labor time necessary for the production and reproduction of it. This reduces to the labor time needed to produce the means of subsistence to support the worker, i.e., the value of the means of subsistence necessary to maintain and reproduce the worker as a laboring individual.

The money owner purchases labor power on the market. He then sets labor power to work on raw material (which he has also purchased in the market) to produce commodities and surplus value. Within Marx's framework, the possessor of labor power has become a laborer; the money owner has finally become a capitalist.

Here we will present an account of the transformation of money into capital, based upon a commodity rather than Marx's labor theory of value. This reworking of this section of Marx results in the following major changes:

1. The ability for money to make more money, that is, for value to self-expand, is not to be found *only* in the use to which the commodity labor power is put. Self-expanding value arises when commodities in general are used to make more commodities than are used up in the production process.[1]

2. Using a commodity theory of value, labor power has no value. This is because labor power is not directly produced by other commodities; instead it is produced largely (though not entirely) in the family.[2]

In spite of these changes (or, alternatively, with these changes), Marx's analysis of the transformation of money into capital may be constructed upon the basis of a commodity theory of value rather than upon his labor theory of value.

Now, the starting point of capital is the circulation of commodities.[3] All new capital begins in the form of money.[4] By a definite process money must be transformed into capital.[5] The first distinction between money that is money only and money that is capital is a difference in their form of circulation. Money as capital takes the form M-C-M, that is, buying in order to sell. Money used in this manner is transformed into capital.[6]

Compare the actions of a merchant with that, for example, of a peasant. A peasant who sells corn and then buys clothes circulates commodities in the form C-M-C. Here the starting and ending points are commodities. This is exchange in pursuit of use value. In contrast to this, the merchant circulates money in the form M-C-M. The merchant as buyer lays out money in order to, as a seller, recover money. The merchant releases money in order to get it back again.[7]

The circuit M-C-M begins and ends with money.[8] The motive behind this is exchange value. To be more precise, the goal of the circuit is to increase exchange value, in order to form the circuit M-C-M', where M' is greater than M:

> This increment or excess over the original value I call 'surplus value.' The value originally advanced, therefore, not only remains intact while in circulation, but adds to itself a surplus-value or expands itself. It is this movement that converts it into capital.[9]

Money can be spent as money in order to buy commodities intended for consumption. In this case it is not capital. Money can also be withdrawn from circulation. In this case it becomes petrified into a hoard. Money can also be used to buy commodities with the aim of selling these commodities to make more money. In this case money is used as capital.[10]

To *sell* commodities in order to *buy* other commodities involves the appropriation of use values and the satisfaction of wants. On the other hand, the circulation of money as capital, money used to make more money, is an end in itself. The possessor of money used in this manner (i.e., to make more money) is a capitalist. To the extent or degree this possessor is a capitalist, "the expansion of value, which is the objective basis or mainspring of the circulation M-C-M, becomes his subjective aim." For this reason, use values are not the real aim of the capitalist (that is, insofar as the person is a capitalist and represents capital).[11]

In the circuit M-C-M, both money and the commodity represent value; indeed, both are value. Money is the general mode of value and the commodity is a particular form of existence of value. Capital is thus both money and commodities.[12] In turn, it constantly assumes the form of money and then of commodities, and yet at the same time it experiences changes in magnitude. That is, capital grows as it changes its form of value.[13]

Value thus becomes the active factor in a process. Value assumes at one time the form of money, at another time the form of commodities. Value in the circulation of M-C-M, i.e., in the circulation of capital, becomes an independent substance. It has a motion of its own. Money and commodities are simply forms which value variously assumes and then casts off. Value thus becomes value in motion, or self-expanding value.[14] As such, value is capital.[15]

A problem arises: How can money make more money? How can there be self-expanding value?

Suppose two owners of commodities buy from each other. As commodity owners, both part with goods which, as use values, are of no service to them. Both receive other goods which they can use. With reference to use value, both parties may gain — otherwise they would not trade.[16]

Yet, it is different with exchange value. The exchange value of two goods traded is the same. Commodities have exchange value because they are produced by other commodities. No exchange value is created in the circulation of commodities. In exchange there is nothing but a metamorphosis, a mere change in the form of the commodity. The exchange value remains the same in the hands of the owner of the commodity, first in the form of that commodity, then in the form of the money for which the original commodity is exchanged, and then in the new commodity. There has been no increase in exchange value, even though, with regards the use values exchanged, both buyer and seller may gain. In its normal state, exchange is the exchange of equivalents and no value is produced.[17]

Marx argues that

> The creation of surplus-value, and therefore the conversion of money into capital, can consequently be explained neither on the assumption that commodities are sold above their value, nor that they are bought below their value.[18]

Within the Marxian framework:

> The conversion of money into capital has to be explained on the basis of the laws that regulate the exchange of commodities, in such a way that the starting point is the exchange of equivalents. Our friend, Moneybags, who as yet is only an embryo capitalist, must buy his commodities at their value, must sell them at their value, and yet at the end of the process must withdraw more value from circulation than he threw into it at starting. His development into a full-grown capitalist must take place, both within the sphere of circulation and without it. These are the conditions of the problem.[19]

Marx argues that the solution to this problem lies in the buying and selling of labor power. According to him, this is the one commodity which can actually create value and surplus value.[20] Actually, according to the commodity theory of value developed herein, the potential capitalist must merely purchase commodities which can create more commodities. The key to the self-expansion of value is that the potential capitalist be able to purchase commodities on the market and then set them to work making *more* commodities.[21]

However, for Marx

> Moneybags, must be so lucky as to find, within the sphere of circulation, in the market, a commodity, whose use-value possesses the peculiar property of being a source of value, whose actual consumption, therefore, is itself an embodiment of labour, and consequently a creation of value.[22]

Marx argues that "the possessor of money does find on the market such a special commodity in capacity of labour or labour power."[23] By labor power or capacity for labor Marx means

> the aggregate of those mental and physical capabilities existing in a human being, which he exercises whenever he produces a use-value of any description.[24]

In a commodity theory of value, Mr. "Moneybags" must simply find those commodities in the market needed to make more commodities. Labor power, of course, will be an important (but not unique) one of these commodities.

The conditions that labour power be actually available on the market have been elaborated by Marx. Labor power appears on the market as a commodity only if its possessor, the person, offers it for sale as a commodity. The possessor of labor power must have certain legal rights. For example, he must be the owner of his capacity to labor, that is, he cannot be a slave to someone else.

The individual selling his labor power is selling a commodity.[25] The owner of the money is also buying a commodity — labor power. In order that they may continue the relationship of buyer and seller, the owner of labor power must sell it only for a definite period of time, not forever. Were the owner to sell this labor power forever, he or she would become a slave. In that case he or she would no longer be the owner of the commodity labor power and could no longer meet in the market place as the equal to the purchaser of labor power.[26]

For the owner of money to find the commodity labor power on the market, the laborer must be obliged to offer labor power for sale as a commodity. Thus, the (potential) worker must have a twofold freedom. As a free person the laborer must be free to sell the commodity labor power to anyone. At the same time the laborer must be forced to sell the commodity labor power because that is the only commodity the laborer has to offer for sale. The laborer must therefore be free from access to the means of production so that he or she is "short of everything necessary for the realization of his labor-power";[27] this will compel the worker to sell his labor power as a commodity.[28]

Consider the point in view of the owner of money. That person does not care why the commodity labor power is available on the market. As far as the owner is concerned, the labor market is simply a branch of the general market for commodities. The fact that there are now two groups of people — one with money which purchases labor power and another selling labor power — is the result of history. Yet, then again, everything discussed so far is the result of history:

> So too, the economical categories, already discussed by us, bear the stamp of history. Definite historical conditions are necessary that a product may become a commodity. It must not be produced as the immediate means of subsistence of the producer himself. Had we gone further, and inquired under what circumstances all, or even the majority of products takes the form of commodities, we should have found that this can only happen with production of a very specific kind, capitalist production.[29]

Capitalist production means production under the direction of capital.[30] Capital is money used to make more money, or, to be more precise, it is self-expanding value.[31] Capitalist production can spring into life only when it uses commodities to produce more commodities.[32] Hence, it is crucially important that capital can confront labor power as a commodity, since labor power is a necessary factor of production. It is for this reason that capital "can spring into life, only when the owner of the means of production and subsistence meets in the market with the free labourer selling his labour-power."[33]

Labor power appears on the market as a commodity. It has a price at which it is sold. Unlike other commodities in capitalism, it is not produced by capitalists or in firms. It is produced outside the firm in families. It has a minimum price below which it cannot fall. This minimum price must be high enough so that the worker may receive enough to support herself and reproduce the class of workers (the reproduction of the class of workers is done outside of the firm).[34] However, although there is a minimum price at which labor power can sell, according to Marx, "In contradistinction . . . to the case of other commodities, there enters into the determination of the value of labour-power a historical and moral element." Yet, in spite of this, "in a given country, at a given period, the average quantity of the means of subsistence necessary for the labourer is practically known."[35]

Any commodity is a nonuse value to its owner; otherwise the owner of the commodity would not want to exchange it. The same is true for the commodity labor power. Since the worker is separated from the means of production, the worker must sell her labor power. The worker is unable to use the labor power personally. Thus,

> if his capacity for labour remains unsold, the labourer derives no benefit from it, but rather he will feel it to be a cruel nature-imposed necessity that this capacity has cost for its production a definite amount of the means of subsistence and that it will continue to do so for its reproduction.[36]

Actually, although it will seem like a "nature-imposed necessity," the imposition on the worker, that is, the necessity of the worker to sell labor power, is not a product of nature per se. Rather, it is the result of the development of human society.

The money owner purchases labor power, raw materials, and other commodities on the market. These commodities are then taken to the money owners' workshops where they are set to work making new commodities. The commodities can be said to be consumed by the money owner, but they are consumed "productively," that is, they are used to make more commodities.

Thus, the creation of surplus value, the ability of money to make more money, or for value to self-expand, involves leaving the sphere of circulation. (This is true using either Marx's labor theory of value or the commodity theory of value formulated here.[37]) The money owner buys what commodities are needed on the market, takes them to the workshop to make more commodities, and then returns to the market to sell them.

Capital, self-expanding value, arises out of the sphere of circulation.[38] It is a certain way of using money; that is, employing money to make more money.[39] Money itself also comes from the sphere of circulation; it represents the value of commodities. Commodities themselves are products which are meant to be exchanged, so that they have both a use value and an exchange value. To put it another way, commodities generate money which in turn generates capital.

The sphere of circulation is, from certain perspectives, a delightful place. In the sphere of circulation, freedom rules, because all people meet as free commodity owners, buying and selling each others' commodities. Also, in the sphere of circulation, everyone is equal. Commodity owners meet as equal contracting parties. They are equal in the eyes of the law, and they exchange equivalents for equivalents.[40]

In the sphere of circulation, each commodity owner looks out for his or her own interest. Commodity owners enter into contracts only if they think they can benefit from the contract. They look out for themselves. Yet, from one point of view, because they each look out for their own interests, it may be said that the interest of society will be furthered:

> The only force that brings them together and puts them in relation with each other, is the selfishness, the gain and the private interests of each. Each looks to himself only, and no one troubles himself about the rest, and just because they do so, do they all, in accordance with the preestablished harmony of things, or under the auspices of an all-shrewd providence, work together to their mutual advantage, for the common weal and in the interest of all.[41]

On the other hand, there are now also two distinct social classes of people. The former money owner has now become a capitalist who uses money in order to make more money (self-expanding value). The seller of labor power has become a worker, working for the capitalist. The worker mixes the commodity labor power with other commodities furnished by the capitalist in order to make more commodities (which are owned by the capitalist). The money which the worker receives from the sale of the commodity labor power is used to support herself or himself and a family, not to make more money.[42]

In summary, Marx has been followed in his development of the theoretical genesis of capital. However, instead of basing the analysis on the labor theory of value, this work has been based on a Sraffian theory of value.

The two theories of value are so similar that very little is changed by the substitution of the commodity theory of value for the labor theory of value. In both cases, commodities generate money which generates capital which is self-expanding value. Capital then seizes hold of the production process and uses commodities (including the commodity labor power) to make more commodities.[43] Thus, using either the labor theory of value or a commodity theory of value, the development of capital leads to a situation where there are two groups of people and where

> On leaving this sphere of simple circulation or of exchange of commodities, . . . we think we can perceive a change in the physiognomy of our dramatis personae. He, who before was the money owner, now strides, in front as capitalist; the possessor of labour-power follows as his labourer. The one with an air of importance, smirking, intent on business; the other, timid and holding back, like one who is bringing his own hide to market and has nothing to expect but — a hiding.[44]

NOTES

1. This point has been argued very forcefully by Roemer: "It must be pointed out that Marx was completely wrong about one thing. Labor power as a commodity is not unique in its magical property of producing more value than it embodies. Indeed, in any economy capable of producing a surplus, any commodity has this magical property." [*New Directions in the Marxian Theory of Exploitation and Class,* p. 273.] Note: Here it may be worthwhile to emphasize that commodities are not paid according to their productivity, using either a labor or a commodity theory of value. Hence, a commodity theory of value does not fall victim to Marx's criticisms of productivity theories of income distribution. See, e.g., *Capital*, Vol. I, p. 584, where Marx disparages these theories: "Instead of the real fact, we have the false semblance of an association, in which labourer and capitalist divide the product in proportion to the different elements which they respectively contribute towards its formation."

2. This interpretation may be controversial, yet it seems to be consistent with how such authors as Ian Steedman, Sraffa, and Dmitriev have treated labor power. (For more on this, see Note 35 below.) It may be noted that there are commodities within the Marxian system which may have a price even though they have no value. For example, for Marx, unworked land, which contains no embodied labor power, has no value, yet may nevertheless have a price. Thus, the fact that labor power has no value, yet, nevertheless, has a price would not

seem to be a major problem when working within a basically Marxian framework grounded upon a commodity theory of value.

It was stated above that labor power is not entirely produced in the family. This is because the socialization of labor power, and the production of it in such a form that it is "suitable" for capitalist production, is an immense and problematical task which is not solely accomplished in the family. This is one of the themes of Antonio Gramsci's work; on this point, see, also, Samuel Bowles and Herbert Gintis, *Schooling in Capitalist America: Educational Reform and the Contradictions of Economic Life* (New York: Basic Books, 1976).

3. Marx, *Capital,* Vol. I. p. 163; "Production based on capital originally came out of circulation." [*Grundrisse,* pp. 542-543.]

4. "Capital comes initially from circulation, and, moreover, its point of departure is money." [*Grundrisse,* p. 253.]

5. "Money as capital is an aspect of money which goes beyond its simple character as money. It can be regarded as a higher realization; as it can be said that man is a developed ape. However, in this way the lower form is posited as the primary subject, over the higher. In any case, money as capital is distinct from money as money." [*Grundrisse,* pp. 250-251.]

6. Marx, *Capital,* Vol. I, p. 164.

7. Ibid., pp. 165-166; "Mercantile capital, or money as it presents itself as merchant wealth, is the first form of capital. i.e., of value which comes exclusively from circulation (from exchange), maintains, reproduces and increases itself within it, and thus the exclusive aim of this movement and activity is exchange value." [*Grundrisee,* p. 856.]

8. "The first quality of capital is, then, this: that exchange value deriving from circulation and presupposing circulation preserves itself within it and by means of it; does not lose itself by entering into it; that circulation is not the movement of its disappearance. . . . " [*Grundrisse,* pp. 259-260.]

9. Marx, *Capital,* Vol. I, p. 168.

10. Ibid., p. 169; "Just as money originates from the bare form of commodity circulation, C-M-C, not only as a measure of value and a medium of circulation, but also as the absolute form of commodity, and hence of wealth, or hoard, so that its conservation and accumulation as money becomes an end in itself, so, too, does money, the hoard, as something that preserves and increases itself through mere alienation, originate from the bare form of the circulation of merchant's capital, M-C-M'." [*Capital,* Vol. III, p. 330.]

11. Ibid. Vol. I, p. 170; "We have demonstrated above, in the development of the concept of capital, that it is value as such, money, which both preserves itself through circulation and also increases itself through exchange with living labour. That, hence, the aim of producing capital is never use value, but rather the general form of wealth as wealth." [*Grundrisse,* p. 600.]

12. "Capital posits the permanence of value (to a certain degree) by incarnating itself in fleeting commodities and taking on their form, but at the same time changing them just as constantly; alternates between its eternal form in money and its passing form in commodities." [*Grundrisse,* p. 646.]

13. Marx, *Capital,* Vol. I, p. 171. It may be pointed out that the theory of capital being developed here is also very similar to Adam Smith's theory of capital. Adam Smith also asserts that both money and commodities are capital. For him, both money and commodities are part of a person's stock, and "His whole stock, therefore, is distinguished into two parts. That part which, he expects, is to afford him this revenue, is called his *Capital.* The other is that which supplies his immediate consumption." [*Wealth of Nations,* pp. 373, ff.; emphasis added.]

14. "Capital as self-expanding value embraces not only class relations, a society of a definite character resting on the existence of labour in the form of wage-labour. It is a movement, a circuit-describing process going through various stages . . . .Therefore it can be understood only as motion, not as a thing at rest . . . .Value here passes through various forms, various movements in which it maintains itself and at the same time expands." [*Capital,* Vol. II, p. 105.]

15. Marx, *Capital*, Vol. I, pp. 172–173.

16. Etienne Bonnot de Condillac pointed this out in the 18th century: "The very fact that an exchange takes place is proof that there must necessarily be profit in it for both the contracting parties; otherwise it would not be made. Hence, every exchange represents two gains for humanity." [Quoted in Hunt, *History of Economic Thought*, p. 157.]

17. Marx, *Capital*, Vol. I, pp. 176–177.

18. Ibid., p. 179.

19. Ibid., pp. 184–185.

20. "The point to remember here is only that capital creates no surplus value as long as it employs no living labour." [*Grundrisse*, p. 670]; "The use value of labour capacity, as value, is itself the value-creating force; the substance of value, and the value-increasing substance." [*Grundrisse*, p. 674.]

21. This is the answer to Alfredo Medio's charge that "The methodological foundations of the neo-Ricardian theory can be traced back to the work of V. K. Dmitriev and L. von Bortkiewicz. . . . The main element that distinguishes the neo-Ricardian from the Marxian approach is a restrictive definition of the concept of "value," which is in fact identified with that of exchange-value or price . . . this approach—contrary to Marx's—does not provide any explanatory theory of capitalist profit." ["Neoclassicals, Neo-Ricardians and Marx" in Schwartz, *The Subtle Anatomy of Capitalism*, p. 386.] This approach does indeed provide an explanatory theory of capitalist profit. The source of capitalist profit is the ability of capitalists to buy commodities in the market (including labor power) and set them to producing more commodities.

22. Marx, *Capital*, Vol. I, p. 186.

23. Ibid. Recall that by Marx's theory of value "machinery, like every other component of constant capital, creates no new value, but yields up its own value to the product that it serves to beget. . . . It never adds more value than it loses, on an average, by wear and tear." [*Capital*, Vol. I, p. 423.] Hence, for Marx, only labor power can *create* value.

24. Ibid., p. 186.

25. "The seller of labour-power, like the seller of any other commodity, realizes its exchange-value, and parts with its use-value." [*Capital*, Vol. I, p. 216.]

26. Marx, *Capital*, p. 186; "As a slave, the worker has exchange value, a value; as a free wage-worker he has no value; it is rather his power of disposing of his labour, effected by exchange with him, which has value. His valuelessness and devaluation is the presupposition of capital and the precondition of free labour in general . . . the worker is thereby formally posited as a person who is something for himself apart from his labour, and who alienates his life-expression only as a means towards his own life." [*Grundrisse*, pp. 288–289.]

27. Marx, *Capital*, Vol. I, p. 188.

28. This point was elaborated in Chapter 5. Karl Polanyi is critical of societies based upon wage labor, and has argued that "To separate labor from other activities of life and to subject it to the laws of the market was to annihilate all organic forms of existence and to replace them by a different type of organization, an atomistic and individualistic one.

Such a scheme of destruction was best served by the application of the principle of freedom of contract. In practice this meant that the non-contractual organizations of kinship, neighborhood, profession, and creed were to be liquidated since they claimed the allegiance of the individual and thus restrained his freedom. To represent this principle as one of noninterference, as economic liberals were wont to do, was merely the expression of an ingrained prejudice in favor of a definite kind of interference, namely, such as would destroy non-contractual relations between individuals and prevent their spontaneous re-formation." [*The Great Transformation*, p. 163.]

29. Marx, *Capital*, Vol. I, p. 188.

30. Thus, "buying in order to sell, which makes up the formal aspect of commerce, of capital as merchant capital, is found in the earliest conditions of economic development; it is

the first movement in which exchange value as such forms the content—is not only the form but also its own content. This motion can take place within peoples, or between peoples for whose production exchange value has by no means yet become the presupposition. The movement only seizes upon the surplus of their directly useful production and proceeds only on its margin. . . . Commercial capital is only circulating capital, and circulating capital is the first form of capital; *in which it has as yet by no means become the foundation of production*." [*Grundrisse,* p. 253; emphasis added.]

31. "As soon as money is posited as an exchange value which not only becomes independent of circulation, but which also maintains itself through it, then it is no longer money, . . . but is capital. That money is the first form in which exchange value proceeds to the character of capital . . ." [*Grundrisse,* p. 259.]

32. That is why ". . . historically, . . . capital did not begin the world from the beginning, but rather encountered production and products already present, before it subjugated them beneath its process. Once in motion, proceeding from itself as basis, it constantly posits itself ahead of itself in its various forms as consumable product, raw material and instrument of labour, in order constantly to reproduce itself in these forms. They appear initially as the conditions presupposed by it, and then as its result. In its reproduction it produces its own conditions." [*Grundrisse,* p. 675.]

33. Marx, *Capital,* Vol. I, p. 189; Marx also adds "And this one historical condition comprises a world's history."

34. ". . . [T]he money which the capitalist pays to the labourer for the use of his labour-power is nothing more or less than the form of the general equivalent for the means of subsistence required by the labourer. To this extent, the variable capital consists *in substance* of means of subsistence." [*Capital,* Vol. II, p. 165; emphasis added.]

35. Marx, *Capital,* Vol. I, p. 190. Actually, to be strictly accurate, the commodity labor power has no value, when using a commodity theory of value. This is because labor power is not directly produced by other commodities. Since labor power has no value, its price is actually *indeterminate.* In view of this, Dmitriev argued that political economy should proceed as follows:

"The quantity denoting the amount of the product consumed per unit of work, when the iron law of wages prevails, will be dependent on the level of needs of the worker and will increase together with them. If we imagine a situation in which the iron law of wages does not hold, the quantity 'a' ['a' is the amount of goods consumed by workers] will in general be determined by the actual struggle of the mutually opposed interest of the capitalists striving to establish the greatest possible value for 'r' ['r' is the rate of profit] and therefore striving to reduce the quantity 'a' to the minimum possible, and of the workers striving conversely to raise 'a' to the greatest possible value. The level of 'a' at which equilibrium is established is a question of fact and is dependent on the strength of the contending parties. In this state of affairs investigations of the conditions affecting the level of 'a' falls outside the scope of political economy and within that of other disciplines; in this case also, as when the iron law of wages prevails and 'a' is determined by the physiological needs of the worker's body, political economy should take the quantity 'a' to be given in its analysis." [*Economic Essays on Value Competition and Utility,* p. 74.]

This would also seem to be consistent with Sraffa's approach (see Chapter 2, No. 8, pp. 9–10.)

36. Marx, *Capital,* Vol. I, pp. 192–193.

37. This is actually also one of the main themes in Adam Smith. For Smith, the wealth of nations lies not in the accumulation of gold or silver, or in foreign trade, but in what is actually produced in society.

38. "It is in the circulation process that money develops into capital. It is in circulation that products first develop as exchange-value, as commodities and as money. Capital can, and must, form in the process of circulation, before it learns to control its extremes—the various spheres of production between which circulation mediates." [*Capital,* Vol. III, p. 328.]

39. "Capital has one single life impulse, the tendency to create value and surplus-value." [*Capital*, Vol. I, p. 257.]

40. Marx, *Capital*, Vol. I, p. 195.

41. Ibid. Irving Kristol, a fashionable "neo-conservative," has grasped this one aspect of capitalist society so well that he censures any economist who dares to forget it. For him, "the bedrock truths about the human condition that were first comprehensively enunciated in *The Wealth of Nations* are (1) The overwhelming majority of men and women are naturally and incorrigibly interested in improving their material conditions; (2) efforts to repress this natural desire lead only to coercive and impoverished polities; (3) when this natural desire is given sufficient latitude so that commercial transactions are not discouraged, economic growth does take place; (4) as a result of such growth everyone does eventually indeed improve his condition, however unequally in extent or time; (5) such economic growth results in a huge expansion of property-owning middle classes. . . . This is not all we need to know, but it is what we do know, and it is surely not asking too much of economic theory that in its passion for sophisticated methodology it not leave this knowledge behind." ["Rationalism in Economics," *The Public Interest* Special Issue (1980), p. 281.] With regard to this "eminent" social theorist, one might agree with Marx when he despairs that "on the level plain, simple mounds look like hills; and the imbecile flatness of the present bourgeoisie is to be measured by the altitude of its great intellects." [*Capital*, Vol. I, p. 568.]

42. "The exchange between capital and labour belongs within simple circulation, does not enrich the worker." [*Grundrisse,* p. 295.]

43. "But capital arises only where trade has seized possession of production itself, and where the merchant becomes producer." [*Grundrisse,* p. 859.]

44. See Marx, *Capital*, Vol. I, p. 196.

11

CONCLUSION

For many years there has been much controversy over the validity and usefulness of Marx's labor theory of value. Much of the *recent* criticism of the labor theory of value has been based upon the work of Sraffa. What has not been very clear in recent debates over the labor theory of value is that many of the criticizers of the labor theory of value have actually been using another theory of value. For Sraffa and his followers, commodities have value because they are produced by other commodities; for Marx and his orthodox followers, commodities have value because they are produced by human workers. The two theories are very similar. In a sense, a Sraffian-based commodity theory of value can be seen to be a generalization of the labor theory of value. Using a commodity theory of value, *any* commodity which is used to create more commodities can be said to create value; whereas, in the Marxian framework, only the commodity labor power creates value.

A key to understanding the commodity theory of value is the full realization that a commodity is both a use value and a value. This value is manifested when the commodity is exchanged for other commodities; hence, it manifests itself in what may be termed exchange value. Since a commodity is both a use value and a value, when commodities produce other commodities, they produce not only use values, but values as well. When commodities produce more commodities than are used up in the production process, they may be said to produce surplus value.

In analyzing Marx's work, it must be kept in mind that although it largely rests upon the labor theory of value, it is not merely a theory of the determination of relative prices and the rate of profit. Rather, Marx seeks to try to determine the laws of motion of capitalist society. This is, of course, a very ambitious undertaking, and in Marx's formulation of the laws of motion of capitalist society, much weight is indeed placed upon the labor theory of value.

This work has shown that it is possible to retrace Marx's analysis of the laws of motion of capitalism using a commodity rather than a labor theory of value. Admittedly, this retracing of Marx's work has been carried out only up to the theoretical development of the concept of capital. However, a foundation has now been laid, and it would not seem to be too difficult an undertaking to retrace the rest of Marx's work basing it upon a commodity rather than the labor theory of value. In the course of this work, it was seen that very little of Marx's analysis of the development of capital is altered by the substitution of a commodity theory of value for the labor theory of value.

Marx's analysis of the development of capital can be schematically shown as in Figure 2.

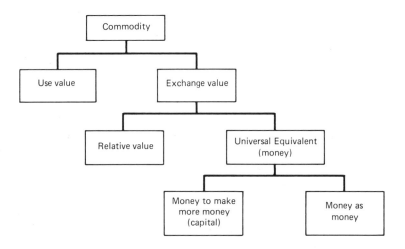

Figure 2. The Genesis of Capital

For Marx, a commodity has two aspects: it is both a use value and an exchange value. Marx analyzes the form of exchange value and finds that it generates both a relative value (i.e., a particular ordinary commodity) and an equivalent value. In time, one commodity always takes the form of the equivalent value and becomes a universal equivalent, that is, it becomes money. Marx then analyzes money and finds that it can either be used as money, to aid in the circulation of commodities, or it can be used to make more money, in which case it becomes capital.

One particularly interesting result emerges from the substitution of the commodity theory of value for the labor theory of value in the theoretical development of capital. It appears that Marx did not sufficiently develop the different uses to which a commodity may be put. A commodity's use value can be employed in two different ways. A commodity may be consumed, in which case it produces no value and drops out of sight, or it may be used to create more commodities. In this case, the commodity creates not only more use values, but more exchange value as well (since a commodity is both a use value and an exchange value).

Using a commodity theory of value, it may be said that value is created when commodities in a given time period are used to create other commodities. Although this is not quite the same as Marx's labor theory of value, it seems to be largely compatible with much of the rest of Marx's analysis, as has been demonstrated in this work. Capital, as in Marx's analysis, has been seen to arise out of the commodity form itself. Capital, using a commodity theory of value, may be viewed as self-expanding value. Capital is a certain way of using commodities (here, money may be viewed as a particular type of commodity, i.e., the universal equivalent, or that commodity whose form represents the value of all other commodities); capital is the use of commodities to make more commodities, or, in Sraffa's words, capital may be viewed as the production of commodities by means of commodities.

The following changes were made in the course of developing Marx's analysis of the theoretical genesis of capital when basing that analysis upon a commodity rather than upon Marx's labor theory of value:

1. The common substance of all commodities which enables them to be compared with one another is that they are produced by other commodities, not that they are all products of human labor.

2. Commodities have value not because they are produced by human labor; instead they have value because they are produced by other commodities.

3. The use value to which a commodity is put is of relatively more importance when using the commodity theory of value than when using the labor theory of value. When commodities are *used* to create other commodities, they may be said to create value.

4. A thing can be a use value without having value, not because it contains no human labor, as Marx argued, but because it is not produced by other commodities.

5. The ability of money to make more money, that is, of value to self-expand, is not to be found *only* in the use to which the commodity labor power is put. Capital, or self-expanding value, arises when commodities in general are used to make more commodities than are used up in the production process.

6. The magnitude of a commodity's value is not determined solely by the amount of socially necessary labor time embodied in that commodity. Instead, the magnitude of a commodity's value is determined by the production process in general.

7. Using a commodity theory of value, labor power has no value. This is because labor power is not directly produced by other commodities; instead, it is produced largely (though not entirely) in the family.

In spite of these changes, this work has shown that it is indeed possible to do what Joan Robinson and others have urged: to build upon Marx's work and perform a Marxian-type analysis without using the labor theory of value. This work has shown that one is not forced to abandon a basically Marxist understanding of capitalism when adopting Sraffa's analysis of equilibrium relative pricing. More specifically, this work has shown how one may reconstruct Marx's account of the theoretical genesis of capital based upon a Sraffian commodity theory of value rather than upon Marx's labor theory of value.

Generally speaking, this work has had two broad goals. It has attempted to show to those economists not directly influenced by Marx's work and who do not subscribe to the labor theory of value that much of Marx's work still stands up, even without the labor theory of value, and is interesting in its own right. It has also been addressed to those economists who have been influenced by Marx's work and are attempting to carry out Marxian-type analyses of capitalist societies. These economists have split into two often hostile camps: those who subscribe to the labor theory of value and those who do not. Hopefully, this work has shown that the two camps are not very far apart. The commodity theory of value is very, very similar to the labor theory of value, and very little of Marx's analysis (particularly so-called qualitative issues, i.e., those issues not dealing with the determination of such things as relative prices and the rate of profit) is effected whether a commodity or the labor theory of value is used. Hopefully, this work will help contribute to a greater understanding between these two camps of economists, both of whom have been largely inspired by, and find much usefulness in, Marx's writings. If this work has contributed to a greater understanding between these two schools of thought, and (optimistically) contributed toward an eventual reintegration of these two schools, then it will have more than served its purpose. Hopefully, it will encourage those economists inspired by Marx's work to spend less time arguing amongst themselves and to get on with the serious business of studying and analyzing the society in which we live.

APPENDIX A

CAPITAL AS SELF-EXPANDING VALUE

"Capitalist production is not merely the production of commodities, it is essentially the production of surplus-value. The labourer produces, not for himself, but for capital. It no longer suffices, therefore, that he should simply produce. He must produce surplus-value. That labourer alone is productive, who produces surplus-value for the capitalist, and thus works for the self-expansion of capital." [*Capital*, Vol. I, p. 558.]

"By turning his money into commodities that serve as the material elements of a new product, and as factors in the labour-process, by incorporating living labour with their dead substance, the capitalist at the same time converts value, i.e., past materialised, and dead labour into capital, into value big with value, a live monster that is fruitful and multiplies." [*Capital*, Vol. I, p. 217.]

"But, so far as he is personified capital, it is not values in use and enjoyment of them, but exchange-value and its augmentation, that spur him into action. Fanatically bent on making value expand itself, he ruthlessly forces the human race to produce for production's sake; he thus forces the development of the productive powers of society, and creates those material conditions, which alone can form the real basis of a higher form of society, a society in which the full and free development of every individual forms the ruling principle . . . competition makes the immanent laws of capitalist production to be felt by each individual capitalist, as external coercive laws. It compels him to keep constantly extending his capital, in order to preserve it . . ." [*Capital*, Vol. I, p. 649]

"Capital as self-expanding value embraces not only class relations, a society of a definite character resting on the existence of labour in the form of a wage-labour. It is a movement, a circuit-describing process going through various stages, which itself comprises three different forms of the circuit-describing process. Therefore it can be understood only as motion. . . ." [*Capital*, Vol. II, p. 105.]

"The process of production appears in the form of a circuit-describing process, formally and explicitly as that which it is in the capitalist mode of production, as a mere means of expanding the advanced value, hence enrichment as such as the purpose of production." [*Capital*, Vol. II, pp. 56–57.]

"The entire character of capitalist production is determined by the self-expansion of the advanced capital-value, that is to say, in the first instance by the production of as much surplus-value as possible; . . ." [*Capital*, Vol. II, p. 78.]

". . . [T]he rate of self-expansion of the total capital, or the rate of profit, being the goal of capitalist production (just as self-expansion of capital is its only purpose), . . ." [*Capital*, Vol. III, p. 241.]

"And the capitalist process of production consists essentially of the production of surplus-value, represented in the surplus-product or that aliquot portion of the produced commodities materialising unpaid labour. It must never be forgotten that the production of this surplus-value—and the reconversion of a portion of it into capital, or the accumulation, forms an integrate part of this production of surplus-value—is the immediate purpose and compelling motive of capitalist production. It will never do, therefore, to represent capitalist production as something which it is not, namely as production whose immediate purpose is enjoyment of the manufacture of the means of enjoyment for the capitalist. This would be overlooking its specific character, which is revealed in its inner essence." [*Capital*, Vol. III, pp. 243-244.]

"The compelling motive of capitalist production is always the creation of surplus-value by means of the advanced value, . . ." [*Capital*, Vol. II, p. 153.]

". . . [T]he characteristic property of capital, that of being a value generating value." [*Capital*, Vol. II, p. 81.]

APPENDIX B

DMITRIEV'S CALCULATION OF THE SUM OF LABOR EXPENDED IN THE PRODUCTION OF A GIVEN PRODUCT

Dmitriev solves this problem through the use of a system of simultaneous equations.

Let N_A be the total amount of labor directly and indirectly expended on the production of a unit of commodity A; let the direct labor consumed in the production of A be n_A; let the various capital goods involved in the production be K_1, K_2, . . ., K_m; let the quantities or amounts of each capital good consumed be a known fraction: $1/m_1$ of K_1, $1/m_2$ of K_2 . . . $1/m_m$; let the amount of labor directly and indirectly expended on the production of the capital K_1 be N_1, on K_2, N_2 . . . K_m, N_m. The total sum of the labor expended in the production of a unit of commodity A will be

$$N_A = n_A + \frac{1}{m_1} N_1 + \frac{1}{m_2} N_2 + \ldots + \frac{1}{m_m} N_m \qquad (1)$$

The quantities n_A and the coefficients m_1, m_2 . . . m_m are given by the technical conditions of production, with assumption that the m's represent known quantities of the intermediate inputs required for the production of A. N_A, N_1, N_2 . . . N_m are the unknowns. Since some capital goods required for A themselves require other capital goods not directly required in the production of A, let the number of all capital goods directly and indirectly required for the production of A be m. The amount of labor directly and indirectly needed to produce the capital good K_1 from the m capital goods, i.e., N_1, will be given by an equation similar to that for N_A; and, a similar equation for each of the m capital goods may be constructed. This gives $m + 1$ equations to solve the $m + 1$ unknowns $(N_A, N_1, \ldots N_M)$, which is precisely soluble. Hence:

Therefore, without any digressions into the prehistoric times of the first inceptions of technical capital, we can always find the total sum of the labour directly and indirectly expended on the production of any product *under present-day production conditions,* both of this product itself and of those capital goods involved in its production. As we have seen, the fact that all capital under *present-day* conditions is itself produced with the assistance of other capital in no way hinders a precise solution of the problem. [*Economic Essays on Value, Competition and Utility,* p. 44.]

APPENDIX C

DMITRIEV'S MODEL OF A
FULLY AUTOMATED SOCIETY

The obscure Russian mathematical economist Vladimir Dmitriev was the first economist to set forth a formal model of a fully automated society which nonetheless had a determinate set of relative prices and a positive rate of profit (see Dmitriev, *Economic Essays on Value, Competition and Utility,* pp. 58-64). He originally set his model forth in terms of "dated quantities of labour," which is very similar to one of Sraffa's models (see Sraffa, *Production of Commodities by Means of Commodities,* Chap. 6, pp. 34-40).

Dmitriev made the following assumptions:

a. goods can be increased without limit by the application of labor and capital goods;

b. separate portions of the goods are produced with identical production costs (this excludes the case of rent);

c. the production and sale of these goods takes place under the influence of unlimited competition;

d. wages are exogenously given; and

e. workers consume only one good (e.g., corn—this assumption is later dropped).

It is assumed that a good sells for its cost (where the rate of profit is a part of the cost and is an endogenous variable to be determined by the model).

Let
X_a = cost of production of one unit of good a;
n_a = the amount of labor directly consumed in the production of one unit of good a;

a = the amount of good a consumed by a worker per day;

r = the rate of profit;

$t_a, t_1, t_2, \ldots$ = time needed for manufacture and delivery to the market of a good a (it is assumed that the product is sold immediately upon delivery to the market) and of capital good K_1 used in the production of a, K_2 used in the production of K_1, K_3 used in the production of K_2, etc.

$n_1, n_2, n_3, \ldots n_m$ = the amounts of labor expended on the production of capital goods $K_1, K_2, K_3, \ldots, K_m$ used in the production of one unit of good a; so

$$X_a = n_a a X_a (1 + r)^{t_a} + n_1 a X_a (1 + r)^{t_a + t_1} + n_2 a X_a (1 + r)$$

$$t_a + t_1 + t_2 + \ldots + n_m a X_a (1 + r) t_a + t_1 + t_2 + \ldots t_m. \qquad (1)$$

Let $t_a + t_1, = t_{a1}, t_a + t_1 + t_2 = t_{a2}, \ldots$; then

$$X_a = n_a a X_a (1 + r)^{t_a} + n_1 a X_a (1 + r)^{t_{a1}} + n_2 a X_a (1 + r)$$

$$t_{a2} + \ldots + n_m a X_a (1 + r) t_a m \qquad (2)$$

where

$$t_a m > t_a (m -) > t_a (m - 2) > \ldots > t_{a2} > t_{a1} > t_a.$$

corresponding for increasingly long periods of time separating the times at which the amounts of labor $n_m, n_{m-1}, \ldots, n_1, n_a$ are expended, from the time at which the finished product is delivered to the market. The rationale for this type of approach has been explained by Sraffa:

> We shall call reduction to dated quantities of labour an operation by which in the equation of a commodity the different means of production used are replaced with a series of quantities of labour, each with its appropriate date. In our earlier equation, we replace the commodities forming the means of production of A with their own means of production and quantities of labour which, as appears from their own respective equations, must be employed to produce those means of production; and they, having been expended a year earlier, will be multiplied by a profit factor at a compound rate for the appropriate period. . . . We next proceed to replace these latter means of production with their own means of production and labour, and to these will be applied a profit factor for one more year. . . . (*Production of Commodities by Means of Commodities*, p. 34.)

Similarly, the price of B, X_B, may be formulated as follows:

$$X_B = m_B a X_a (1 + r)^{t_B} + m_1 a X_a (1 + r)^{t_{B1}} + \ldots$$

$$+ m_p a X_a (1 + r) t^{Bp} \qquad (3)$$

where $m_B, m_1, m_2, \ldots, m_p$ is the amount of current labor expended in the the production of B and in the capital goods used up in the production of B, and $t_B, t_{B1}, \ldots, t_{Bp}$ is the length of times needed for the manufacture and delivery to the market for good B and of the capital goods used up in the production of good B. The exchange value of a to B is X_a/X_B or

$$X_{aB} = \frac{n_a (1 + r)^{t_a} + n_1 (1 + r)^{t_{a1}} + \ldots + n_m (1 + r)^{t_{am}}}{m_B (1 + r)^{t_B} + m_1 (1 + r)^{t_{B1}} + \ldots + n_p (1 + r)^{t_{Bp}}} . \qquad (4)$$

Note that the terms $a X_a$ drop out.

Thus, the relative price of a to B,

$$X_{aB} = f(n_a, n_1, n_2, \ldots; m_B, m_1, m_2, \ldots; t_a, t_{a1}, t_{a2}, \ldots; t_B, t_{B1}, t_{B2}, \ldots; r). \qquad (5)$$

If $n_a, n_1, \ldots, m_B, m_1, \ldots, t_a, t_{a1}, \ldots, t_B$ and $t_{B1} \ldots$ have been adopted as quantities dependent on the technical conditions of production of the products a and B, $X_{aB} = f(r)$ is obtained, where X_{aB} will be a determined quantity when r is given. By the same assumptions, the same will hold for any X_{MN}:

$$X_{MN} = \frac{n_M (1 + r)^{t_M} + n_1 (1 + r)^{t_{M1}} + \ldots + n_k (1 + r)^{t_{Mk}}}{m_N (1 + r)^{t_N} + m_1 (1 + r)^{t_{N1}} + \ldots + m_p (1 + r)^{t_{Np}}} \qquad (6)$$

so that, given the technical conditions of production (including the wage rate), once the rate of profit is known all relative prices may be determined.

In a society with n goods, there will be n production cost equations, such as (2) and (3) above, to solve $n + 1$ unknowns (the prices of the n goods and the rate of profit). However, one good N may be taken as the unit of value (e.g., gold) so that

$$X_N = a X_a [P_N (+ r)^{t_N} + p_1 (1 + r)^{t_{N1}}$$

$$+ p_2 (1 + r)^{t_{N2}} + \ldots + p_s (1 + r)^{t_{Ns}}] = 1 \qquad (7)$$

thus reducing the number of unknowns by one (the price of N).

Furthermore, the rate of profit can be determined *solely* from (2), the equation which gives the production conditions of the product a (which is the only product consumed by the workers) and to which in the final analysis the expenditure in all the other products can be reduced. If each side of (2) is divided by X_a, and 1 is subtracted from each side, then

$$a[n_a(1 + r)^{t_a} + n_1(1 + r)^{t_{a1}}$$

$$+ n_2(1 + r)^{t_{a2}} + \ldots + n_m(1 + r)^{t_{am}}] - 1 = 0 \qquad (8)$$

and determining r from this equation,

$$r = F(n_a, n_1, n_2, \ldots, n_m; t_a, t_{a1}, t_{a2}, \ldots, t_{am}; a). \qquad (9)$$

Since $n_a, n_1, \ldots; t_a, t_{a1}, \ldots;$ and a are given quantities dependent upon the technical conditions of production of the product a (i.e., the product forming the essential means of existence of the worker), r is a given magnitude. Knowing r, insert it into the production equations to find $X_B, X_C, \ldots,$ and the corresponding $X_{aB}, X_{aC}, \ldots$ as functions of the same *given* quantities n, $m, \ldots$ (with the appropriate indices), t's . . . (with the appropriate indices) and of the quantity a (see Dmitriev, *Economic Essays on Value, Competition and Utility*, p. 59). Thus, there is a determinate system, solving for all relative prices as well as the average rate of profit, based on the exogenously given wage rate and the technical conditions of production.

The situation is not fundamentally altered when workers consume more than one good. Let $A, B, C, \ldots$ be products consumed by the workers. Let the daily consumption of a single worker be a for the product A, b for the product B, c for the product $C, \ldots$ The production costs equations will then be:

$$X_A = n_A(aX_A + bX_B + cX_C \ldots)(1 + r)^{t_A} + n_{A1}(aX_A + bX_B$$

$$+ cX_C \ldots)(1 + r)^{t_{A1}} + \ldots \qquad (10)$$

$$X_B = n_B(aX_A + bX_B + cX_C \ldots)(1 + r)^{t_B} + n_{B1}(aX_A + bX_B$$

$$+ cX_C \ldots)(1 + r)^{t_{B1}} + \ldots \qquad (11)$$

$$X_C = n_C(aX_A + bX_B + cX_C \ldots)(1 + r)^{t_C} + n_{C1}(aX_A + bX_B$$

$$+ cX_C \ldots)(1 + r)^{t_{C1}} + \ldots \tag{12}$$

$$\vdots$$

Multiply both parts of (10) by a, both parts of (11) by b, both parts of (12) by c and so on, and add up all the equations:

$$(aX_A + bX_B + cX_C \ldots) = an_A(aX_A + bX_B + cX_C \ldots)(1 + r)^{t_A}$$

$$+ an_{A1}(aX_A + bX_B + cX_C \ldots)(1 + r)^{t_{A1}} + \ldots$$

$$+ bn_B(aX_A + bX_B + cX_C \ldots)(1 + r)^{t_B}$$

$$+ bn_{B1}(aX_A + bX_B + cX_C \ldots)(1 + r)^{t_{B1}} + \ldots \tag{13}$$

$$+ cn_C(aX_A + bX_B + cX_C \ldots)(1 + r)^{t_C}$$

$$+ cn_{C1}(aX_A + bX_B + cX_C \ldots)(1 + r)^{t_{C1}} + \ldots$$

Divide both sides of (13) by $(aX_A + bX_B + cX_C, \ldots)$:

$$1 = an_A(1 + r)^{t_A} + an_{A1}(1 + r)^{t_{A1}} + \ldots + bn_B(1 + r)^{t_B}$$

$$+ bn_{B1}(1 + r)^{t_{B1}} + \ldots + cn_C(1 + r)^{t_C} + cn_{C1}(1 + r)^{t_{C1}} + \ldots \tag{14}$$

Consequently,

$$r = f(n_A, n_{A1}, \ldots; n_B, n_{B1}, \ldots; n_C, n_{C1}, \ldots; a, b, c, \ldots;$$

$$t_A, t_{A1}, \ldots; t_B, t_{B1}, \ldots; t_C, t_{C1}, \ldots; \ldots). \tag{15}$$

Thus, the rate of profit is fully determined and is a function of given quantities dependent on the technical conditions of production in the products consumed by workers, as well as the given real wage rate.

Now, to simplify matters, return to the assumption that workers consume only one good. Set the magnitudes an_a, an_1, an_2, $\ldots$ in equation (2) equal to A_a, A_{a1}, A_{a2}, and the magnitudes am_B, am_1, $\ldots$ in equation (3) equal to A_B, A_{B1}, $\ldots$, etc. In this case A_a, A_{a1}, $\ldots$, A_B, A_{B1}, $\ldots$ will denote the quantity of some good q to the expenditure of which may, in the final analysis, reduce the production costs of the products A, B, $\ldots$.

The production cost of that product q is

$$X_q = A_q X_q (1 + r)^{t_q} + A_{q1} X_q (1 + r)^{t_{q1}} \ldots \tag{16}$$

Divide both sides by the price of q:

$$1 = A_q (1 + r)^{t_q} + A_{q1} (1 + r)^{t_{q1}} + \ldots \tag{17}$$

Since the periods of production $t_q, t_{q1}, \ldots$ are always finite, it follows that when

$$A_q + A_{q1} + A_{q2} + \ldots \text{ is less than 1,} \tag{18}$$

r is greater than zero.

Solving (17) with respect to r,

$$r = f(A_q, A_{q1}, \ldots; t_q, t_{q1}, \ldots). \tag{19}$$

Equation (19) does not contain the quantities $n_q, n_{q1}, \ldots$, i.e., it does not contain the quantity of *labor* used in the production of q. It yields r as a function only of the *production period* and the *quantity of good q* expended in production.

Equations (18) and (19) show that whenever a known quantity of some product q has been used up in the production of q and can obtain a *larger* quantity of the same product within some finite period of time as a result of the production process, the profit rate in the given branch of industry will be a fully determined quantity, greater than zero, irrespective of the price of the product q:

> If the production costs of the other goods, A, B, C, . . . are reduced in the *final analysis* to the same product q, the same profit rate should also be established in these branches under conditions of free mobility from one branch of production to another (irrespective of what the ratios $X_{Aq}, X_{Bq}, \ldots$, will be). The essence of the production process by means of which a 'production good' q yields as a result the products A, B, C, . . . and new quantitites of the same good q, is a matter of *complete indifference* for determination of the rate of profit. Whether the potential energy incorporated in the product good *a* is released and used in production in the form of *human labor* as happens at present, or by means of some other process (*not involving the participation of human labor*) is a matter of indifference. [Dmitriev, *Economic Essays on Value, Competition and Utility*, pp. 62–63; emphasis in the original.]

Therefore, suppose a machine M is able, without participation of human labor, and using natural forces as a motor, to produce machines of the following orders: $M_1, M_2, M_3, \ldots$; let these machines singly or in combination produce machines of a higher order $M_1', M_2', M_3', \ldots$ until ultimately there are machines $M_A, M_B, M_C, \ldots$ which produce the consumer products $A, B, C, \ldots$.

In this case, $A, B, C, \ldots$ may always be reduced in the final analysis to the number (or parts) of machines M consumed in the production of products $A, B, C, \ldots$. Suppose M itself is capable of reproduction. Then

$$X_A = n_M' X_M (1 + r)^{t_A} + n_M'' X_M (1 + r)^{t_{A1}} \ldots$$

$$\vdots \qquad\qquad (20)$$

$$X_M = N_M' X_M (1 + r)^{t_M} + N_M'' X_M (1 + r)^{t_{M1}} \ldots$$

where $n_M', n_M'', \ldots, N_M', N_M'', \ldots$ will denote the number of machines M used up in the production of units of the products $A, B, C, \ldots, M, \ldots$. If $N_M' + N_M'' + \ldots < 1$ in the equation for M, then r will be greater than zero and a fully defined quantity, provided that the quantities $N_M', N_M'', \ldots, t_M, t_{M1}, \ldots$ are given. Thus, there can indeed be a rate of profit in a fully automated society.

Dmitriev concludes that

> Conceivably a state of technology could exist where the profit level is determined in a production process where *no 'living' power is involved at all* and 'reproduction' of goods (including machines) is effected by machines driven by free 'inanimate' natural forces. Therefore, we can imagine a state of society where *wage labour is not used* in production, but where *'surplus value' will nevertheless arise, and where,* consequently, *there will be profit on capital.* [Dmitriev, *Economic Essays on Value, Competition and Utility,* p. 214, emphasis in original.]

APPENDIX D

ARISTOTLE AND MARX ON THE ORIGINS OF CAPITAL

It has been argued that Parts I and II of Volume I of *Capital* are trying to answer the question: Why is there capital? From this point of view, approximately the first 150 pages of *Capital* do not comprise some kind of abstract history of the development of capitalism. Rather, it is an attempt to explain theoretically why there is capital in the first place. Moreover, a close reading of Marx shows that he does not start with the realm of production, as is commonly supposed. The position that Marx starts with simple commodity *production* has been put forward by Paul Sweezy in his deservedly popular textbook *The Theory of Capitalist Development*:

> Marx begins by analyzing 'simple commodity production,' that is to say a society in which each producer owns his own means of production and satisfies his manifold needs by exchange with other similarly situated producers.[1]

The source of this dominant interpretation of Marx[2] is no doubt Frederick Engels. In his "Preface" to Volume III of *Capital,* Engels asserts that

> in the beginning of his first book Marx proceeds from the simple production of commodities as the historical premise, ultimately to arrive from this basis to capital . . . he proceeds from the simple commodity instead of a logically and historically secondary form—from an already capitalistically modified commodity.[3]

In contradistinction to this point of view, the interpretation offered in this work is that Marx starts with the realm of circulation.[4] At a certain point in time, products take the form of commodities. Commodities generate money which in turn generates capital. Support for this interpretation of Marx (that he starts with circulation) comes from a close reading of the relevant sections of the 1859 *Critique, Capital,* and the *Grundrisse.* Indirect support also comes from a reading of Aristotle's *The Politics.* By this interpretation, it turns out that approximately the first 150 pages of *Capital* are to a large extent an elaboration and development of several pages of Book I of *The Politics.* This is because, there, in a few passages, Aristotle argues that commodities generate money which in turn may be used to make more money. Therefore, a key to understanding the first part of *Capital* can be found by studying Aristotle. The purpose of this appendix is to substantiate this claim.

In *The Politics,* Aristotle argues that although individual people and families exist in time before the polis does, the polis must be assumed to exist prior to individuals and families:

> We may now proceed to add that though the individual and the family are prior in the order of time the polis is prior to the order of nature to the family and the individual. The reason for this is that the whole is necessarily prior in nature to the part.[5]

The reason for this is further explained by the translator in a footnote:

> The whole is prior to the part in the sense that the part presupposes it; the idea of the whole must first be there before the part can be understood, and the whole itself must be there before the part can have or exercise a function.[6]

This is very similar to Marx's approach to the study of the capitalist mode of production. As argued earlier (see Chapter 5), Marx begins his study by assuming that the capitalist mode of production already exists. It is this whole which conditions and determines all other aspects of Marx's theoretical system. Thus, given the existence of the capitalist mode of production, Marx begins his analysis by asking how such things as commodities and money interact in such a way as to generate capital, which is self-expanding value.[7] Just as (for Aristotle) individuals and families exist historically prior to the polity, so money and commodities exist historically prior to the capitalist mode of production. Yet, Marx starts with these concepts not for historical reasons, but so as to explain why there is capital (or self-expanding value); at the same time Marx is always assuming the existence of the capitalist mode of production. In this fashion, Marx's method is similar to that of Aristotle, who assumes the polity is theoretically prior to individuals and families even though this is not historically true.

In the course of his analysis Aristotle discovers that there are different ways to acquire property. One form of acquiring property may be called the hunting form, and this is a form of acquiring property which Aristotle considers to be natural or just:

> It follows that one form of acquisition, i.e. what may be called the 'hunting form' is naturally a part of the art of household management. . . . It is clear that there is a natural art of acquisition which has to be practised by managers of households and statesmen; and the reason for its existence is also clear, the reason being that it is natural for man to acquire what is naturally provided for his use.[8]

However, there is another form of acquiring property which Aristotle does not consider to be natural.[9] This is the use of money to make more money. In Chapter IX of Book I of *The Politics,* Aristotle briefly considers how this second (unnatural) form of acquiring property develops.

In order to explain how a second form of acquiring property comes about, Aristotle starts with the observation that every article of property has two uses:

> We may start our discussion of this from the following point of view. All articles of property have two possible uses. Both of these uses belong to the article as such, but they do not belong to it in the same manner or to the same extent. The one use is proper and peculiar to the article concerned; the other is not. We may take a shoe as an example. It can be used for wearing and for exchange.[10]

In Marxian terminology, it may be said that each article of property has a use value and an exchange value:

> Even the man who exchanges a shoe, in return for money or food, with a person who needs the article, is using the shoe as a shoe; but since the shoe has not been made for the purpose of being exchanged, the use which he is making of it is not its proper and peculiar use. The same is true of all other articles of property.[11]

Aristotle then inquires under what circumstances the exchange of articles of property develops.[12] He holds that

> exchange simply served in the first beginnings to satisfy the natural requirements of sufficiency. None the less it was from exchange, as thus practiced, that the art of acquisition in its second sense developed, in the sort of way we might reasonably expect.[13]

Articles of property were originally exchanged between villages in the form of barter.[14] In time foreign trade developed and people began to depend on the foreign trade for the provisioning of some of their needs.[15] This exchange of articles of property generated the use of a money currency, or of a universal equivalent:

The reason for this institution of a currency was that all the naturally necessary commodities were not easily portable; and men therefore agreed, for the purpose of their exchanges, to give and receive some commodity i.e. some form of more or less precious metal which itself belonged to the category of useful things and possessed the advantage of being easily handled for the purpose of getting the necessities of life.[16]

Thus, rather than one article of property being exchanged (bartered) for another, one article of property was exchanged for money which in turn could be exchanged for another. Hence, out of exchange arose money, or in Marx's terminology, a universal equivalent.

At first the article which served as money was actually weighed and measured at every transaction. In time however, "a stamp was imposed on the metal which, serving as a definite indication of the quantity, would save men the trouble of determining the value on each occasion."[17]

After accounting for the origin of money, Aristotle then accounts for that other form of acquisition (which he considers unnatural), the use of money to make more money. This other form of acquisition also *arose out of exchange*:

When, in this way, a currency had once been instituted, there next arose, *from the necessary process of exchange, i.e. exchange between commodities,* with money serving merely as a measure, the other form of the art of acquisition, which consists in retail trade conducted for profit.[18]

For Aristotle the other form of acquisition consisted of retail trade, that is, the buying and selling of commodities. People could make a profit from the buying and selling of commodities; in this way money could be used to make more money. In this form of acquisition, money, instead of serving merely to facilitate the exchange of commodities, becomes the goal and end in itself. Thus:

The natural form of the art of acquisition is connected with the management of the household which in turn is connected with the general acquisition of all the resources needed for its life; but the other form is a matter only of retail trade, and it is concerned only with getting a fund of money, and that only by the method of conducting the exchange of commodities. This latter form may be held to turn on the power of currency; for currency is the starting point, as it is also the goal, of exchange.[19]

The second form of acquisition, the use of money to make more money, knows no limits. The object of this form of acquisition is not to satisfy wants: it is merely to make more money. Therefore, "the wealth produced by this latter form of the art of acquisition is unlimited,''[20] This form of acquisition leads only to more acquisition, to the desire of money itself, and to the never ending desire for *more* money.

Aristotle concludes that the second form of acquisition, the use of money to make more money, is unnatural.[21] It arises out of the use of currency or money, which in turn "came into existence merely as a means of exchange.''[22] That is to say, money itself came out of the exchange of articles of property.[23]

This brief review of a section of Aristotle's *Politics* shows that his account of the origins of the second form of acquisition was remarkably similar to Marx's account of the genesis of capital. Parts I and II of *Capital* can be viewed largely as an extended elaboration of this part of Aristotle. Of course, there are important differences between Marx and Aristotle on this issue. Most importantly, Aristotle himself had no theory of value.[24] Aristotle also did not talk about capitalist *production*. In this form of production, which is the subject matter of Marx's *Capital*, money is used to purchase commodities; the commodities are then used to make more commodities; finally, the output is sold for a profit.

Clearly, Marx himself had a theory of value—a labor theory of value. On the basis of this theory, Marx followed Aristotle by showing that commodities generate money which in turn generates capital. For Marx, this capital then seizes a hold of the production process, transforms an entire class of people into wage laborers, and organizes the entire society around the needs of capital, i.e., around the needs of self-expanding value.

To conclude this appendix, Marx's account of the genesis of capital can be seen to be an elaboration of a few pages in Aristotle. Furthermore, it has been shown above that the same process (i.e., the theoretical genesis of capital) can be analyzed using a commodity theory of value. By this theory commodities have value because they are produced by other commodities; surplus value arises because commodities can produce more commodities as output than are used up as inputs. The capitalist mode of production can then be viewed as a society based upon production by capital, i.e., production based upon self-expanding value. Following Marx (who in turn apparently followed Aristotle), it has also been shown that capital arises out of the circulation process; it arises out of money, which in turn arises out of commodities.

NOTES

1. Sweezy, *Theory of Capitalist Development,* p. 23.

2. See, also, e.g., Shaik: "The struggle for production is the fundamental social practice in all human society; hence the analysis of production is the beginning point of Marxist analysis." (In Schwartz, *The Subtle Anatomy of Capitalism,* p. 110); or Meek, *Studies in the Labour Theory of Value,* especially pp. 305–306.

3. Engels, "Preface" to *Capital,* Vol. III, p. 14. Engels was consistent in his interpretation of Marx's work. See, also, "Law of Value and Rate of Profit," "Supplement to *Capital,* Vol. III,"" pp. 891–907, and his review of Marx's *Contribution to Critique of Political Economy,* reprinted in *Critique,* pp. 218–227.

4. This interpretation is clearly and succinctly stated in Uno, *Principles of Political Economy: Theory of a Purely Capitalist Society.*

5. Book I, Chapter II, No. 12–13.

6. Ibid., p. 6.

7. Although there may be disagreement as to where and how Marx begins his analysis in *Capital,* there is little disagreement that for Marx capital is indeed self-expanding value. See, e.g., Sweezy and Magdoff: "Capital is not a thing, nor a sum of money, nor even only a social relation—though it partakes of all of these. It is above all *self-expanding value.*" ["The Present Stage of the Global Crisis of Capitalism," in *The Deepening Crisis of U.S. Capitalism,* p. 54; emphasis in original.]

8. I, viii No. 13–15.

9. I, ix, No. 1.

10. I, ix, No. 2.

11. I, ix, No. 3.

12. I, ix, No. 5–6.

13. I, ix, No. 6–7.

14. Ibid.

15. I, ix, No. 7.

16. I, ix, No. 8.

17. Ibid.

18. Ibid.; emphasis added.

19. I, ix, No. 12.

20. I, ix, No. 13.

21. I, x, No. 4.

22. I, x, No. 5.

23. Money itself was often looked down upon by the Greeks. See, for example, Sophocles:

> Nothing in use by man, for power of ill,
> Can equal money. This lays cities low,
> This drives men forth from quiet dwelling-place
> This warps and changes minds of worthiest stamp
> To turn to deeds of baseness.
> —*Antigone,* 295.

24. Marx points this out; *Capital,* p. 69.

APPENDIX E

SOME UNRESOLVED QUESTIONS RAISED BY THE COMMODITY THEORY OF VALUE

A major problem with economic theory is that in a very real sense everything depends upon everything else. A work of the sort which this study represents, dealing as it does with such fundamental issues as the nature of value, the determination of relative prices, the question of how to correctly pose the concepts money and capital, etc., will necessarily raise many other issues which cannot be adequately dealt with within the scope of only *one* study. The purpose of this appendix[1] is to briefly deal with several issues which were raised in the study itself, which would not be fully developed in the main text, but which nevertheless are highly interesting in their own right. This appendix will deal with what is meant by created versus determined value, the role of general equilibrium analysis in Marxian theory, and the need to introduce monetary analysis into the framework proposed in the main text. These issues are all interrelated; all of them are unresolved and controversial. Nevertheless, none of them seem to contradict the main theme of the study, which is that one may reconstruct Marx's theory of the genesis of capital (i.e., Parts I and II of *Capital*) when using a commodity theory of value.

Now, from a certain point of view, one may draw a distinction between what determines value and what creates value. Admittedly, this may not be a distinction which immediately leaps to the attention of the mathematically minded economist.[2] Nonetheless, there are times when this may be a useful distinction. As an example of this approach, Joseph Schumpeter has argued that this was indeed the method taken by Bohm-Bawerk in his work concerning interest. According to Schumpeter, Bohm-Bawerk

> was out to 'explain' or 'understand' the phenomenon of interest. This task seemed to him to involve two different things. First, it seemed obviously necessary to unearth the '*cause*' or 'source' or 'nature' of interest. Second, after this had been done . . . there arose the problem of what determines the rate of interest.[3]

132

Without getting into a discussion of Bohm-Bawerk's work, one may posit that a similar type of distinction may be made with regard to Marx's work. For Marx, labor and the exploitation of labor power is the source or cause of value: only labor *creates* value; but Marx also goes further than this, and argues that labor *determines* the amount of value which a commodity has. For Marx, the value of a commodity is determined by the amount of socially necessary labor time embodied within that commodity.

Unfortunately, things are a bit more complicated when using a commodity theory of value. It is true that one may say that commodities have value because they are produced by other commodities, or that commodities create value when they are used to make other commodities. One may go on to say that surplus value is created when commodities are used to create more commodities as output than are used up as inputs. However, it does not seem to make much sense to say that the value of a commodity is *determined* by the amount of commodities embodied within that commodity. Rather, it seems that, when using the commodity theory of value, the value of a commodity must be determined within the production process as a whole. Hence, there is no simple equivalent in the commodity theory of value to the orthodox Marxist statement that the value of a commodity is determined by the amount of labor embodied within that commodity. Some may see this as a drawback to the commodity theory of value. Whether or not it is a drawback, the question of the determination of value when using a commodity theory of value does point to the need to look at the production process in its entirety. This then leads to a consideration of what is known as general equilibrium theory and its role within Marxian theory. However, before taking up this issue, let us consider a case where the distinction between the creation and to determination of value could be crucial.

Samuel Hollander is an economist at the University of Toronto who takes what may be termed a "Marshallian" position with regard to the classical economists. His viewpoint is that there is no fundamental difference between classical and neoclassical economics; for him, neoclassical economics can be seen to be a relatively smooth progression and improvement upon classical economics. To support his position, he has undertaken lengthy studies of Adam Smith, David Ricardo, and is now apparently working on Karl Marx. In an article in *History of Political Economy*,[4] Hollander has put forth the rather surprising position that within Marx's theoretical system, the mass of profits is *determined* by both surplus labor time and the "abstinence" of capitalists. From this, Hollander concludes that

> Marx did not succeed in his fundamental objective, which was to demonstrate, by his preliminary formulation in *Capital* of a value structure, that the capitalist has a personally functionless role.[5]

This is not the place to go into a thorough critique of this position.[6] However, let us assume that Hollander's position is correct, and that even within Marx's system the mass of profits is partly determined by the "abstinence" of capitalists. Even if that were true, then using *either* a labor theory of value or a commodity theory of value, it is clear that capitalists in their role as capitalists do not work. They do not produce commodities, and they do not *create* value. As far as human beings are concerned, only workers (using either a commodity or a labor theory of value) work; only workers create value. Within the Marxian framework, using either a labor or a commodity theory of value, capitalists do indeed have a personally functionless role with regard to the *creation* of value.

With regard to the determination of value, the Sraffian system and the commodity theory of value suggests that one must look at the production process *as a whole*. This raises another question: Does this then mean that the Sraffian analysis is a subset of neoclassical general equilibrium modelling, only without equations of demand? Now, without going into this point in detail, I would argue that this appears to be an unwarranted interpretation of Sraffa's work. As John Roemer has argued, the use of general equilibrium models does not lead to the assimilation of the Sraffian or classical models into neoclassical models. The reason for this is due to the importance of the specification of property rights and of property relations in the analyses performed by Sraffa as well as in the classical general equilibrium models.[7]

Yet, even if Roemer's interpretation is correct, one is then led to another question. If one needs to look at the production process as a whole in order to *determine* the value of a commodity when using the commodity theory of value, and if this is then seen to be some kind of general equilibrium theory (although not necessarily neoclassical general equilibrium theory), then in what sense is this compatible with Marx's work? May it not be that Marx's work is necessarily incompatible with any kind of general equilibrium theory? This is the view taken by some. Aglietta, for example, asserts that "general equilibrium theory . . . (is) quite foreign to the developmental logic of the basic concepts of Marxism" and that therefore the "theoretical universe of general equilibrium . . . is totally foreign to the law of capitalist accumulation."[8] Moreover, it must be admitted that, as Schumpeter has pointed out, in Marx's work, "disequilibrium prevails throughout, but Marx saw that this disequilibrium is the very life of capitalism. . . ."[9]

On the other hand others have actually argued that Marx is really a general equilibrium theorist. Hollander, in the article cited above, claims that

> Marx too is in the general-equilibrium tradition. . . . Any notion of a
> sharp duality between a Ricardo–Marx tradition, on the one hand, and
> a neoclassical or general-equilibrium tradition, on the other, must be
> abandoned.[10]

Yet, the issue of Marx's relationship to general equilibrium theory is a much more complex one than the above quotes imply. The interpretation offered here is that Marx may be classified as a general equilibrium theorist, but only in a restricted sense of the term. Marx may indeed be considered to be one of the founders of general equilibrium theory, but he used his general equilibrium models to show why in capitalist societies "equilibrium" is nearly impossible to achieve. Hence, the philosopher David Hawkins is correct when he states that

> Simple mechanical models, defined by linear differential equations, have been described repeatedly since the time of Marx's *Capital,* Vol. III. These are usually known as general equilibrium models, although the term "equilibrium" is somewhat misleading.[11]

The term equilibrium is somewhat misleading because one may use a so-called general equilibrium model without arguing that the system will ever reach equilibrium.[12]

Marx's relationship to general equilibrium theory is thus very similar to that of Joseph Schumpeter, one of the great economists of the 20th century and perhaps the most well-read economist since Karl Marx himself.[13]

Schumpeter clearly appreciated the value and usefulness of equilibrium theory.[14] Nonetheless, he still felt that one should "look to business cycles for material with which to build the fundamental theory of capitalist reality," and this is what he did indeed do in his own creative work.[15]

I would suggest that the situation with Marx is very similar. Marx appreciated general equilibrium theory and was one of its founders, but he used it to show why equilibrium would *not* be achieved in capitalist societies. This relatively complex relationship between Marx and general equilibrium theory has been well clarified in a recent article by Peter Groenewegen in the journal, *Australian Economic Papers.*[16] Groenewegen argues that Marx was a skillful equilibrium economist, as particularly exemplified by Part II of Volume II of *Capital.* Here Groenewegen is referring to Marx's schemes of simple and expanded reproduction.[17] Nonetheless, Groenewegen argues that ". . . the purpose of Marx's analysis of reproduction was to illuminate aspects of the theory of crises."[18] Groenewegen concludes that

> Marx fully realised the theoretical importance of equilibrium analysis—as he also realised the importance of mathematical modelling—for which his work in the theory of reproduction provides the perfect illustration. However, unlike many modern equilibrium economists, Marx was fully aware of the limitations of equilibrium analysis arising from the conflict between history and equilibrium. He therefore valued equilibrium propositions for what they denied rather than for what they affirmed. Marx's careful inferences from

equilibrium analysis therefore reveal the possibilities of a peaceful co-existence of history and equilibrium.[19]

The following inferences may now be made. The interpretation offered here is that Marx may be viewed as a general equilibrium theorist, although with qualifications; with reference to the work done in the study, one must indeed look at the production process as a whole in order to determine the value of a commodity when using the commodity theory of value; this may then be seen to entail the use of some kind of general equilibrium theory; yet, nonetheless, this does not mean that Sraffa's work and the commodity theory of value is not compatible with Marx's work, since in crucial respects Marx himself may be viewed as a general equilibrium theorist.

Yet, even granted this interpretation, this then raises another set of questions: How does a full monetary analysis effect the determination of values when using a commodity theory of value? Also, how will this then effect things when the commodity theory of value is used as a foundation upon which to build Marx's analysis?

These are very difficult and important questions. Much more work needs to be done before these questions can be completely answered. This appendix will not attempt to answer these questions. However, a few notes and suggestions will be given as a guide to future research and as a way to clarify a few preliminary issues.

First, it must be emphasized that Marx, in Volume I of *Capital,* is not giving a full account of the functions and role of money in a capitalist society. This point was made in Chapter 9, but its importance merits repetition as well as elaboration. For Marx, money used as credit only arises on any extensive scale when there is capitalist production. Hence, money used as credit can only be fully discussed after Marx has discussed capital. Thus, while Marx needs to discuss money before he can discuss capital, money when used as credit cannot be extensively discussed until after he has developed his concept of capital. Marx makes this point in the *Grundrisse*:

> Finally, credit. This form of circulation etc. directly posited by capital—which arises, hence, specifically from the nature of capital, this specific characteristic of capital.[20]

As a second point, which merits clarification, Marx may be called a theoretical metallist. Marx derives the necessity of money from the circulation of commodities themselves, and from the role which one particular commodity comes to assume in the circulation of commodities. For reasons concerning the use values of metals, the particular commodity which comes to serve as money or as the universal equivalent is usually a precious metal (gold or silver). It is for this reason that Marx may be termed a theoretical metallist, a term apparently "coined" by Schumpeter:

By Theoretical Metallism we denote the *theory* that it is logically essential for money to consist of, or to be 'covered' by, some commodity so that the logical source of the exchange value or purchasing power of money is the exchange value or purchasing power of that commodity, considered independently of its monetary role.[21]

Yet note that this does not *necessarily* mean that Marx was a practical metallist. Again, following Schumpeter:

By Practical Metallism . . . sponsorship of . . . the principle that the monetary unit 'should' be kept firmly linked to, and freely interchangeable with, a given quantity of some commodity.[22]

As Schumpeter points out, one may be a theoretical metallist, but not necessarily a practical metallist, and vice versa.[23]

In spite of the fact that Marx is a theoretical metallist, this does not mean that Marx would develop the theory of credit, or money used as credit, from the concept of money itself. Rather, credit money may be developed from the concept of capitalist production. Indeed, Joseph Schumpeter also seems to be pointing in this direction (and to be in agreement with Marx) when he suggests that

logically, it is by no means clear that the most useful method is to start from the coin—even if, making a concession to realism, we add inconvertible government paper—in order to proceed to the credit transactions of reality. It may be more useful to start from these in the first place, to look upon capitalist finance as a clearing system that cancels claims and debts and carries forward the differences—so that 'money' payments come in only as a special case without any particularly fundamental importance. In other words: practically and analytically, a credit theory of money is possibly preferable to a monetary theory of credit.[24]

Yet note that while credit can and should (according to Marx) be developed from the concept of capitalist production, this is not incompatible with also being a theoretical metallist (which Marx is).

Finally, it should be noted that thus far money, with all its ramifications, has not been *fully* incorporated into the Sraffian framework. Thus, so far the Sraffian framework has been largely confined to what Schumpeter has called "Real Analysis":

Real Analysis proceeds from the principle that all the essential phenomena of economic life are capable of being described in terms of goods and services. . . . Money enters the picture only in the modest role of a technical device that has been adopted in order to facilitate transactions. . . . Thus, money has been called a 'garb' or 'veil' of the things that really matter. . . . Not only *can* it be discarded whenever we are analyzing the fundamental features of the economic process but it *must* be discarded. . . . Accordingly, money prices must give way to the exchange ratios between the commodities that are the really important thing 'behind' money prices. . . . The specifically monetary problems can then be treated separately. . . .[25]

Few economists today would subscribe to what Schumpeter has called Real Analysis. Consequently, monetary phenomena must be more fully integrated into the Sraffian framework. A start has recently been made in this direction. In a recent article in *Australian Economic Papers,* Geoff Hodgson has attempted to include money in the Sraffian framework.[26] He finds that prices, wages, and profits all depend, to some extent, on variables that pertain to the monetary side of the economy.[27] Monetary phenomena will change relative prices as well as the maximum rate of profit. In spite of these findings, Hodgson argues that

The monetised Sraffa model should not be conceived as either a simple amendment, or a fundamental critique, of Sraffa's original long-run model. . . . With a monetised model changing expectations of the future are likely to influence current economic behaviour, through, in part, changes in liquidity preference. . . . The original Sraffa system is not invalidated, more it is complemented, by the approach adopted in this paper.[28]

This seems to be a reasonable approach to take. Furthermore, it may serve as a guide to future research in this area.

All of the issues discussed in this appendix are controversial and have not been resolved at the time of this writing. They are all important in their own right, and more work needs to be done to clear up problems which they pose. These are all issues which are brought up when an attempt is made to base Marx's work upon a commodity rather than upon his labor theory of value. However, none of these issues seem to contradict the basic point made in the text which is that Marx's account of the theoretical genesis of capital (i.e, Parts I and II of *Capital*) remains basically intact when it is based upon a commodity theory of value rather than upon Marx's labor theory of value.

NOTES

1. This appendix draws heavily upon Schumpeter's *History of Economic Analysis.*
2. See Schumpeter, *History of Economic Analysis,* pp. 968-971.
3. Ibid., p. 968; emphasis added.
4. Hollander, "Marxian Economics as 'General Equilibrium' Theory," *History of Political Economy* **13**, No. 1 (1981): 121-155.
5. Ibid., p. 154.
6. Actually, this position is not quite as iconoclastic as it at first appears. As Hollander correctly notes, it is also the position held by no less an authority than Joseph Schumpeter (*History of Economic Analysis,* pp. 661-662). However, it may be noted that this interpretation turns Marx into some sort of "pre-Keynesian." (Here the term pre-Keynesian is being used in the sense that it is used in macroeconomic textbooks.) For the pre-Keynesians, the mass of investment largely depends upon the mass of savings; hence, the aggregate demand for labor, the wealth of nations, and the mass of profits in turn largely depend upon the savings proclivities or "abstinence" of capitalists. On the other hand, for Keynes, the line of causation is essentially reversed. Since savings is largely a function of income and income is largely a function of investment, one may say that the amount of savings (or "abstinence") in an economy is largely determined by the amount of investment undertaken by capitalists, rather than vice versa. Now, admittedly, the exact relationship between Marx and Keynes is controversial. Yet, attempts to transform Marx into some sort of "pre-Keynesian," as the term is used in macroeconomic textbooks, seem rather strained, to say the least. For a diametrically opposite interpretation of Marx, see Sweezy's *Theory of Capitalist Development.*
7. See John Roemer, *A General Theory of Exploitation and Class,* especially Chap. 7, pp. 194-237, and his articles in *Politics and Society* **11**, No. 3 (1982).
8. Michel Aglietta, *A Theory of Capitalist Regulation* (New Left Books, 1979); the quotes are from pp. 18 and 354, respectively.
9. Schumpeter, *History of Economic Analysis,* p. 1051.
10. Hollander, "Marxian Economics as 'General Equilibrium' Theory," p. 123. Georgescu-Roegen also sees Marx to be in the tradition of general equilibrium theory. (*The Entropy Law and the Economic Process,* Harvard University Press, 1971, p. 18) A major difference between Hollander and Georgescu-Roegen is this: Hollander seems to think that it is a point in Marx's favor that he can be put in the general equilibrium tradition; Georgescu-Roegen has the opposite opinion.
11. Hawkins, *The Language of Nature,* p. 337.
12. As Hawkins does. See Hawkins, *Some Conditions of Macroeconomic Stability.*
13. For support of this assertion see approximately the first 1000 pages of Schumpeter, *History of Economic Analysis.*
14. See Chapters 7 and 8 of Part IV of Schumpeter, *History of Economic Analysis,* pp. 951-1135.
15. The quote is from p. 1135 of Schumpeter, *History of Economic Analysis.* For support of the above statement, see the editor's footnote on that same page as well as Part II of Schumpeter, *Capitalism, Socialism and Democracy.*
16. Groenewegen, "History and Political Economy: Smith, Marx and Marshall," *Australian Economic Papers* **21**, No. 38 (1982): 1-17.
17. Ibid., p. 9.
18. Ibid., p. 10 fn.
19. Ibid., p. 11.
20. Marx, *Grundrisse,* p. 672. See, also, p. 535 of *Grundrisse*; emphasis in original: "It thus appears as a matter of chance for production based on capital whether or not its essential condition, the continuity of the different processes which constitute its process as a whole, is

actually brought about. The suspension of this chance element by capital itself is *credit*. (It has other aspects as well; but this aspect arises out of the direct nature of the production process and is hence the foundation of the necessity of credit.) Which is why *credit* in any developed form appears in no earlier mode of production. . . . And credit as an essential, developed relation of production appears *historically* only in circulation based on capital or on wage labour.''

21. Schumpeter, *History of Economic Analysis,* p. 288; emphasis in original.

22. Ibid.

23. Ibid.

24. Ibid., p. 717.

25. Ibid., p. 277.

26. Hodgson, "Money and the Sraffa System", *Australian Economic Papers,* 20, No. 36, (1981): 83-95.

27. Ibid., p. 92.

28. Ibid., p. 93.

SELECTED BIBLIOGRAPHY

Abraham-Frois, G. and Berrebi, E. *Theory of Value, Prices and Accumulation: A Mathematical Integration of Marx, von Neumann and Sraffa,* Cambridge, England: Cambridge University Press, 1979.

Aglietta, Michel. *A Theory of Capitalist Regulation.* London: New Left Books, 1979.

Albritton, Robert. "The Theoretical and Historical in Marxian Political Economy." Unpublished.

Althusser, Louis. *For Marx.* Middlesex, England: Penguin Press, 1969.

Althusser, Louis and Balibar, Etienne. *Reading Capital.* London: Verso Edition, 1979.

Aristotle. *The Politics of Aristotle,* translated by Ernest Barker, Oxford, England: Oxford University Press, 1946.

Armstrong, Philip; Glyn, Andrew; and Harrison, John. "In Defense of Value: A Reply to Ian Steedman." *Capital and Class* No. 6, (1978): 1–31.

Arrow, Kenneth. "Real and Nominal Magnitudes in Economics." *The Public Interest* Special Issue (1980): 139–150.

Arthur, Chris. "Dialectic of the Value-form," In Diane Elson, *Value, The Representation of Labour in Capitalism.* London: CSE Books, 1979, pp. 67–81.

Aumeeruddy, Aboo and Tortajada, Ramon. "Reading Marx on Value: A Note on the Basic Texts." In Diane Elson, *Value, The Representation of Labour in Capitalism.* London: CSE Books, 1979, pp. 1–13.

Banaji, Jairus. "From the Commodity to Capital: Hegel's Dialectic in Marx's Capital." In Diane Elson, *Value, The Representation of Labour in Capitalism.* London: CSE Books, 1979, pp. 14–45.

Bandyopadhyay, Pradeep. "Who's Afraid of the 'Neo-Ricardians'?: Some Notes on the Jousting." Unpublished.

———. "New Methods on Modes of Production." Paper presented to Graduate Seminar, Department of Anthropology, University of Toronto, Toronto, March 1978.

———. "The Renewal of Marx's Economics." *Catalyst* No. 12 (1978); 22–40.

———. "Further on the Renewal of Marx's Economics: A Reply to Thompson." *Catalyst* No. 14 (1981): 72–91.

———. "In Defense of a Post-Sraffian Approach." In I. Steedman, P. M. Sweezy *et al., The Value Controversy.* London: New Left Books, 1981, pp. 100–129.

———. "Neo-Ricardianism in Urban Analysis." *The International Journal of Urban and Regional Research* 6 (1) (1982).

———. "Marxist Urban Analysis and the Economic Theory of Rent." *Science and Society* 46 (1) (1982).

———. "Looking for Social Abstract Labour," 1983. Unpublished.

Baran, Paul A. *The Political Economy of Growth.* New York: Monthly Review Press, 1957.

Baran, Paul A. and Sweezy, Paul M. *Monopoly Capital.* New York: Monthly Review Press, 1966.

Baran, Paul. *The Longer View.* New York: Monthly Review Press, 1969.

Baumol, W. "The Transformation of Values: What Marx 'Really' Meant (An Interpretation)." *Journal of Economic Literature* 12, No. 1 (1974): 51–62.

_____. "Comment." *Journal of Economic Literature* 12, (March 1974): 74–75.

_____. "A New Critique of Marx's Economics," *Monthly Review* 26, No. 9 (1975): 57–64.

_____. *Economic Theory and Operations Analysis.* 4th edition. Englewood Cliffs, N.J.: Prentice-Hall, 1977.

Becker, Gary. *Human Capital.* New York: Columbia University Press, 1964.

_____. *The Economic Approach to Human Behavior.* Chicago: University of Chicago Press, 1976.

Bell, Daniel. "Models and Reality in Economic Discourse." *The Public Interest* Special Issue (1980): 46–80.

Bell, Peter. "Marxist Theory, Class Struggle, and the Crisis of Capitalism." In Jesse Schwartz, *The Subtle Anatomy of Capitalism.* Santa Monica, Calif.: Goodyear Publishing Co., 1977, pp. 170–194.

Blake, William J. *Elements of Marxian Economic Theory and Its Criticism.* New York: Cordon Company, 1939.

Blaug, Mark. *Economic Theory in Retrospect.* 3rd edition. Cambridge, England: Cambridge University Press, 1978.

Bliss, Christopher. *Capital Theory and the Distribution of Income.* New York: American-Elsevier, 1975.

Bohm-Bawerk. *Karl Marx and the Close of His System,* edited by Paul Sweezy. New York: Augustus M. Kelley, 1966.

Bortkiewicz, Ladislaus von. "On the correction of Marx's Fundamental Theoretical Construction in the Third Volume of Capital," 1907. Reprinted in English in Bohm-Bawerk, *Karl Marx and the Close of His System,* edited by Paul Sweezy. New York: Augustus M. Kelley, 1966.

_____. "Value and Price in the Marxian System." *International Economic Papers* No. 2, (1952).

Bose, Arun. *Marxian and Post-Marxian Political Economy.* Middlesex, England: Penguin Books, 1975.

_____. *Marx on Exploitation and Inequality.* Oxford, England: Oxford University Press, 1980.

Boulding, Kenneth. *Economics as a Science.* New York: McGraw-Hill, 1970.

Bowles, Samuel and Gintis, Herbert. *Schooling in Capitalist America: Educational Reform and the Contradictions of Economic Life.* New York: Basic Books, 1976.

Bowles, Sam and Gintis, Herbert. "The Marxian Theory of Value and Heterogeneous Labour: A Critique and Reformation." *Cambridge Journal of Economics,* Vol. I, (1977).

_____. "Structure and Practice in the Labor Theory of Value." *Review of Radical Political Economy* 12, No. 4 (1981).

Brady, Barbara. "The Remystification of Value." *Capital and Class* (Summer 1982): 114–133.

Braverman, Harry. *Labor and Monopoly Capital.* New York: Monthly Review Press, 1974.

Brody, Andras. *Proportions, Prices and Planning: A Mathematical Restatement of the Labor Theory of Value*. New York: American Elsevier, 1970.

Bronfenbrenner, Martin. "A 'Middlebrow' Introduction to Economic Methodology." In Sherman Krupp, editor, *The Structure of Economic Science: Essays on Methodology*. Englewood Cliffs, N.J.: Prentice-Hall, 1966, pp. 5–24.

_____ . "The Vicissitudes of Marxian Economics." *History of Political Economy* 2 (1970): 205–224.

_____ . "Samuelson, Marx, and Their Latest Critics." *Journal of Economic Literature* 11 (1973): 58–63.

_____ . "Review of Walsh and Gram, 'Classical and Neoclassical Theories of General Equilibirum. '" *History of Political Economy* 12, No. 4 (1980): 620–621.

Brown, Murray, Sato, Kazuo, and Zarembka, Paul, editors. *Essays in Modern Capital Theory*. New York: American-Elsevier, 1976.

Brunhoff, S. de. "Marx as an A-Ricardian, Value, Money and Price at the Beginning of Capital." *Economy and Society* II (1973): 421–430.

_____ . "Controversies in the Theory of Surplus Value: A Reply of John Eatwell." *Science and Society* 38, No. 4 (1974): 478–482.

_____ . *Marx on Money*. Boston: Urizen Books, 1976.

Burns, Scott. *The Household Economy*. Boston: Beacon Press, 1977.

Chace, Susan. "Tomorrow's Computer May Reproduce Itself, Some Visionaries Think." *Wall Street Journal*. January 6, 1983, p.1

Chattophadhyay, Paresh. "Political Economy: What's in a Name?" *Monthly Review* 25, No. 11 (1974): 23–33.

Churchman, C. W. "On the Intercomparison of Utilities." In Sherman Roy Krupp, *The Structure of Economic Science: Essays on Methodology*. Englewood Cliffs, N.J.: Prentice-Hall, 1966, pp. 243–256.

Clarke, Simon. "The Value of Value: Rereading 'Capital.'" *Capital and Class* (Spring 1980): 1–18.

Cleaver, Harry. *Reading Capital Politically*. Austin: University of Texas Press, 1979.

Cochrane, Peter. "Gold: The Durability of a Barbarous Relic." *Science and Society* XLIV, No. 4 (1980): 385–400.

Cohen, G. A. "Karl Marx and the Withering Away of Social Science." *Philosophy and Public Affairs* I, No. 2 (1972): 182–203.

_____ . *Karl Marx's Theory of History: A Defense*. Princeton, N.J.: Princeton University Press, 1978.

_____ . "The Labor Theory of Value and the Concept of Exploitation." In Marshall Cohen, Thomas Nagel, and Thomas Scanlon, editors, *Marx, Justice and History*. Princeton, N.J.: Princeton University Press, 1980, pp. 135–157.

Colletti, Lucio. *From Rousseau to Lenin*. New York: Monthly Review Press, 1972.

_____ . *Marxism and Hegel*. London: New Left Books, 1973.

Darity, William A. "The Simple Analytics of Neo-Ricardian Growth and Distribution." *American Economic Review* 71, No. 5 (1981): 978–993.

Dean, James W. "The Dissolution of the Keynesian Consensus." *The Public Interest* Special Issue (1980): 19–34.

Denis, Henri. "Postface: V. K. Dmitriev ou les Malheurs de la Sagesse Mathématique." In Dmitriev, V. K., *Essais Economiques*. Paris: Editions du Centre National de la Recherche Scientifique, 1968, pp. 261–269.

Dmitriev, V. K. *Economic Essays on Value, Competition and Utility.* Cambridge, England: Cambridge University Press, 1974.

Dobb, Maurice. *Political Economy and Capitalism.* London: George Routledge and Sons, 1937.

_____ . "Introduction" to Karl Marx, *A Contribution to the Critique of Political Economy.* New York: International Publishers, 1970, pp. 5–16.

_____ . "The Sraffa System and Critique of the Neo-Classical Theory of Distribution." *De Economist* **118** (1970): 347–362. Reprinted in E. K. Hunt and Jesse Schwartz, editors, *A Critique of Economic Theory.* Middlesex, England: Penguin Education, 1972, pp. 205–221.

_____ . *Theories of Value and Distribution Since Adam Smith: Ideology and Economic Theory.* Cambridge, England: Cambridge University Press, 1973.

Dragstedt, Albert, editor. *Value: Studies by Karl Marx.* New York: Labor Publications, 1976.

Drucker, Peter. "Towards the Next Economics." *The Public Interest* Special Issue (1980): 4–18.

Eatwell, John "Controversies in the Theory of Surplus Value, Old and New." *Science and Society* **38**, No. 3 (1974): 281–303.

_____ . "On the Theoretical Consistency of Theories of Surplus Value, A Comment on Savran." *Capital and Class* (Spring 1980): 155–158.

Echevarria, Rafael. "Critique of Marx's 1857 Introduction." *Economy and Society* 7, No. 4 (1978): 333–366.

Eichner, Alfred S., editor. *A Guide to Post-Keynesian Economics.* White Plains, N.Y.: M. E. Sharpe, 1978.

Elson, Diane. "The Value Theory of Labour." In Diane Elson, *Value, The Representation of Labour in Capitalism.* London: CSE Books, 1979, pp. 115–180.

Elson, Diane, editor. *Value, The Representation of Labour in Capitalism.* London: CSE Books, 1979.

Engels, Frederick. "Introduction" to Karl Marx, *The Poverty of Philosophy.* New York: International Publishers, 1963, pp. 7–25.

_____ . "Preface" to Karl Marx, *Capital.* Vol. II. New York: International Publishers, 1967, pp. 1–19.

_____ . *The Origin of the Family, Private Property and the State.* New York: International Publishers, 1972.

England, Richard. "Morishima on Marx: A Retrospective Review." 1978. Unpublished.

Ernst, John. "Simultaneous Valuation Extirpated: A Contribution to the Critique of the Neo-Ricardian Concept of Value." *Review of Radical Political Economics* **14**, No. 2 (1982): 85–94.

Federal Reserve Bank of Minneapolis. "Eliminating Policy Surprises: An Inexpensive Way to Beat Inflation." In *1978 Annual Report.* Reprinted in Robert Puth, editor, *Current Issues in the American Economy.* Lexington, Mass.: D. C. Heath and Co., 1980–1981, pp. 131–136.

Feiwel, George. *The Intellectual Capital of Michal Kalecki.* Knoxville: University of Tennessee Press, 1975.

Ferguson, C. E. *The Neoclassical Theory of Production and Distribution.* Cambridge, England: Cambridge University Press, 1969.

Ferguson, C. E. and Gould, J. *Microeconomic Theory.* 4th edition. Homewood, Il.: Irving, 1975.

Fine, B. and Harris, L. "Controversial Issues in Marxist Economic Theory." *The Socialist Register* (1976): 141–178.

Fischer, Norman. "The Ontology of Abstract Labor." *Review of Radical Political Economics* 14, No. 2 (1982): 27–35.

Foley, Duncan. "The Value of Money, The Value of Labor Power and the Marxian Transformation Problem." *Review of Radical Political Economics* 14, No. 2, (1982): 37–47.

Ganssmann, Heiner. "Transformations of Physical Conditions of Production: Steedman's Economic Metaphysics." *Economy and Society* 10, No. 4 (1981): 403–422.

Garegnani, Pierangelo. "Heterogeneous Capital, The Production Function, and the Theory of Distribution." *Review of Economic Studies* 37 (1970): 407–436. Reprinted in E. K. Hunt and Jesse Schwartz, *A Critique of Economic Theory.* Middlesex, England: Penguin Education, 1972, pp. 245–291.

_____. "Sraffa's Revival of Marxist Economic Theory." *New Left Review,* No. 112 (Nov.-Dec. 1978): 71–75.

Georgescu-Roegen, N. *The Entropy Law and the Economic Process.* Cambridge, Mass.: Harvard University Press, 1971.

Geras, N. "Essence and Appearance: Aspects of Fetishism in Marx's 'Capital.'" *New Left Review,* No. 65 (Jan.-Feb. 1971): 69–85.

Gerstein, I. "Production, Circulation and Value." *Economy and Society* 5, No. 3 (1976): 243–291.

Godelier, Maurice. "System, Structure and Contradiction in Capital." *Socialist Register* (1967): 91–119.

Goldway, David. "Appearance and Reality in Marx's Capital." *Science and Society* (1967): 428–447.

Gordon, David. *Theories of Poverty and Underemployment.* Lexington, Mass.: D. C. Heath and Co., 1972.

Graham, Frank. "The Theory of International Values." *Quarterly Journal of Economics* 46 (1932): 581–616.

Gray, Alexander. *The Development of Economic Doctrine.* London: Lowe and Brydone, 1931.

Gramsci, Antonio. *Prison Notebooks.* New York: International Publishers, 1971.

Groenewegen, Peter D. "History and Political Economy: Smith, Marx and Marshall." *Australian Economic Papers* 21, No. 38 (1982): 1–17.

Gudeman, Stephen. "Anthropological Economics: The Question of Distribution." *Annual Review of Anthropology* 7 (1978): 347–379.

_____. *The Demise of a Rural Economy: From Subsistence to Capitalism in a Latin American Village.* London: Routledge and Kegan Paul, 1978.

Hahn, Frank. "General Equilibrium Theory." *The Public Interest* Special Issue (1980): 123–138.

Harcourt, G. C. "Some Cambridge Controversies in the Theory of Capital." *Journal of Economic Literature* 7 (1969): 369–405.

Harcourt, G. C. and Laing, N. F., editors. *Capital and Growth: Selected Readings.* London, England: Penguin Books, 1971.

Harcourt, G. C. *Some Cambridge Controversies in the Theory of Capital.* Cambridge, England: Cambridge University Press, 1972.

_____ . "The Theoretical and Social Significance of the Cambridge Controversies in the Theory of Capital: An Evaluation." *Revue d'Economie Politique* (1977). In Jesse Schwartz, *The Subtle Anatomy of Capitalism.* Santa Monica, Calif.: Goodyear Publishing Co., 1977, pp. 285–303.

Harris, Donald J. "Introduction" to Nikolai Bukharin, *Economic Theory of the Leisure Class.* New York: Monthly Review Press, 1972, pp. vii–xvi.

_____ . *Capital Accumulation and Income Distribution.* Palo Alto, Calif.: Stanford University Press, 1978.

Harris, Laurence. "The Science of the Economy." *Economy and Society* 7, No. 3 (1978): 284–320.

Hawkins, David. "Some Conditions of Macroeconomic Stability." *Econometrica* 16 (October 1948): 309–322.

Hawkins, David and Simon, Herbert. "Note: Some Conditions of Macroeconomic Stability." *Econometrica* 17 (July–October, 1949): 245–248.

Hawkins, David. *The Language of Nature: An Essay on the Philosophy of Science.* San Francisco: W. H. Freeman and Co., 1964.

Heilbroner, Robert L. *The Worldly Philosophers.* 3rd edition. New York: Simon and Schuster, 1967.

_____ . *Between Capitalism and Socialism.* New York: Vintage Books, 1970.

Henderson, James M. and Quandt, Richard E. *Microeconomic Theory, A Mathematical Approach* 2nd edition. New York: McGraw-Hill, 1971.

Hicks, J. R. *Value and Capital* 2nd edition. Oxford, England: Oxford University Press, 1946.

Hilferding, Rudolf. "Bohm-Bawerk's Criticism of Marx." In Bohm-Bawerk, *Karl Marx and the Close of His System,* edited by Paul Sweezy. New York: Augustus M. Kelley, 1966, pp. 121–196.

Hirschman, Albert O. *The Passions and the Interests, Political Arguments for Capitalism Before Its Triumph.* Princeton, N.J.: Princeton University Press, 1977.

Hodgson, Geoff. "A Theory of Exploitation Without the Labor Theory of Value." *Science and Society* XLIV, No. 3 (1980): 257–273.

_____ . "Money and the Sraffa System." *Australian Economic Papers* 20, No. 36, (1981): 83–95.

_____ . "Marx Without the Labor Theory of Value." *Review of Radical Political Economics* 14, No. 2 (1982): 59–66.

Hollander, Samuel. "Marxian Economics as 'General Equilibrium' Theory." *History of Political Economy* 13, No. 1 (1981): 121–155.

Hollis, M. and Neil, E. *Rational Economic Man.* Cambridge, England: Cambridge University Press, 1975.

Holton, Gerald. *Thematic Origins of Scientific Thought: Kepler to Einstein.* Cambridge, Mass.: Harvard University Press, 1973.

Horowitz, David. "Introduction" to David Horowitz, editor, *Marx and Modern Economics.* New York: Monthly Review Press, 1968, pp. 11–17.

Horowitz, David, editor. *Marx and Modern Economics.* New York: Monthly Review Press, 1968.

Hsieh, Ching-Yao, Abushaikha, Ahmad A., and Richards, Anne. *A Short Introduction to Modern Growth Theory*. Washington, D.C.: University Press of America, 1978.

Hunt, E. K. and Schwartz, Jesse, editors. *A Critique of Economic Theory*. Middlesex, England: Penguin Education, 1972.

Hunt, E. K. *History of Economic Thought: A Critical Perspective*. Belmont, Calif.: Wadsworth Publishing Co., 1979.

_____. "Marx's Concept of Human Nature and the Labor Theory of Value." *Review of Radical Political Economics* 14, No. 2 (1982): 7-25.

Hussain, Athar. "Misreading Marx's Theory of Value: Marx's Marginal Notes on Wagner." In Diane Elson, *Value, The Representation of Labour in Capitalism*. London: CSE Books, 1979, pp 82-101.

Itoh, Makoto. *Value and Crisis*. New York: Monthly Review Press, 1980.

Jauch, J. M. *Are Quanta Real?* Bloomington, Ind.: Indiana University Press, 1973.

Johansen, Leif. "Labour Theory of Value and Marginal Utilities." *Economics of Planning* 3 (1963). Reprinted in E. K. Hunt and Jesse Schwartz, editors, *A Critique of Economic Theory*. Middlesex, England: Penguin Education, 1972, pp. 295-311.

Johnson, Harry and Johnson, Elizabeth. *The Shadow of Keynes: Understanding Keynes, Cambridge and Keynesian Economic*. Chicago: University of Chicago Press, 1978.

Kay, Geoffrey. "Why Labour Is the Starting Point of Capital." In Diane Elson, *Value, The Representation of Labour in Capitalism*. London: CSE Books, 1979, pp. 46-66.

Kayali, Resad. "Neoclassical Theory Revisited." *Review of Radical Political Economy* (Winter 1978): 61-65.

Kellner, Douglas. "Human Nature and Capitalism in Adam Smith and Karl Marx." In Jesse Schwartz, *The Subtle Anatomy of Capitalism*. Santa Monica, Calif.: Goodyear Publishing Co., 1977, pp. 66-85.

Kemp, Jack. "The Renewal of Western Monetary Standards." *Wall Street Journal*, April 7, 1982.

Keynes, John Maynard. *The General Theory of Employment, Interest, and Money*. New York: Harcourt, Brace and World, 1964.

Klein, Lawrence. "Theories of Effective Demand and Employment." *Journal of Political Economy* (April 1947). Reprinted in David Horowitz, editor, *Marx and Modern Economics*. New York: Monthly Review Press, 1968, pp. 138-175.

Koopmans, Tjalling. *Three Essays on the State of Economic Science*. McGraw-Hill, 1957.

Kregel, J. S. *The Reconstruction of Political Economy: An Introduction to Post-Keynesian Economics*. London: Macmillan, 1973.

Kristol, Irving. "Rationalism in Economics." *The Public Interest* Special Issue (1980): 201-218.

Krupp, Sherman Roy. *The Structure of Economic Science: Essays on Methodology*. Englewood Cliffs, N.J.: Prentice-Hall, 1966.

Laibner, David. "Values and Prices of Production: The Political Economy of the Transformation Problems." *Science and Society* XXXVII (Winter 1974): 404-436.

_____ . "Controversies in the Theory of Surplus Value: A Comment" *Science and Society* **38**, No. 4 (1975): 482–487.

_____ . "Exploitation, Commodity Relations and Capitalism: A Defense of the Labor-Value Formulation." *Science and Society* **XLIV** No. 3 (1980): 274–288.

_____ . "Technical Change, the Real Wage and the Rate of Exploitation: The Falling Rate of Profit Reconsidered." *Review of Radical Political Economics* **14**, No. 2 (1982): 95–105.

Lange, Oskar and Taylor, Fred. *On the Economic Theory of Socialism*. New York: McGraw, 1956.

_____ . "Marxian Economics and Modern Economic Theory." *Review of Economics Studies* (June 1935). Reprinted in David Horowitz, *Marx and Modern Economics*. New York: Monthly Review Press, 1968, pp. 68–87.

Lebowitz, M. "The Current Crisis of Economic Theory." *Science and Society* **37** (Winter 1974): 385–403.

Lenin, V. I. *Imperialism, The Highest Stage of Capitalism*. Moscow: Progress Publishers, 1975.

Leontief, W. *The Structure of the American Economy, 1919–1939*. New York: Oxford University Press, 1951.

_____ . "The Significance of Marxian Economics for Present-day Economic Theory," Proceedings of the 50th Annual Meeting of the American Economic Association, 1937. *American Economic Review Supplement* (March, 1938). Reprinted in David Horowitz, *Marx and Modern Economics*, pp. 88–99.

_____ . "Preface" to Andras Brody, *Proportions, Prices and Planning: A Mathematical Restatement of the Labor Theory of Value*. New York: American-Elsevier, 1970, pp. 7–8.

Lerner, Abba. "A Note on Understanding the Marxian Notion of Exploitation." *Journal of Economic Literature* **10** (1972): 50–51.

Lippi, Marco. *Value and Naturalism in Marx*. London: New Left Books, 1979.

Locke, John. *Two Treatises of Government*. Cambridge, England: Cambridge University Press, 1980.

Lowe, Adolph. *On Economic Knowledge*. New York: Harper & Row, 1965.

Luxemburg, Rosa. *The Accumulation of Capital* London: Routledge and Kegan Paul, 1951.

Maarek, Gérard. *An Introduction to Karl Marx's Das Kapital: A Study in Formalisation*. New York: Oxford University Press, 1979.

Macpherson, C. B. *The Political Theory of Possessive Individualism: Hobbes to Locke*. London: Oxford University Press, 1962.

_____ . *The Real World of Democracy*. Canadian Broadcasting Corporation, 1965.

_____ . *Democratic Theory: Essays in Retrieval*. London: Oxford University Press, 1973.

Macpherson, C. B., editor. *Property: Mainstream and Critical Positions*. Toronto: University of Toronto Press, 1978.

Maddock, Rodney and Carter, Michael. "A Child's Guide to Rational Expectations." *Journal of Economic Literature* **XX**, No. 1 (1982): 39–51.

Magdoff, Harry and Sweezy, Paul. *The Deepening Crisis of U.S. Capitalism*. New York: Monthly Review Press, 1981.

Mandel, Ernest. *Late Capitalism*. London: New Left Books, 1975.

Mansfield, Edwin. *Microeconomics*. 2nd edition. New York: W. W. Norton and Co., 1975.

Marshall, Alfred. *Principles of Economics*. 8th edition. London: Macmillan, 1948.

Marx, Karl. *Capital*, Vol. I. Chicago: Charles H. Kerr and Co., 1906.

_____. *Wages, Price and Profit*. Moscow: Progress Publishers, 1947.

_____. *The Poverty of Philosophy*. New York: International Publishers, 1963.

_____. *Capital*, Vol. II and Vol. III. New York: International Publishers, 1967.

_____. *A Contribution to the Critique of Political Economy*. New York: International Publishers, 1970.

_____. "Critique of the Gotha Program." In Saul Padover, editor, *Karl Marx on Revolution*. New York: McGraw-Hill, 1971, pp. 488–506.

_____. *Grundrisse: Foundations of the Critique of Political Economy*, New York: Random House, 1973.

Mattick, Paul. *Marx and Keynes: The Limits of the Mixed Economy*. Boston: Extending Horizon Books, 1969.

_____. "Samuelson's 'Transformation' of Marxism and Bourgeois Economics." *Science and Society* 36 (Fall 1973): 258–273.

_____. "Review of Maurice Dobb, 'Theories of Value and Distribution Since Adam Smith'." *Science and Society* 38, No. 2 (1975): 220–223.

McLachlan, Hugh, O'Donnell, A. T., and Swales, J. K. "On the Logical Consistency of Sraffa's Economic Theory: A Comment on Savran and Steedman." *Capital and Class* (Spring 1980): 159–165.

Medio, Alfredo. "Profits and Surplus-Value: Appearance and Reality in Capitalist Production." In E. K. Hunt and Jesse Schwartz, editors, *A Critique of Economic Theory*. Middlesex, England: Penguin Education, 1972, pp. 312–346.

_____. "Neoclassicals, Neo-Ricardians, and Marx." In Jesse Schwartz, *The Subtle Anatomy of Capitalism*. Santa Monica, Calif.: Goodyear Publishing Co., 1977, pp. 381–411.

Meek, Ronald. "Mr. Sraffa's Rehabilitation of Classical Economics." *Science and Society* (Spring, 1961).

_____. "The Law of Value in Ricardo and Marx: A Reply to Mr. Pilling." *Economy and Society* II, (1973): 499–502.

_____. *Studies in the Labor Theory of Value*. 2nd edition. New York: Monthly Review Press, 1976.

Mepham, John. "The Grundrisse: Method or Madness." *Economy and Society* 7, No. 4 (1978): 430–444.

Mitchell, Wesley. *Lecture Notes on Types of Economic Theory*. New York: Augustus M. Kelly, 1949.

Mohtadi, A. "Negative Labor Values and the Joint Production Technique: A Debate in the Marxian Transformation Problem." *Review of Radical Political Economics* 13, No. 4 (1981): pp. 33–37.

Morishima, Michio. *Marx's Economics: A Dual Theory of Value and Growth*. Cambridge England: Cambridge University Press, 1973.

Morishima, M. "The Fundamental Marxian Theorem: A Reply to Samuelson." *Journal of Economic Literature* 12 (March 1974): 71–74.

_____. "Marx in the Light of Modern Economic Theory." *Econometria* **42**, No. 4 (1974): 611–632.

Morishma M. and Catephores, G. "Is There an Historical Transformation Problem?" *Economic Journal* **85** (June, 1975): 309–328.

Morishima, M. "Marx from a von Neumann Viewpoint." In Brown et al., *Essays in Modern Capital Theory*. New York: American-Elsevier, 1976, pp. 233–263.

_____. *The Economic Theory of Modern Society*. Cambridge, England: Cambridge University Press, 1976.

_____. *Walras' Economics*. Cambridge, England: Cambridge University Press, 1977.

Morishima, M. and Catephores, G. *Value, Exploitation and Growth*. New York: McGraw-Hill, 1978.

Morris, Jacob. "Marx as a Monetary Theorist." *Science and Society* (Fall 1967): 404–427.

_____. "Some Comments on Marx's Value Theory." *Science and Society* **36** (1972): 341–343.

Mundell, Robert. "Gold Would Serve Into the 21st Century." *Wall Street Journal,* September 30, 1981, p. 29.

_____. "The Debt Crisis: Causes and Solutions." *Wall Street Journal*, January 31, 1983.

Myrdal, Gunnar. *An International Economy*. New York: Harper and Brothers, 1956.

Napoleoni, Claudio. "Sraffa's 'Tabula Rosa'." *New Left Review* (November-December 1978): 75–77.

Needham, W. Robert. "Some Comments on the Cambridge Paradigm: An Introduction to Modern Economics." In Jesse Schwartz, *The Subtle Anatomy of Capitalism*. Santa Monica, Calif: Goodyear Publishing Co., 1977, pp. 304–326.

Nell, E. J. "Property and the Means of Production: A Primer on the Cambridge Controversy." *Review of Radical Political Economics* **10**, No. 2 (1972): 1–27.

_____. "Value and Capital in Marxian Economics." *The Public Interest* Special Edition (1980): 174–200.

Neumann, J. von. "A Model of General Economic Equilibrium." Review of Economic Studies **13** (1945): 1–9.

Newman, Peter. "Production of Commodities by Means of Commodities: A Review." *Schweizerische Zeitschrift für Volkswirtschaft und Statistik* **98** (1962): 58–75. Reprinted in Jesse Schwartz, *The Subtle Anatomy of Capitalism* Santa Monica, Calif: Goodyear Publishing Co., 1977, pp. 346–362

Nicholson, Walter. *Intermediate Microeconomics*. Hinsdale, Ill.: Dryden Press, 1975.

Nicolaus, Martin. "Foreward" in Karl Marx, *Grundrisse: Foundations of the Critique of Political Economy*. New York: Random House, 1973, pp. 7–63.

Nordahl, Richard. "Marx on the Use of History in the Analysis of Capitalism." *History of Political Economy* **14**, No. 3 (1982): 342–365.

Nuti, D. M. "'Vulgar Economy' in the Theory of Income Distribution." *De Economist* **118** (1970): 363–369. Reprinted in editors, E. K. Hunt and Jesse Schwartz, *A Critique of Economic Theory*. Middlesex, England: Penguin Education, 1972, pp. 222–232.

_____ . "V. K. Dmitriev: A Biographical Note." In V. K. Dmitriev, *Economic Essays on Value, Competition and Utility*. Cambridge, England: Cambridge University Press, 1974, pp. 29–32.

_____ . "Introduction" to V. K. Dmitriev, *Economic Essays on Value, Competition and Utility*. Cambridge, England: Cambridge University Press, 1974, pp. 7–28.

_____ . "The Transformation of Labour Values in Production Prices and the Marxian Theory of Exploitation." In Jesse Schwartz, *The Subtle Anatomy of Capitalism*, Santa Monica, Calif: Goodyear Publishing Co., 1977, pp. 88–105.

Okishio, Nobuo. "A Mathematical Note on Marxian Theorems." *Weltwirtschafliches Archiv* **91** (1963): 287–299.

Pack, Spencer. "Cambridge Theories of Underdevelopment." *Presentation to International Workshop*, University of New Hampshire, Spring 1981.

Panico, Carlo. "Marx's Analysis of the Relationship Between the Rate of Interest and the Rate of Profits." *Cambridge Journal of Economics* **4**, (1980): 363–378.

Parys, Wilfried. "The Deviation of Prices from Labor Values." *American Economic Review* (December 1982): 1208–1212.

Pasinetti, Luigi. *Lectures on the Theory of Production*. New York: Columbia University Press, 1977.

_____ , editor. *Essays on the Theory of Joint Production*. New York: Columbia University Press, 1980.

_____ . *Structural Change and Economic Growth*. Cambridge, England: Cambridge University Press, 1981.

Patinkin, Don. "Frank Knight as a Teacher." *American Economic Review* **LXIII**, No. 5, (1973): 787–810.

Perlman, Freddy. "The Reproduction of Daily Life." in Jesse Schwartz, *The Subtle Anatomy of Capitalism*. Santa Monica, Calif: Goodyear Publishing Co., 1977, pp. 51–65.

Polanyi, Karl. *The Great Transformation*. Boston: Beacon Press, 1957.

_____ . "Aristotle Discovers the Economy." in George Dalton, editor, *Primitive, Archaic, and Modern Economies: Essays of Karl Polanyi*. Garden City, N.Y.: Anchor Books, 1968, pp. 78–115.

Puth, Robert C., editor *Current Issues in the American Economy*. 1980–1981 edition. Lexington, Mass.: D. C. Heath and Co., 1980.

Ricardo, David. *The Principles of Political Economy and Taxation*. London: J.M. Dent and Sons, 1973.

Robbins, Lionel. *An Essay on the Nature and Significance of Economic Science*. 2nd edition. London: Macmillan and Co., 1949.

Robinson, Joan. "The Labour Theory of Value." In *Collected Economic Papers*. New York: Augustus M. Kelly, 1951, pp. 145–151.

_____ . *An Essay on Marxian Economics*. 2nd edition. London: Macmillan, 1966.

_____ . "Prelude to a Critique of Economic Theory." *Oxford Economic Papers* **13** (1961): 7–14. Reprinted in E. K. Hunt and Jesse Schwartz, editors, *A Critique of Economic Theory*. Middlesex, England: Penguin Education, 1972, pp. 197–204.

_____ . "Marx and Keynes." In David Horowitz, *Marx and Modern Economics*. New York: Monthly Review Press, 1968, pp. 103–116.

_____ . "Capital Theory up to Date." *Canadian Journal of Economics* **3** (1970): 309–317. Reprinted in E. K. Hunt and Jesse Schwartz editors, *A Critique of Economic Theory*. Middlesex, England: Penguin Education, 1972, pp. 233–244.

_____ . "The Relevance of Economic Theory." *Monthly Review* (1971). Reprinted in Jesse Schwartz, *The Subtle Anatomy of Capitalism*. Santa Monica, Calif.: Goodyear Publishing Co., 1977, pp. 16–21.

_____ . "The Labor Theory of Value." *Monthly Review* **29**, No. 7 (1977): 50–59.

_____ . "Ideology and Analysis". In Jesse Schwartz, *The Subtle Anatomy of Capitalism*. Santa Monica, Calif.: Goodyear Publishing Co., 1977, pp. 364–370.

_____ . "What are the Questions?" *Journal of Economic Literature* (December 1977): 1318–1339.

_____ . *Aspects of Development and Underdevelopment*. Cambridge, England: Cambridge University Press, 1979.

Robinson, Joan and Bhaduri, Amit. "Accumulation and Exploitation: An Analysis in the Tradition of Marx, Sraffa and Kalecki." *Cambridge Journal of Economics* **4**, No. 2 (1980): 103–115.

Roemer, John. "A General Equilibrium Approach to Marxian Economics." *Econometrica* **48**, No. 2, (1980): 505–530.

Roemer, John E. *A General Theory of Exploitation and Class*. Cambridge, Mass.: Harvard University Press, 1982.

_____ . "New Directions in the Marxian Theory of Exploitation and Class." *Politics and Society* **11**, No. 3 (1982): 253–288.

_____ . "Reply." *Politics and Society* **11**, No. 3 (1982): 375–394.

Roncaglia, Alessandro. "Sraffa and Price Theory: An Interpretation." In Jesse Schwartz, *The Subtle Anatomy of Capitalism*. Santa Monica, Calif.: Goodyear Publishing Co., 1977, pp. 371–380.

_____ . *Sraffa and the Theory of Prices*. New York: John Wiley and Sons, 1978.

Roosevelt, Frank. "Cambridge Economics as Commodity Fetishism." *Review of Radical Political Economics* **7**, No. 4 (1975). Reprinted in Jesse Schwartz, *The Subtle Anatomy of Capitalism*, Santa Monica, Calif.: Goodyear Publishing Co., 1977, pp. 412–457.

Rosdolsky, Roman. *The Making of Marx's "Capital."* London: Pluto Press, 1977.

Rosen, Sam. "An Overview of Marxian Economics." 1978. Unpublished.

Rothenberg, Jerome. "Values and Value Theory in Economics." In Sherman Roy Krupp, *The Structure of Economic Science: Essays on Methodology*, Englewood Cliffs, N.J.: Prentice-Hall, 1966, pp. 221–242.

Rothschild, K. W. "Price Theory and Oligopoly." *The Economic Journal* **LVII**, (1952): 229–320. Reprinted in George Stigler and Kenneth Boulding, *A. E. A. Readings in Price Theory*. Vol. VI. Homewood, Il.: Irwin 1952, pp. 440–464.

Rowthorn, R. E. "Neo-Classicism, Neo-Ricardianism and Marxism." *New Left Review* No. 86 (1974): 63–87.

Rubin, I. I. *Essays on Marx's Theory of Value*. Montreal: Black and Red Press, 1972.

Samuelson, Paul Anthony. *Foundations of Economic Analysis*. Cambridge, Mass.: Harvard University Press, 1947.

_____ . "Understanding the Marxian Notion of Exploitation: A Summary of the So-Called Transformation Problem Between Marxian Values and Competitive Prices." *Journal of Economic Literature* **IX**, No. 2 (1971): 399–443.

_____ . "The Economics of Marx: An Ecumenical Reply." *Journal of Economic Literature* **X** (June 1972): 51–57.

_____ . *Economics*. 9th edition. New York: McGraw-Hill, 1973.

_____ . "Reply on Marxian Matters." *Journal of Economic Literature* **XI** (1973): 64–68.

_____ . "Insight and Detour in the Theory of Exploitation: A Reply to Baumol." *Journal of Economic Literature* **XII** (March 1974): 62–70.

_____ . "Rejoinder: Merlin Unclothed, A Final Word." *Journal of Economic Literature* **XII** (March 1974): 75–77.

_____ . "Review of 'Economic Essays on Values, Competition, and Utility' by V. K. Dmitriev." *Journal of Economic Literature* **XIII** (1975): 491–495.

Savran, Sungur. "On the Theoretical Consistency of Sraffa's Economics." *Capital and Class* (Spring 1979): 131–140.

_____ . "Confusions Concerning Sraffa (and Marx): Reply to Critics." *Capital and Class,* (Winter 1980/81); 85–98.

Schaik, A. *Reproduction and Fixed Capital.* Tilburg, Netherlands: Tilburg University Press, 1976.

Schumpeter, Joseph. *Capitalism, Socialism and Democracy.* 3rd edition. New York: Harper & Row, 1950.

_____ . *History of Economic Analysis.* Oxford: Oxford University Press, 1954,

_____ . "The Crisis in Economics—Fifty Years Ago." *Journal of Economic Literature* **XX**, No. 3 (1982): 1049–1059.

Schwartz, Jesse. "There Is Nothing Simple About a Commodity." In Jesse Schwartz, editor, *The Subtle Anatomy of Capitalism.* Santa Monica, Calif.: Goodyear Publishing Co., 1977, pp. 474–500.

_____ , editor. *The Subtle Anatomy of Capitalism.* Santa Monica, Calif.: Goodyear Publishing Co., 1977.

Sekine, Thomas. "Uno-Riron: A Japanese Contribution to Marxian Political Economy." *Journal of Economic Literature* **XIII**, No. 3 (1975): 847–877.

_____ . "The Necessity of the Law of Value." *Science and Society.* **XLIV**, No. 3 (1980): 289–304.

Sen, Amartya. "On the Labour Theory of Value: Some Methodological Issues." *Cambridge Journal of Economics* **2** (1978): 175–190.

Shaikh, Anwar. "Marx's Theory of Value and the 'Transformation Problem'." In Jesse Schwartz, *The Subtle Anatomy of Capitalism.* Santa Monica, Calif.: Goodyear Publishing Co., 1977, pp. 106–139.

_____ . "The Transformation from Marx to Sraffa (Prelude to a Critique of the Neo-Ricardians)." 1980, manuscript.

_____ . "Neo-Ricardian Economics: A Wealth of Algebra, a Poverty of Theory." *Review of Radical Political Economics* **14**, No. 2 (1982): 67–83.

Sherman, Howard. "The Marxist Theory of Value Revisited." *Science and Society* **34** (1970): 257–292. Reprinted in E. K. Hunt and Jesse Schartz, editors, *A Critique of Economic Theory.* Middlesex, England: Penguin Education, 1972, pp. 347–364.

Simmel, Georg. *The Sociology of Georg Simmel,* edited by Kurt Wolff. New York: The Free Press, 1950.

Smith, Adam. *The Wealth of Nations.* Middlesex, England: Pelican Books, 1970.

Somerville, H. "Marx's Theory of Money." *The Economic Journal* **43** (June 1933): 334–337.

Sowell, Thomas. *Say's Law: An Historical Analysis.* Princeton, N.J.: Princeton University Press, 1972.

——— . "Marx's Capital After One Hundred Years." *Canadian Journal of Economics and Political Science* (February 1976): 50–74.

Sraffa, Piero. "Introduction" to David Ricardo, *On The Principles of Political Economy and Taxation*, Vol. I of *Works and Correspondence of David Ricardo.* Cambridge, England: Cambridge University Press, 1951, pp. xiii–lxii.

——— . "The Laws of Returns under Competitive Conditions." *The Economic Journal* **XXXVI** (1926): 535–550. Reprinted in George Stigler and Kenneth Boulding, *A.E.A. Readings in Price Theory.* Vol. VI. Homewood, Il.: Irwin, 1952, pp. 180–197.

——— . *Production of Commodities by Means of Commodities.* Cambridge, England: Cambridge University Press, 1960.

Steedman, Ian. *Marx After Sraffa.* London: New Left Books, 1977.

——— . "On an Alleged Inconsistency in Sraffa's Economics." *Capital and Class* (Autumn 1979): 71–74.

——— , editor. *Fundamental Issues in Trade Theory.* New York: St. Martins Press, 1979.

——— . *Trade Amongst Growing Economies.* Cambridge, England: Cambridge University Press, 1980.

Steindl, J. *Maturity and Stagnation in American Capitalism.* Oxford, England: Blackwell, 1952.

Stigler, George and Boulding, Kenneth, editors. *A.E.A. Readings in Price Theory.* Vol. VI. Homewood, Il.: Irwin, 1952.

Sweezy, Paul. *The Theory of Capitalist Development.* New York: Monthly Review Press, 1942.

——— . "Editors Introduction" to Bohm-Bawerk, *Karl Marx and the Close of His System,* edited by Paul Sweezy. New York: Augustus M. Kelley, 1966, pp. v–xxx.

——— . *Modern Capitalism and Other Essays.* New York: Monthly Review Press, 1972.

——— . "Monopoly Capital and the Theory of Value." *Monthly Review* **28**, No. 8 (1974): 31–32.

——— . "Dobb on Ideology and Economic Theory." *Monthly Review* **27**, No. 9 (1976): 51–55.

——— . "Marxian Value Theory." *Monthly Review* **31**, No. 3 (1979): 1–17.

Takayama, Akira. *Mathematical Economics.* Hinsdale, ILL.: The Dryden Press, 1974.

Thomas, Clive. "Marxism: Looking Backward and Forward." *Monthly Review 26*, No. 2 (1974): 72–78.

Thurow, Lester. "Economics." *Daedalas* **II** (Fall 1977): 79–94.

Uno, Kozo. *Principles of Political Economy: Theory of a Purely Capitalist Society.* Sussex, 1980.

Valiente, Wilfred Santiago. "Is Frank Knight the Victor in the Controversy Between the Two Cambridges?" *History of Political Economy* **12**, No. 1 (1980): 41–64.

Veblen, Thorstein. "The Socialist Economics of Karl Marx." In Max Lerner, editor, *The Portable Veblen*. New York: The Viking Press, 1948, pp. 275–296.

Vroey, Michel de. "On the Obsolence of the Marxian Theory of Value: A Critical Review." *Capital and Class* (Summer 1982): 34–59.

Walsh, V. C. and Gram, H. N. *Classical and Neo-Classical Theories of General Equilibrium: Historical Origins and Mathematical Structure.* Oxford: Oxford University Press, 1980.

Ward, Benjamin. "Institutions and Economic Analysis." In Sherman Krupp, *The Structure of Economic Science: Essays on Methodology.* Englewood Cliffs, N.J.: Prentice-Hall, 1966, pp. 184–200.

_____. *What's Wrong with Economics?.* New York: Basic Books, 1972.

Weizsacker, C. C. "Morishima on Marx." *Economic Journal* (December 1973): 1245–1254.

Wicksteed, Philip H. "The Scope and Method of Political Economy." *The Economic Journal* **XXIV** (1914). Reprinted in George Stigler and Kenneth Boulding, *A.E.A. Readings in Price Theory.* Vol. VI. Richard D. Irwin, 1952, pp. 3–26.

Wolff, Robert Paul. "A Critique and Reinterpretation of Marx's Labor Theory of Value." *Philosophy and Public Affairs* (Spring 1981): 89–120.

Wolfstetter, E. J. "Surplus Labour, Synchronised Labour Costs, and Marx's Labour Theory of Value." *Economic Journal* (September 1973): 787–809.

Wright, Erik Olin. "Alternative Perspectives in Marxist Theory of Accumulation and Crisis." In Jesse Schwartz, *The Subtle Anatomy of Capitalism.* Santa Monica, Calif.: Goodyear Publishing Co., 1977, pp. 195–231.

_____. "The Value Controversy and Social Research." *New Left Review* (July–August 1979): 53–82.

Zauberman, Alfred. "Presentation" to V. K. Dmitriev, *Essais Economiques.* Paris: Editions du Centre National de la Recherche Scientifique, 1968, pp. 5–13.

INDEX

ABOUT THE AUTHOR

Spencer J. Pack is Assistant Professor of Economics at Connecticut College, New London, Connecticut.

Dr. Pack holds a B. A. in Social Theory from Franconia College, Franconia, New Hampshire, an M. A. in Political Science from the University of Toronto, and a Ph.D. in Economics from the University of New Hampshire.

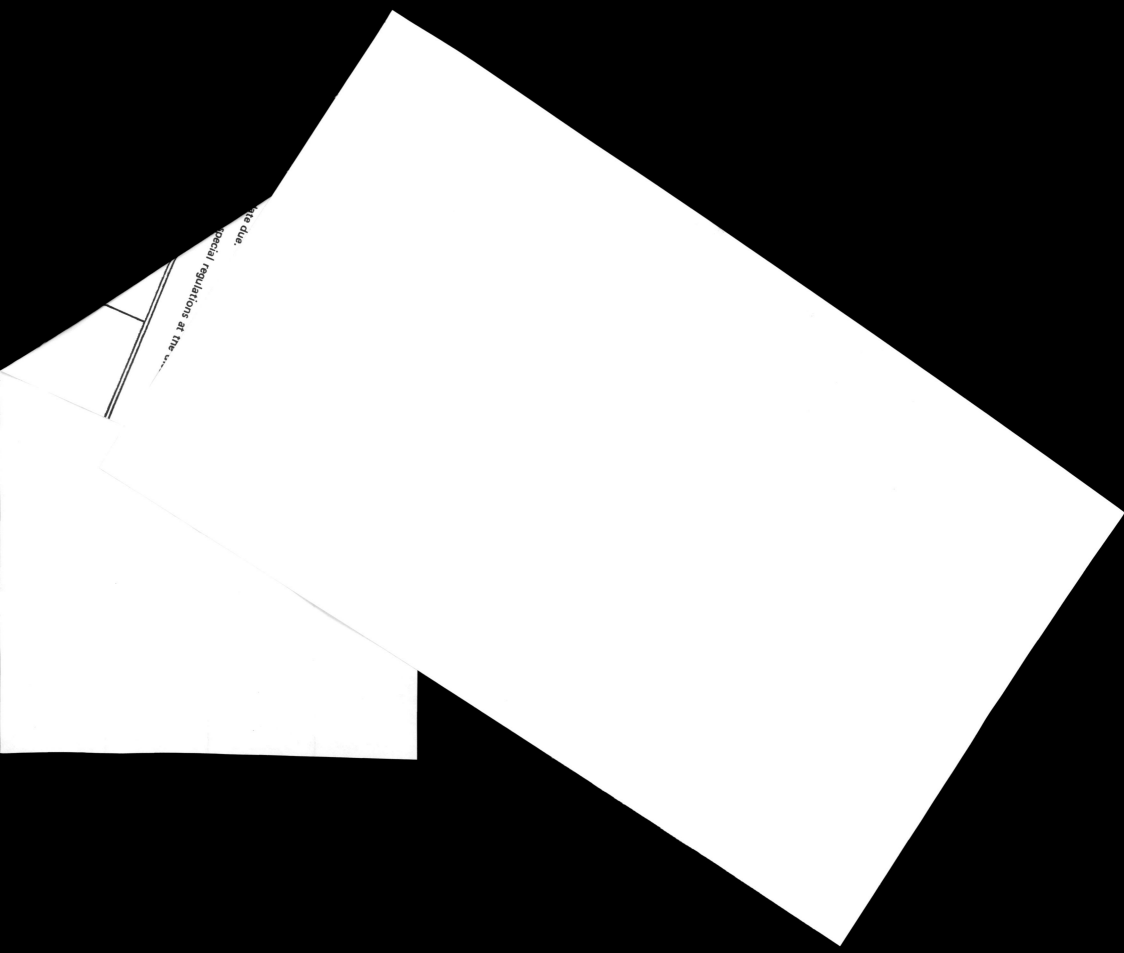

te due.

special regulations at the